IMAGES
of America

CHALDEAN CATHOLIC CHURCH

On the Cover: The Chaldean community of Detroit celebrates the 12th anniversary of the priesthood of Father Thomas (Toma) Bidawid on May 15, 1947. See page 67. (Courtesy of Margaret Gabbara Atto, Chaldean Cultural Center.)

IMAGES
of America

CHALDEAN CATHOLIC CHURCH

Bishop Bawai Soro and Jacob Bacall
Foreword by Bishop Ibrahim N. Ibrahim

ARCADIA
PUBLISHING

ISBN 978-1-4671-6019-3

Published by Arcadia Publishing
Charleston, South Carolina

Printed in the United States of America

Library of Congress Control Number: 2025935424

For all general information, please contact Arcadia Publishing:
Telephone 843-853-2070
Fax 843-853-0044
E-mail sales@arcadiapublishing.com

Visit us on the Internet at www.arcadiapublishing.com

We dedicate this book to the memory of our forefathers and foremothers who for centuries suffered massacres at the hands of savage people, endured torture and persecution, and tolerated humiliation and excessive taxation only to safely hand to their descendants the glorious Christian faith and the cultural values we so proudly embrace today. Pray for us, O Saints of Christ.

One hundred percent of the authors' royalties from the sale of this book will be donated to the Library Fund of The Chaldean Catholic Church of the USA in Southfield, Michigan.

Contents

Foreword

The story of the Chaldean Church in the United States is the story of the immigrant Chaldean people who came to America. The Church, of course, is People of God. In Matthew 18:20, Jesus tells his disciples, "For wherever two or three are gathered together in my name, there am I in the midst of them."

In 1904, members of the Chaldean Church from Iran established a foothold in Chicago, and they were later supported by a Chaldean priest from Iran. Today, the epicenter of the Chaldean Church in the USA is in Detroit, Michigan, where the first North American diocese was established in 1982. I was privileged to be ordained the first bishop of the Chaldean Diocese of Saint Thomas the Apostle.

When I was ordained in 1962, I had no other thoughts beyond being a parish priest in Iraq. As a young man, my view of the United States of America was not that positive, primarily based on the politics of the time. But that all changed when I had the opportunity to visit San Diego in 1976. I was shortly after assigned there to serve the blossoming Chaldean community in Southern California. Soon after, with only $9,600 at hand and the support of a few families, we succeeded in establishing Saint Paul's Chaldean Church in Los Angeles.

I never expected to be a bishop. Several other qualified priests had been in the United States longer than me and were more familiar with the large community in Detroit. During my first 10 years as a bishop, I struggled to establish my bona fides with the Chaldean people. But thankfully, as time passed, my tenure as bishop coincided with the tremendous growth of our Chaldean population, not only in Michigan but in California and Canada as well. Ultimately, the Chaldean Patriarchate divided Saint Thomas Diocese into two more jurisdictions, one in San Diego and one in Toronto, to offer sounder pastoral care and more resounding spiritual support for our Chaldeans in all those areas.

Meanwhile, in Detroit, there was much work to do. The community grew exponentially as the second and third generations of Chaldean Americans established families. The community also began to understand American-style success and how to create wealth. Thus, the second decade of my tenure required growth. We needed more churches, priests, and other ancillary activities to support the mission of the church.

Ultimately, we established 12 new parishes, a seminary fund to help support the education and formation of young men called to the priesthood, and a priest retirement fund to sustain the living income of the elderly priests who would retire in the United States. In 2007, we purchased a 164-acre campground from the City of Detroit and built a small church on those grounds, now bustling with summer camps and other activities. In 2022, the Chaldean diocese purchased an additional 54-acre parcel of property to be used for future development and expansion. This purchase increased the size to 218 acres. There are plans underway as of this writing to establish a brand-new retreat center there as well.

During this time, we always enjoyed the collaboration and synodality of all the Latin archbishops of Detroit, from when our churches were part of the Detroit Latin Rite diocese to the establishment of our own Chaldean Rite diocese. Acknowledging these brothers who supported the Chaldean Church during our formative years is very appropriate. They are Cardinal Edmund Szoka, Cardinal Adam Maida, and Archbishop Allen Vigneron.

Finally, I'd like to thank Bishop Bawai Soro and Jacob Bacall for the critical undertaking of this book to tell the story of the Chaldean Church in the United States and Canada and for offering me the opportunity to make this contribution.

—Ibrahim N. Ibrahim
Bishop Emeritus of Saint Thomas Chaldean Diocese in the USA
Southfield, Michigan
July 2024

Acknowledgments

Writing this book has been a labor of love—a sacred pilgrimage through the corridors of time, where the enduring echoes of the Chaldean Catholic Church resound with glory, sacrifice, and unshakable faith. With every word typed, I felt the presence of our Church fathers—pillars of wisdom and holiness—whose voices still rise in the sacred Chaldean liturgy, ancient yet ever renewed. It has been an indescribable joy to reflect upon their legacy, to walk in their footsteps, and to draw spiritual breath from the living tradition they entrusted to us.

My heartfelt gratitude is especially extended to Jacob Bacall of Michigan—my dear friend, brother in faith, and now my coauthor. Jacob generously invited me to join this endeavor, and it was his vision and tireless dedication that kindled the flame of this work. I am equally grateful to his daughter, Christina Bacall Oraha, whose editorial precision and secretarial support have been a true blessing to the completion of this publication.

I also wish to acknowledge with deep appreciation all those who shared their insights, opened their archives, and entrusted their memories to this project: contributing photographs, documents, and sacred images. First and foremost, I offer my gratitude to His Beatitude Patriarch-Cardinal Louis Raphaël Sako, Bishop Basilius Yaldo, the late Bishop Sarhad Jammo of Blessed memory, Chorbishop Andrew Younan, Abbot Ankido Sipo, Father Hermiz Haddad, and Father Simon Esshaki. Thank you for allowing this book to speak not only through words but also through visual beauty, reverently preserved and remembered. To another cherished group of collaborators and friends who offered invaluable support, I extend my sincere thanks to Samad Attisha, Vincent Kattoula, Samir and Rawa Razooki, and James Shamon.

Finally, I offer my deepest reverence to our forefathers and foremothers of the Chaldean Church, the faithful sons and daughters of the whole Church of the East—those valiant souls who bore the weight of history with grace and devotion. With hearts ablaze for Christ, they carried the torch of faith through fire and silence, through exile and hope, so that future generations might know the saving name of Jesus. Their lives were prayers. Their footsteps, hymns. Their legacy, a living testament to God, family, and the Church.

May this book stand as a tribute to all who came before us and as an inspiration to all who will follow.

—Bawai Soro
Bishop Emeritus of the Chaldean Eparchy of Mar Addai of Toronto
San Diego, California
March 2025

ACKNOWLEDGMENTS

Writing a book is truly not a simple task, and a work like this does not come together without the support and contributions of many people. First and foremost, I am deeply grateful to my dear brother and friend, Bishop Bawai Soro, for accepting my invitation to coauthor this book. Thank you, *Sayidna*! A heartfelt thanks to Bishop Ibrahim Ibrahim for writing the foreword and always being a steadfast source of support.

A special thank-you to my wife, Anne, for being so patient and my sons, Mark and Joseph, for tolerating my work schedule while I worked on this book. I am forever indebted to my daughter, Christina Oraha, for her unconditional love and support in helping fulfill Arcadia Publishing's stringent guidelines and rules. Once again, I will say what I wrote in my last book—Christina is the daughter every father wishes to have. To her husband, Saifee, and my lovely granddaughters, Simone, Aubrey, and "little wise professor" Carmen, thank you for your encouragement. A warm thank-you to my other daughter Caroline, who also helped greatly.

Additionally, I extend my gratitude to Bishop Francis Kalabat and Bishop Emanuel Shaleta for their valuable insights. Father John Jwad, your diligent work and contribution is greatly appreciated. I would also like to thank Dr. Stefan Galyana, and Shamasha Khairy Tomika for their invaluable assistance. A special thanks to Father Michael Bazzi for providing my coauthor and I a wealth of information and images, always reminding us to be proud of our heritage. Many thanks to Shamasha Khairy Foumia, as well as to the Chaldean Cultural Center and their dedicated staff, especially Weam Namou and Judy Jonna. I owe a particular debt of gratitude to my uncle, Akram F. Kareem, for providing a treasure trove of historical information, especially regarding the pope's visit to Iraq, from his book *Peace, Peace, Peace*. Thank you, *Khalu*. I would also like to express my thanks to my longtime friends Salem Dawood Elia, Amir Sitto, the late Samir Mattia, and his brother, the late Nabil Mattia; Father Sabri Kejbo; Father Philip Najim; my dear friend and brother Samad Attisha; Sr. Alexandra Matti; my *amu* Salim Najor and his brother Frank; Basil Zetouna; Roy Gessford, Isaam Garmo, and my longtime friend John Zia Oram.

Many thanks to my Shenandoah Club comrade Raad Kathawa, community die-hard leader Martin Manna, Sharkey Haddad, Dr. Adhid Miri, Morey Gergis, Zuhair Kenaya, John Khami, and specifically Paul Manni for his generous contributions of historical information and images. I am also thankful to Lamar Sulaka, Hend Abro, Nadia Kallabat, Najat M. George, Crystal Kassab-Jabiro, Michael J. Yono, and Patrick Kakos, a fine gentleman. My sincere thanks to Joyce Wiswell for editing the book, my dear friend Joe Grimm for his continued support, and Osama Siblani for his true friendship. Finally, I would like to thank my editor, Caitrin Cunningham, and Arcadia Publishing for their patience and support during this project.

For those who are not mentioned but provided images and valuable information, a heartfelt thanks to all.

—Jacob Bacall
April 2025

Introduction

Among the ancient civilizations in Mesopotamia, the Chaldeans were the last native empire to rule before the Persians began a long series of foreign dominations in 539 BCE. This foreign rule continued until 1958 CE. The Sumerians, who first flourished in that land around 4500 BCE, innovated in agriculture, writing, literature, and urban planning for over 2,000 years. Their advancements laid the groundwork for subsequent empires like the Akkadians, Babylonians, Assyrians, and finally, the Chaldeans, ensuring rapid and secure growth in Mesopotamia. The legacy of Mesopotamia still lives on throughout the world as the "Cradle of Civilization."

The Church of the East, also known as the Chaldean Catholic Church, originated in the first century when the apostles from Jerusalem began evangelizing native Chaldeans and Assyrians. A major attraction for the apostles was the large, stable Jewish communities in Mesopotamia, brought there by the Assyrians and Babylonians since the eighth century BCE. The Church of the East prays in Aramaic, the language Jesus spoke. It has its own liturgical, theological, patristic, and canonical traditions, which, while distinct from Latin and Byzantine traditions, are the same in substance. This church never had an emperor like Constantine to defend it, which is why its adherents always trusted and relied upon the Lord Jesus Christ, who blessed them with the gifts of spiritual awareness, mission, and endurance.

Islam arrived in Mesopotamia around 1,000 years after Babylon's fall to the Persians. The Islamic conquest claimed Mesopotamia following the Battle of Al-Qadisiyya in 636 CE, marking a decisive victory over the Sassanian Empire. The Islamic Age significantly impacted Mesopotamia's history and its Christian communities. Despite enormous taxation, consistent persecution, and massacres, the Church of the East persisted, achieving scientific progress and expanding to the Far East. Chapter Three delves into major events and the Islamic caliphates and dynasties that governed Mesopotamia from the seventh century to the abolition of the Ottoman Empire in the 20th century.

Chapter four covers the modern history of the Chaldeans. Between 1920 and 1979, Iraq endured 22 revolutions or coups d'état, plunging the nation into chronic political instability that severely impacted its people and resources. This unrest, led by the Muslim majority (Arabs and Kurds), resulted in widespread destruction, including the decimation of numerous villages in northern Iraq, particularly in Erbil—many of which were predominantly Christian.

The Gulf War marked a turning point for Christianity in Iraq. Churches were bombed, Christian-owned businesses became targets, and the community faced growing suspicion, with their loyalties unfairly questioned as being aligned with the so-called "new crusaders."

The Chaldeans are Eastern Catholic faithful who settled in Detroit in the early 20th century and have since established a strong community focused on family, church, and the workplace. The Catholic Eparchy of Saint Thomas the Apostle was established in 1982 to serve the Chaldean population. Known for their entrepreneurial spirit and continued focus on education, Chaldeans in America pursue careers in various fields while maintaining their tradition of business acumen and trade.

The early Chaldean pioneers in San Diego, California, were led by Dr. Joseph Jibran and other families such as the Thomases, Najors, and Deddehs. Together, they established a thriving community in the 1950s and 1960s. The community has grown significantly following the establishment of Saint Peter Chaldean Catholic Church in 1973, which initially attracted Chaldeans from Detroit seeking safety, a moderate climate, and new business opportunities. Some Chaldeans also settled in Arizona, drawn by a climate reminiscent of their homeland, Mesopotamia (Iraq). Others initially settled in Mexico before making their way north into the United States, creating a unique Chaldean Mexican community. Today, the Eparchy of Saint Peter in San Diego serves over 55,000 Chaldean/ Assyrian Catholics across 26 western states.

Canada holds a significant place in history as the first country in North America with the largest Chaldean group, initially surpassing even the United States and Mexico. In the early 20th century, the city of Fort William (Thunder Bay), Ontario, had over 30 Aramaic-speaking families. Early Chaldean immigrants like Sadiq Damman and Yousif Shammam played key roles in establishing the Chaldean community, with many eventually moving to Detroit due to the automobile industry boom. The Chaldean community in Toronto celebrated mass in rented spaces until the construction of their first church in 2001. The Eparchy of Mar Addai of Toronto of the Chaldeans (geographically one of the largest jurisdictions in the world) was established in 2011, covering the entire country of Canada and serving 13 parishes, with Windsor housing a fast-growing Chaldean community.

Pope Francis made history with the first-ever papal visit to Iraq, a country with a rich Christian history and significant religious sites but with an extremely dwindling number of native Christians. Despite challenges and a global pandemic, the Holy Father accepted the invitation from the Republic of Iraq and the Patriarchate of the Chaldean Catholic Church. During his four-day visit, Pope Francis met with key Muslim leaders, urged Christians not to abandon their homeland, and called for peaceful coexistence in the face of terrorism and fundamentalism. His visit to the birthplace of Abraham in ancient Mesopotamia marked a significant milestone in his mission to promote unity and understanding between the world's different cultures and religions. "We are all brothers" was the theme of his visit to Iraq.

One

Chaldeans before the Christian Era

Today's Chaldean people are the direct descendants of the indigenous civilizations of the Sumerians, Akkadians, Babylonians, Assyrians, and Chaldeans. These ancient kingdoms and empires reigned in Mesopotamia, the land between the Tigris and Euphrates Rivers, located in modern-day Iraq and parts of Turkey and Syria. Since time immemorial, Mesopotamia has been renowned as the Cradle of Civilization. It was the site of history's first urban experience, which attracted migrant groups from surrounding regions due to its geographical conditions and human inventiveness. The excellent fertile land, favorable temperature, and steady flow of fresh water through the Tigris and Euphrates Rivers enabled agricultural growth, which led to the creation of city-states and, finally, to the rise of several formidable empires.

Sumerian history in Mesopotamia started around 4500 to 4000 BCE. They made pioneering contributions throughout the centuries that became pivotal and groundbreaking for all who inhabited Mesopotamia. Ruling for almost 2,000 years, they advanced in agricultural techniques, invented writing systems, produced literature, and established a complex society with laws and urban infrastructure. These accomplishments laid the foundation for the subsequent empires in Mesopotamia to rise and prosper even more rapidly and securely than other nations elsewhere. And so, the legacy of an impressive Sumerian civilization would be re-created, time and again, by those who followed, such as the Akkadians, Babylonians, Assyrians, and Chaldeans, for many centuries at a time.

Conversely, the Chaldean Empire was the last native group among the indigenous dynasties to rule in Mesopotamia before the Persians sacked Babylon in 539 BCE. The fall of Babylon marked the end of the reign of its native empires. The fall of Babylon was a fundamental turning point that marked the beginning of 25 centuries of invasion, persecution, and conquest by foreign powers in Mesopotamia. This age ended on July 14, 1958, when modern-day Iraq became an independent republic under an Iraqi-born leader, Gen. Abdul Kareem Kassem.

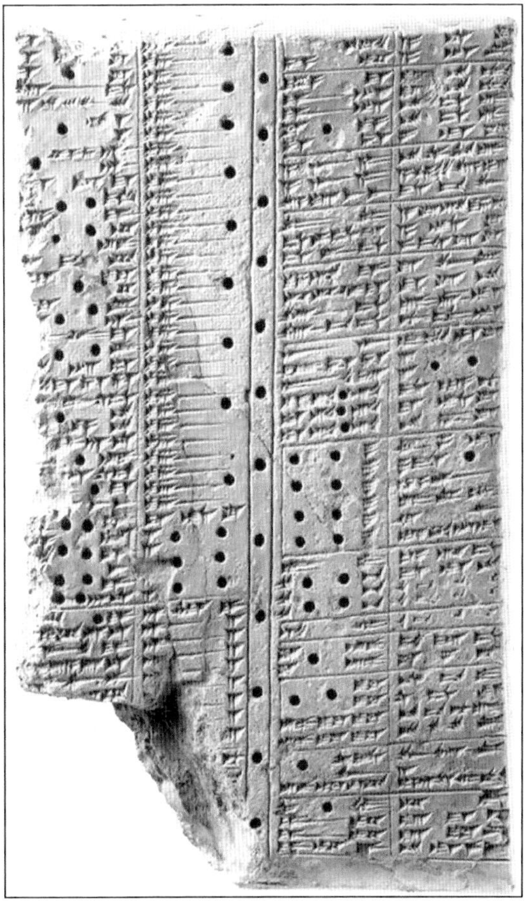

Cracking the Code. Cuneiform is an ancient writing system developed around 3000 BCE by the Sumerians of Mesopotamia and used by the Akkadians, Babylonians, Assyrians, and Chaldeans. The term "cuneiform" comes from the Latin words *cuneus*, meaning "wedge," and *forma*, meaning "shape," referring to the wedge-shaped stylus used to make impressions on clay tablets. It is considered a true foundation in the history of writing. (Courtesy of the *Chaldean News*.)

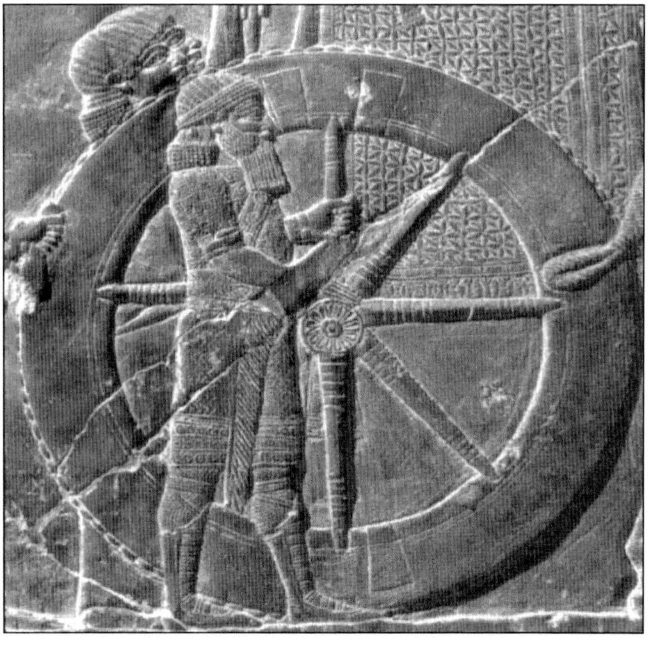

The Birthplace of the Wheel. The wheel was believed to be independently developed in different regions worldwide, although the invention is attributed to the Sumerians of Mesopotamia. The oldest known depictions appear on pictographs and pottery that date back to around 3500 BCE (and Central Europe around 3200 BCE). The wheel revolutionized transportation, trade, and agriculture, impacting society's evolution and marking a significant technological advancement for humanity. This is a depiction of an onager-drawn cart on the Sumerian "War" panel of the standard of the city of Ur. (Courtesy of Selim Matar.)

The Epic of Gilgamesh. It is considered one of history's oldest remaining works of literature, portrayed on 11 cuneiform clay tablets. The story is based on early Sumerian poems. It follows the adventures of Gilgamesh, the legendary king of Uruk (27th century BCE), and his companion Enkidu. Gilgamesh was a powerful and tyrannical ruler who sought fame, glory, and immortality. But his arrogance led the gods to create Enkidu, a wild man, to challenge him. After a fierce battle, Gilgamesh and Enkidu become close friends and set out on a series of heroic quests together. This story tells us about human limits, wisdom, and acceptance. (Courtesy of Jacob Bacall.)

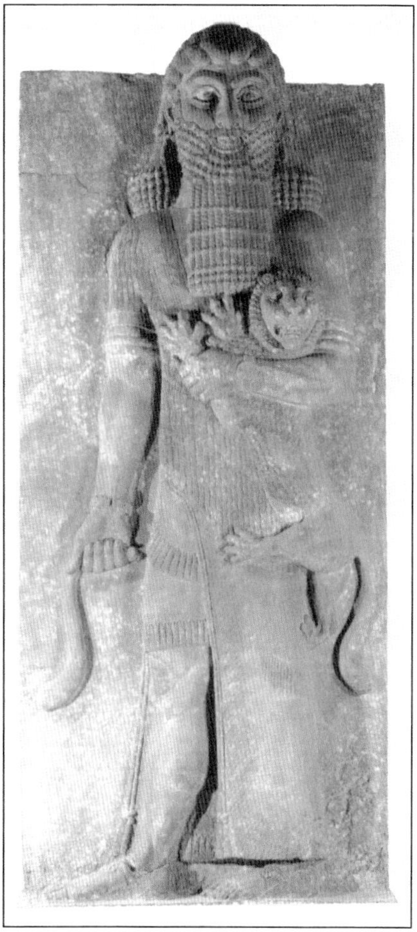

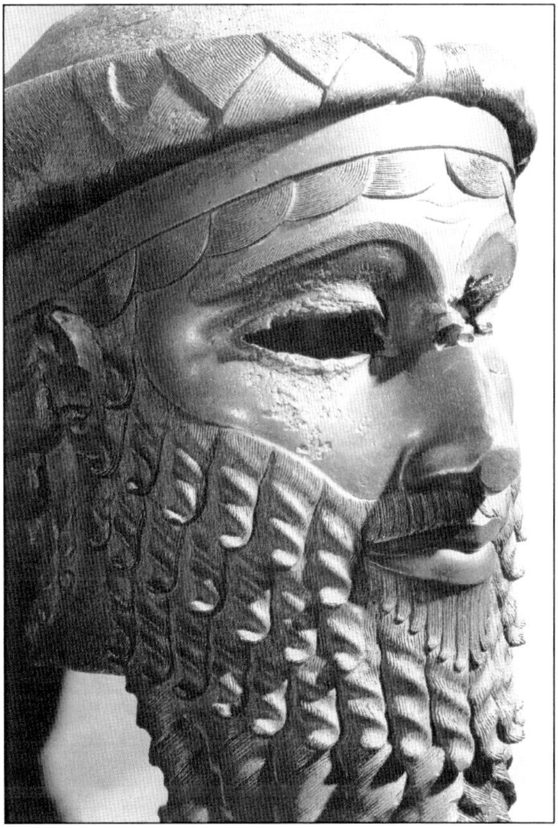

Transforming a Kingdom to an Empire. Around 2300 BCE, the Akkadian people gained power in Mesopotamia. Their king, Sargon the Great (2334 to 2279 BCE), conquered all of the region of Babylonia and Northern Mesopotamia, founding the dynasty of Akkad, which lasted only 150 years. Mesopotamia became two countries: Sumer in the southeast and Akkad in the northwest. King Sargon created a government that became the model for all Middle Eastern civilizations. Akkadian became the culture, arts, and language of Mesopotamia. Today, modern Chaldeans and Assyrians still use many Akkadian words in their spoken dialects. (Courtesy of Selim Matar.)

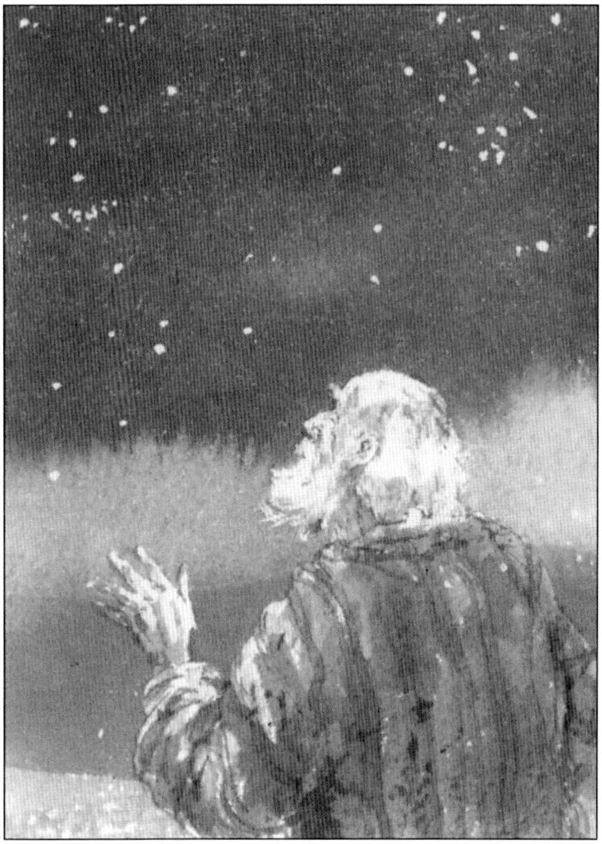

Abraham of Ur of the Chaldees. Abraham is one of the most prominent personalities in the Old Testament because he was given a unique awareness of the divine powers. According to Genesis 11, Abraham rejected the notion of worshipping idols. So God called him to leave his father's homeland, Ur (present-day Iraq), and settle in the land of Canaan (present-day Israel). Abraham was to leave Ur in order for God to bless him and make him the father of a great nation. Abraham, his wife, Sarah, his father, Terah, and his nephew Lot left Ur and traveled to Haran (present-day Turkey). After his father's death, Abraham continued his journey to Canaan. In Canaan, God made a covenant with Abraham, promising him many descendants and a homeland there as an everlasting possession and a unique role in the history of salvation for him and his posterity. (Both, courtesy of Father Michael Bazzi.)

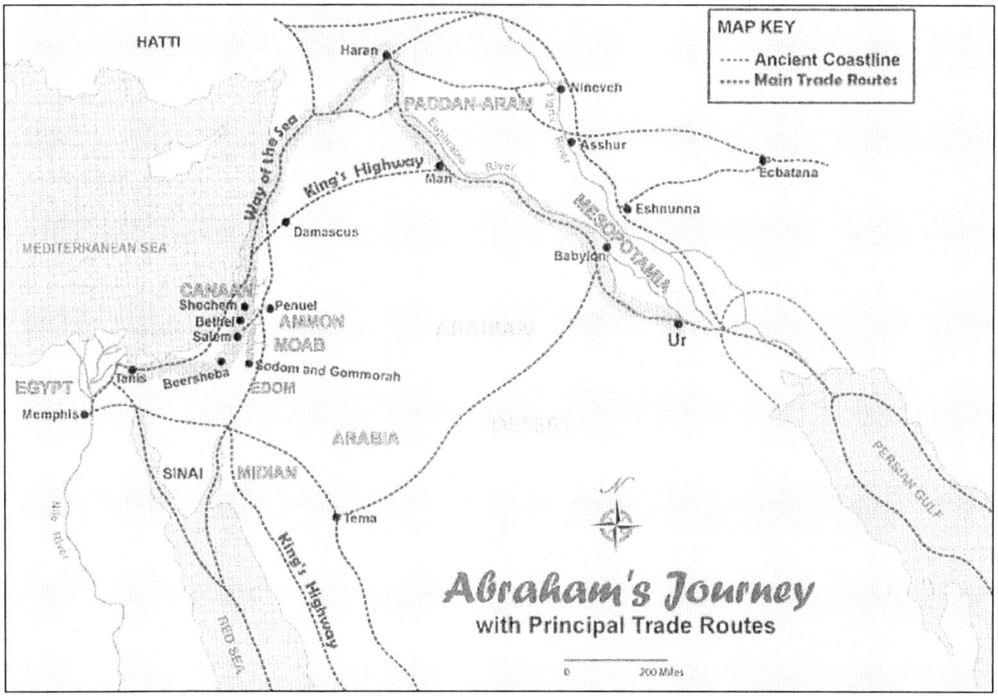

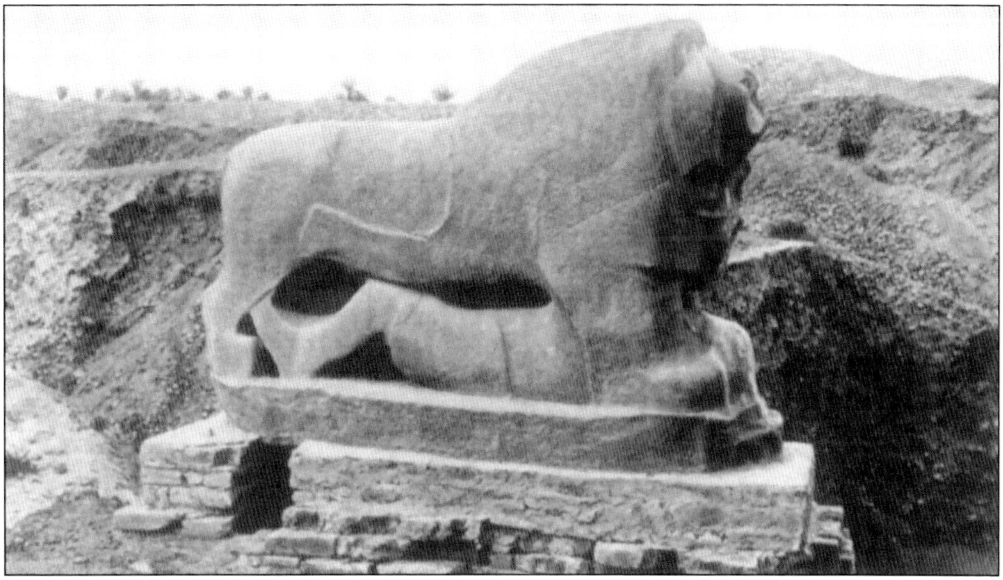

Babylon: The Jewel of Mesopotamia. Babylon, founded in the 20th century BCE on the Euphrates River, became a major center under King Hammurabi (1792–1750 BCE). Known for its urban planning, architecture, and culture, it was a prosperous metropolis. Later, a new dynasty of kings established the rule of the Neo-Babylonian Empire, which spanned from the Persian Gulf to the Mediterranean Sea. Under King Nebuchadnezzar II (605–562 BCE), Babylon became famous for its architecture, including the Hanging Gardens, the Ishtar Gate, and the Tower of Babel. (Courtesy of Bryon Perry.)

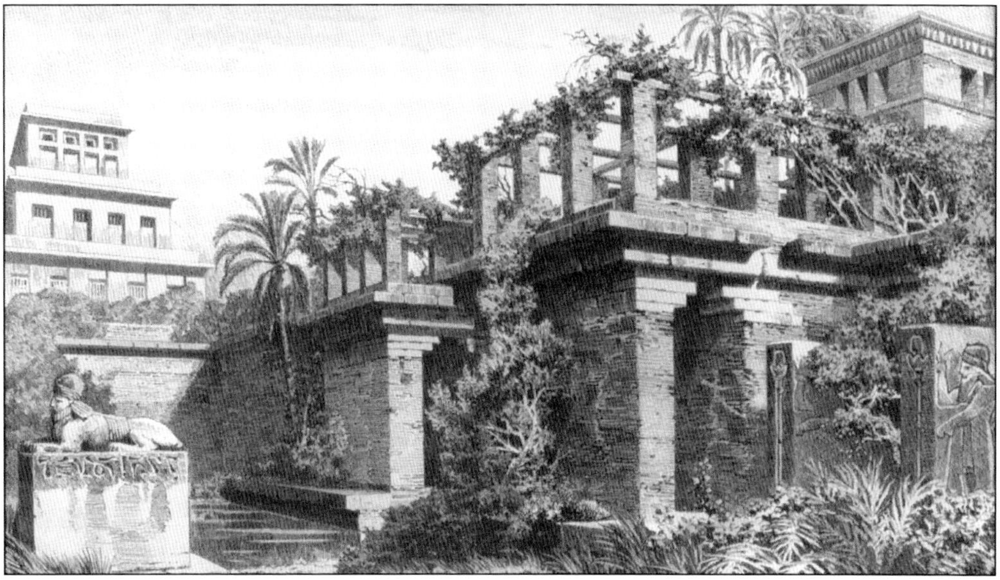

The Hanging Gardens of Babylon. The Hanging Gardens were a complex system of terraced gardens believed to have been built by King Nebuchadnezzar II. They were a stunning engineering marvel featuring lush plants and vibrant flowers irrigated by a system of canals, one of the world's seven wonders. It is said that King Nebuchadnezzar built the gardens to please his homesick wife, Amytis of Media, who longed for her homeland's lush, green mountains. (Courtesy of Chaldean Catholic Diocese of Saint Thomas the Apostle.)

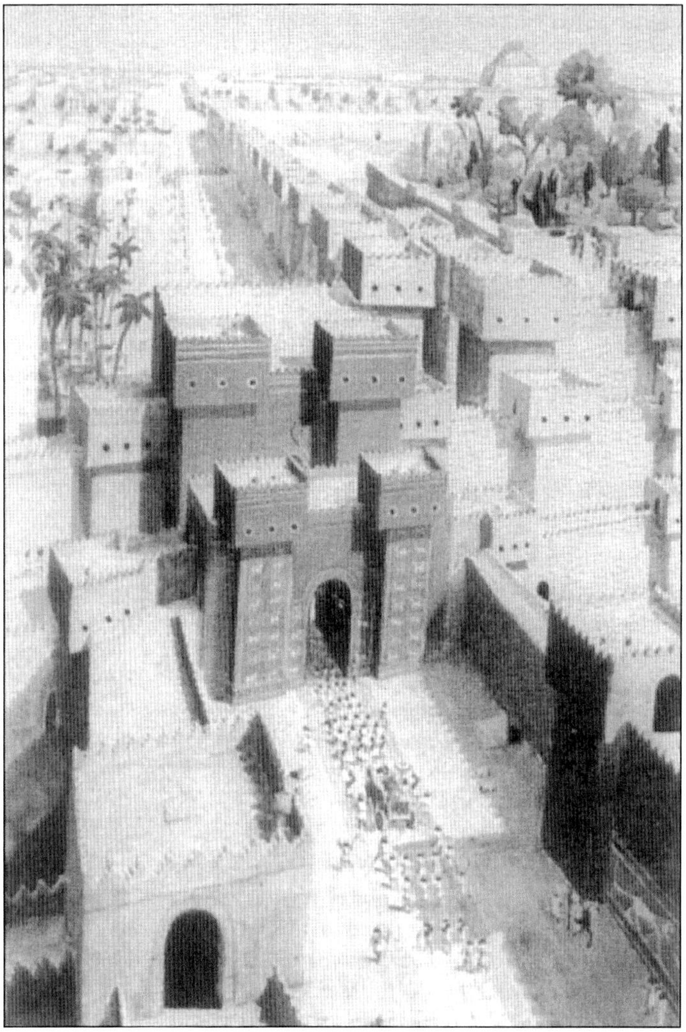

Babylon: The Gate of God. Babylon was Mesopotamia's political, economic, cultural, intellectual, and religious epicenter. During the sixth century BCE, its kings built several remarkable structures to symbolize its power, wealth, and culture: the Lion of Babel (Lion of Al-lāt), the Tower of Babel, the Gate of Ishtar, and the Hanging Gardens of Babylon. Ancient Babylon maintained its vitality and stamina centuries after the fall of the Neo-Babylonian Empire, but its eventual decline and abandonment occurred around the first century CE. (Courtesy of Chaldean Cultural Center.)

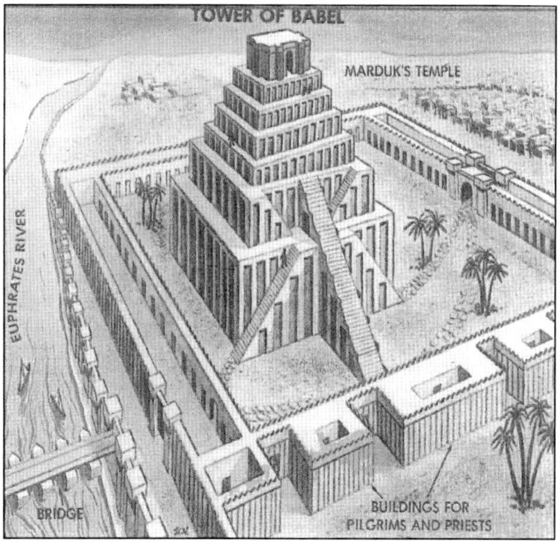

One-of-a-Kind Infrastructure. Babylon was renowned for its well-laid-out streets and complex network of canals for transportation and irrigation. It boasted wide boulevards, bustling markets, and magnificent public buildings, showcasing the city's advanced urban planning and infrastructure. More importantly, Babylon's prime was marked by its role as a trade and cultural exchange center, attracting scholars, merchants, and artists from around the ancient world. The city's diverse population and fostering an environment of innovation and exchange of ideas made it a hub of economic and cultural activity. (Courtesy of Chaldean Catholic Diocese of Saint Thomas the Apostle.)

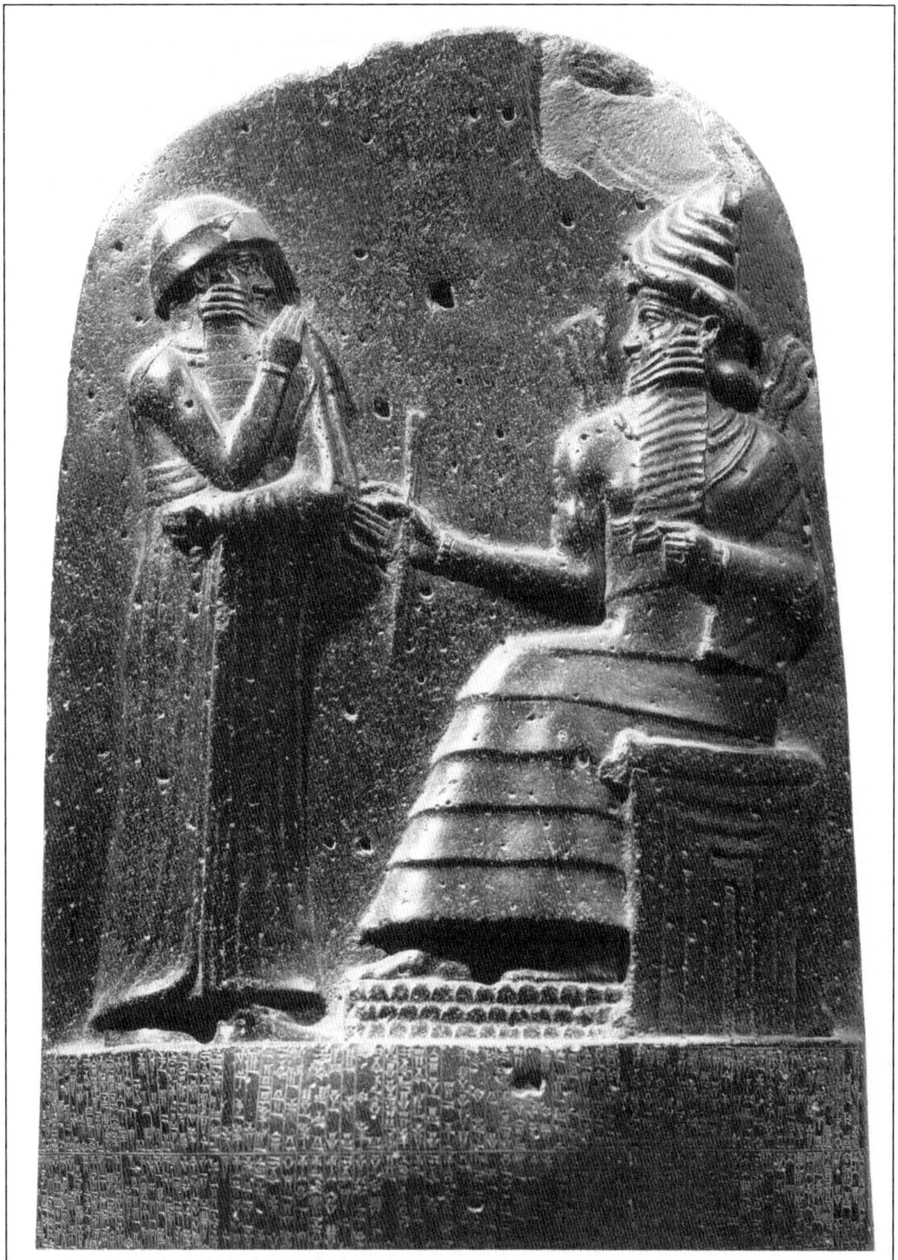

HAMMURABI: A TRUE STATESMAN KING. King Hammurabi was renowned for his Code of Hammurabi, one of the earliest written legal codes with 282 laws covering family, property, trade, and justice. His reign brought stability and prosperity to Babylonia, influencing future legal systems in Mesopotamia and elsewhere. The code was discovered on a seven-foot black pillar carved with an image of Hammurabi receiving the laws from Shamash, the Babylonian god of justice, a key figure in Mesopotamian religion. King Hammurabi improved infrastructure, promoted trade, and fostered cultural and literary development, making Babylon a hub of education and intellectual pursuits. Hammurabi's contributions laid the foundation for governance, commerce, and justice systems that continue to influence the modern world. (Courtesy of Jacob Bacall.)

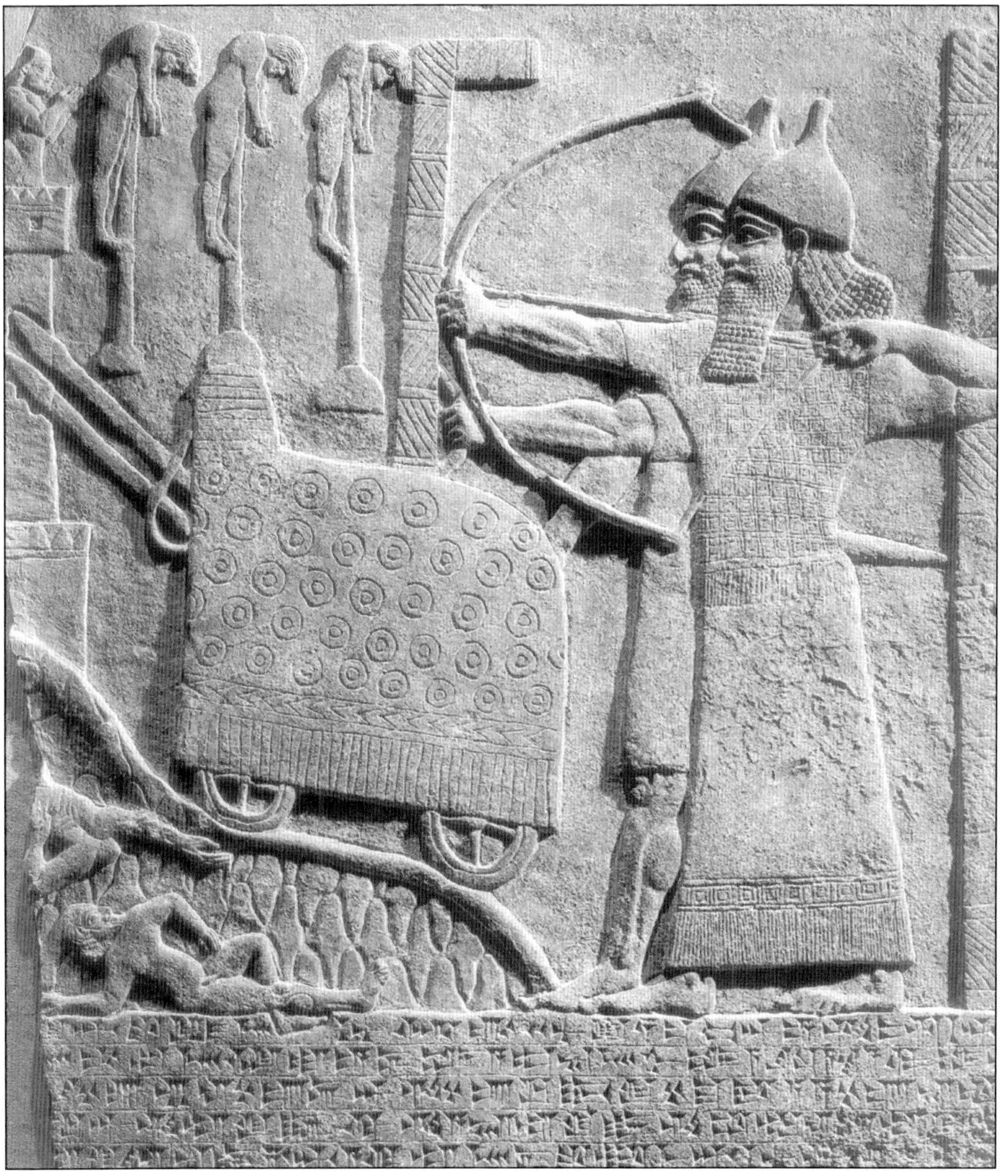

ASSYRIANS: FURIOUS FIGHTERS. The Assyrians were renowned for their military skill, advanced warfare tactics, and disciplined army, enabling them to conquer vast territories and establish a powerful empire in the ancient Near East. Feared for their ferocity and brutal tactics, including siege warfare and mass deportations, they also built a robust civilization. Their architectural achievements included grand cities, palaces, and intricate temples, while their efficient bureaucracy and organized military strengthened their empire. The Assyrians excelled in trade and made significant contributions to literature, science, and mathematics. Their advancements in governance, engineering, and the arts influenced subsequent civilizations. Despite their reputation for conquest, the Assyrians' legacy is marked by cultural, scientific, and administrative innovations that shaped the ancient world and left a lasting impact. (Both, courtesy of Bryon Perry.)

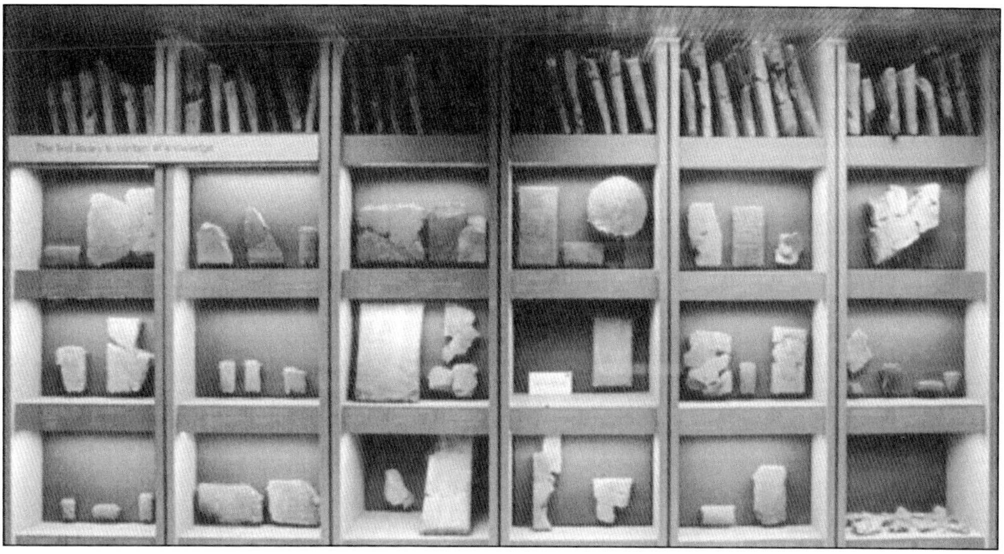

THE LIBRARY OF ASHURBANIPAL. The Ashurbanipal Library, established by King Ashurbanipal (668–627 BCE) in Nineveh, was among the ancient world's most significant libraries. It contained thousands of cuneiform tablets with literary, religious, historical, and scientific texts, such as the *Epic of Gilgamesh*. Organized as a knowledge center, it preserved Mesopotamian culture. Though it was destroyed during Nineveh's sacking in 612 BCE, many tablets have been recovered by archaeologists, offering invaluable insights into ancient history and literature. (Courtesy of Chaldean Cultural Center.)

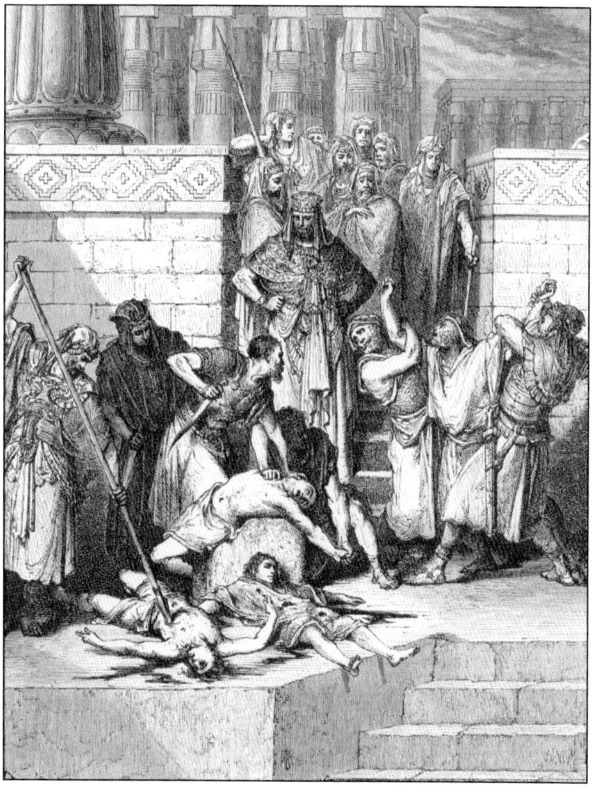

NEBUCHADNEZZAR II: THE VISIONARY KING. During his reign over the Neo-Babylonian Empire, Babylon thrived with remarkable military, scientific, and architectural achievements, including the Hanging Gardens, one of the seven wonders of the ancient world. The Chaldean king also helped Babylon to excel in astronomy, recording lunar and planetary positions. With its central location and control over trade routes, Babylon also became a vital commercial hub, fostering trade and cultural exchanges. (Courtesy of Selim Matar.)

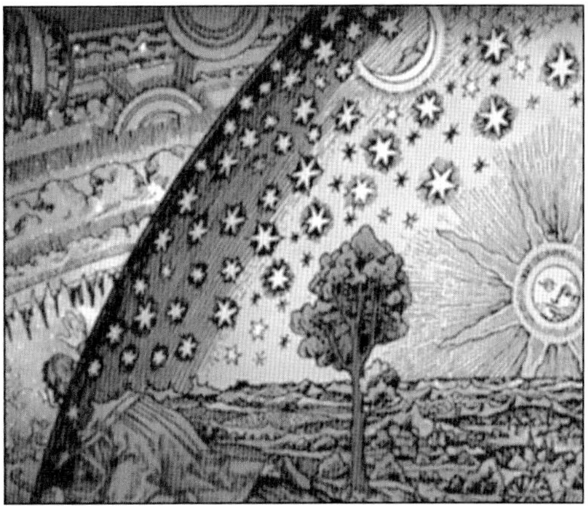

BABYLONIANS: MASTERS OF ASTROLOGY. Astrology is another science that emerged independently in various cultures around the world. In Mesopotamia, the practice was known as Babylonian astrology. Mesopotamian records dating back to the second millennium BCE indicate that priests and scholars dedicated significant time to observing and interpreting celestial phenomena. They believed that celestial events and the positioning of celestial bodies could provide insight into human affairs and the future. (Courtesy of Bryon Perry.)

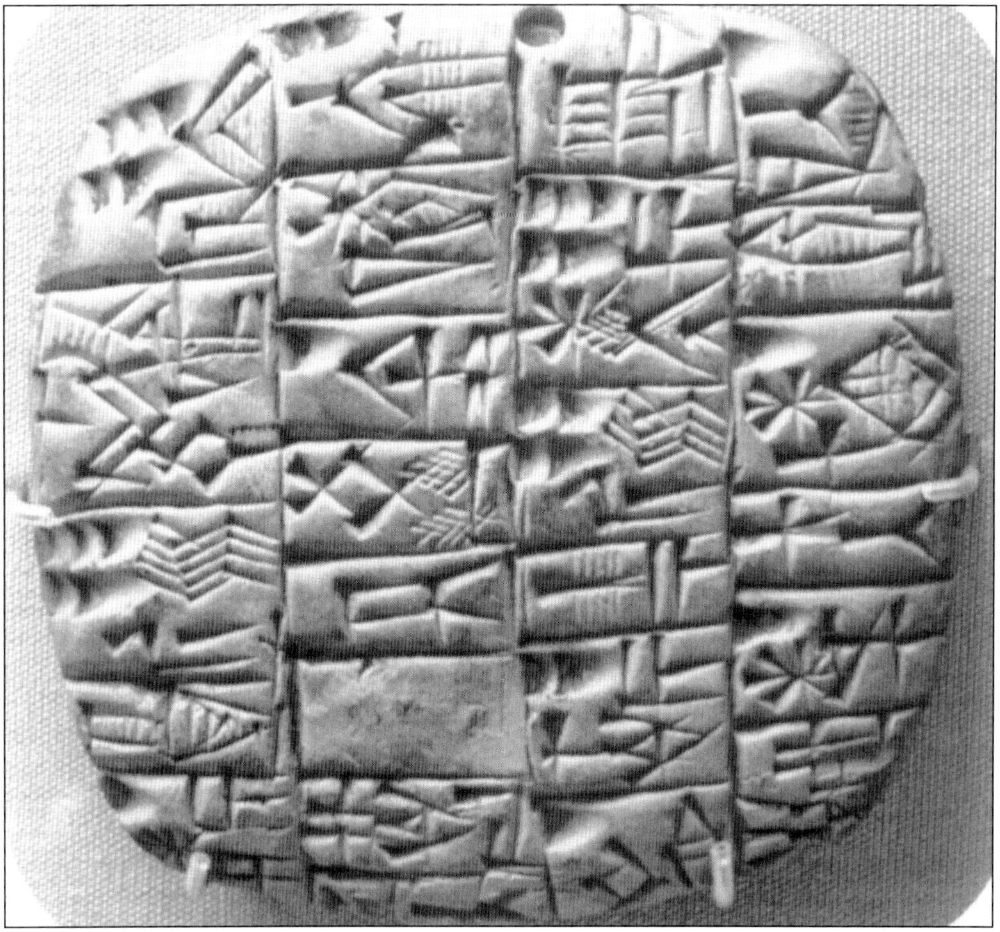

BABYLON OR ATHENS? In 1922, archaeologists in the city of Larsa, southern Iraq, found a cuneiform clay tablet demonstrating knowledge of the Pythagorean triples that predated the Greek mathematician Pythagoras by 11 centuries. This 4,000-year-old artifact, today at Columbia University and named Plimpton 322, highlights the sophistication of Babylonian mathematical practices and remains a fascinating link to humanity's early understanding of numbers and geometry. (Courtesy of Father Michael Bazzi.)

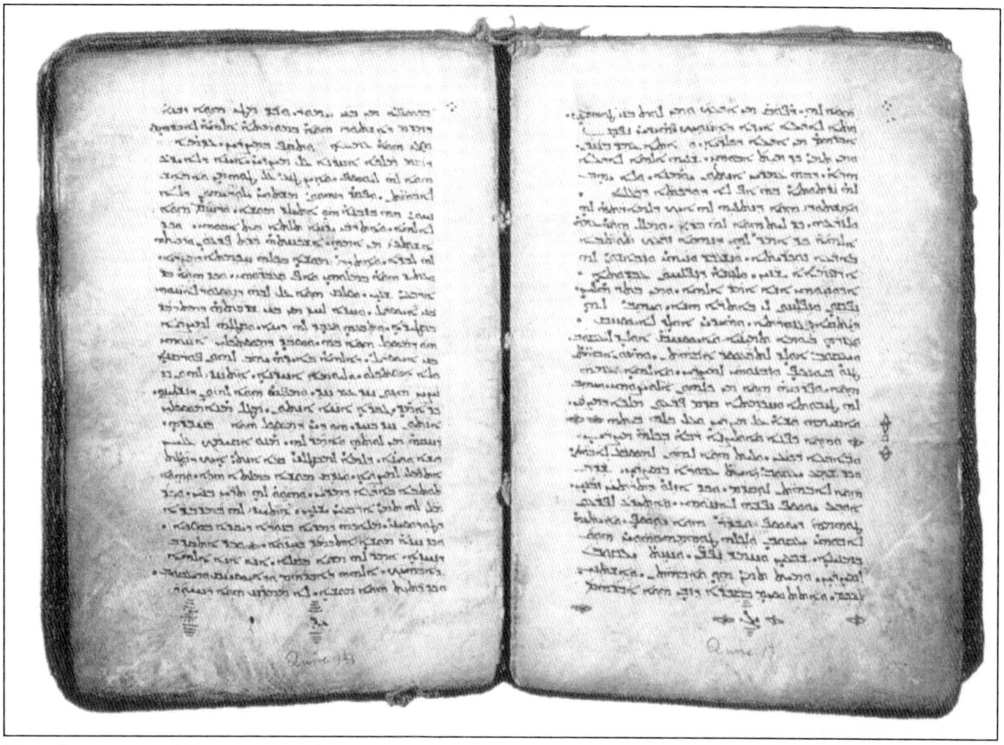

The Chaldeans: Pioneers in Astrology and Astronomy. Astronomy evolved over millennia with contributions from various civilizations, including the Chaldeans of Babylon. Chaldean astronomers, skilled in philosophy, prophecy, and religion, sought the "star" prophesied in Numbers 24:17, later linked to the Messiah's birth in Bethlehem. By the seventh century BCE, they combined religious beliefs with scientific methods to track celestial bodies. Their legacy influenced Islamic astronomy and beyond. For example, a cuneiform text from 164 BCE documented Halley's Comet centuries before Edmond Halley confirmed its recurring return. (Courtesy of Bryon Perry.)

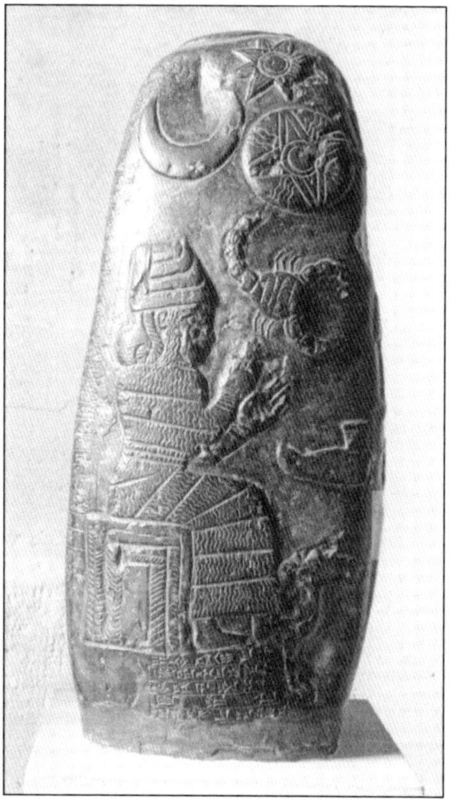

Zodiac: Mesopotamian Origins. The Greek zodiac originated in Mesopotamia, tracing back to the Sumerians, who built the world's first civilization in present-day Iraq. The concept evolved throughout Mesopotamia before reaching the Hellenistic culture. The zodiac took its recognizable form under the Babylonians in the first millennium BCE. Shown here is a stone sculpture from the 14th century BCE known as *Kurdura* with a scorpion at top center marking the autumn equinox. (Courtesy of AramcoWorld.)

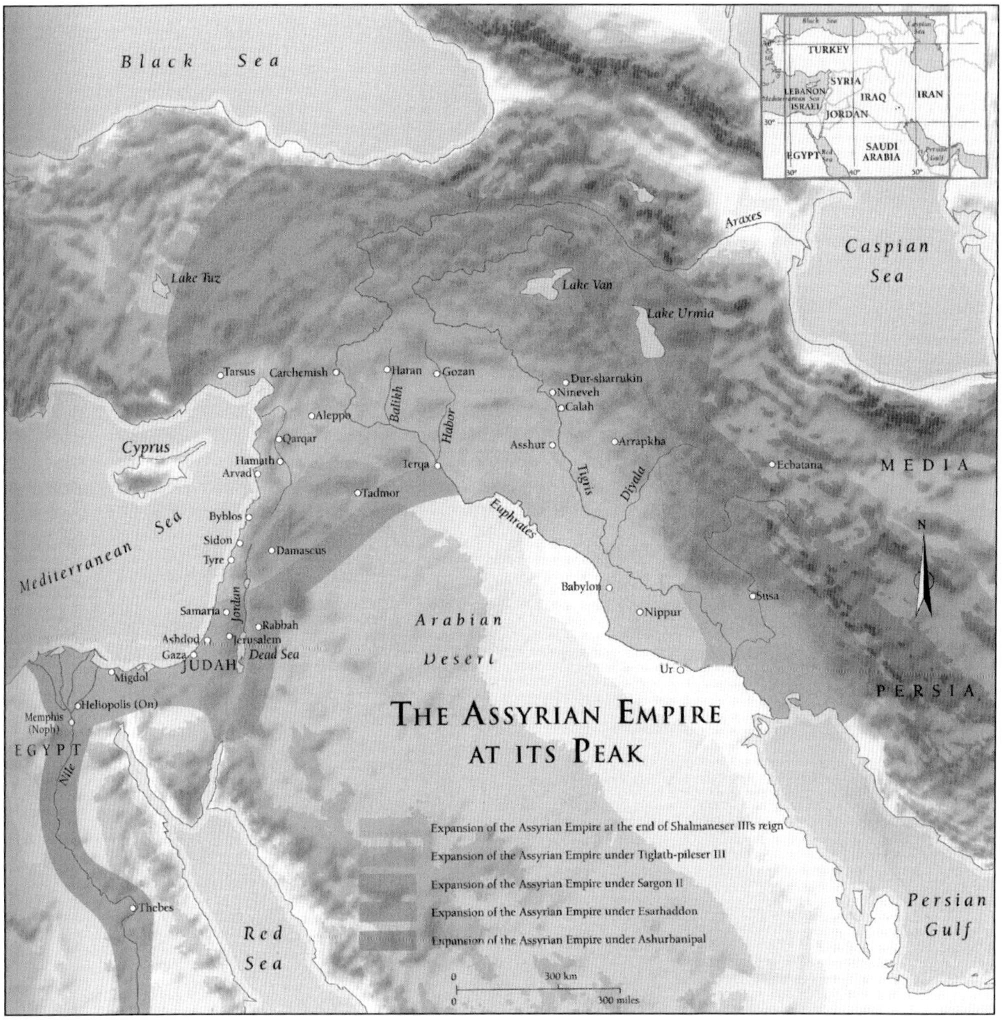

ANCIENT ASSYRIA VERSUS THE JEWISH PEOPLE. Four rulers of the Neo-Assyrian Empire significantly impacted the northern Kingdom of Israel and the Kingdom of Judah, leading to the exile of many Israelites and Jews. King Tiglath-Pileser III (ruled 745–727 BCE) conquered parts of Israel and deported its inhabitants to prevent rebellion. King Shalmaneser V (ruled 727–722 BCE) invaded Israel's capital, aiming to annex it into the empire. King Sargon II (ruled 722–705 BCE) completed the conquest, deporting Israelites and transforming Israel into "the Lost Tribes of Israel." Sennacherib (ruled 705–681 BCE) focused on Judah, capturing many cities but failing to take Jerusalem due to potential disease and negotiations. The outcome was devastating. The fall of the northern Kingdom of Israel scattered the 10 tribes across the Assyrian Empire, reducing their regional political and military powers. Subsequently, the Neo-Assyrian Empire's captivity also led to the Babylonian captivity of the Jews of the southern Kingdom of Judah decades later. Both empires' combined military strategies and expansionist policies reshaped the ancient Near East's political and cultural landscape, with significant historical consequences for the Israelite and the Jewish people. (Courtesy of Selim Matar.)

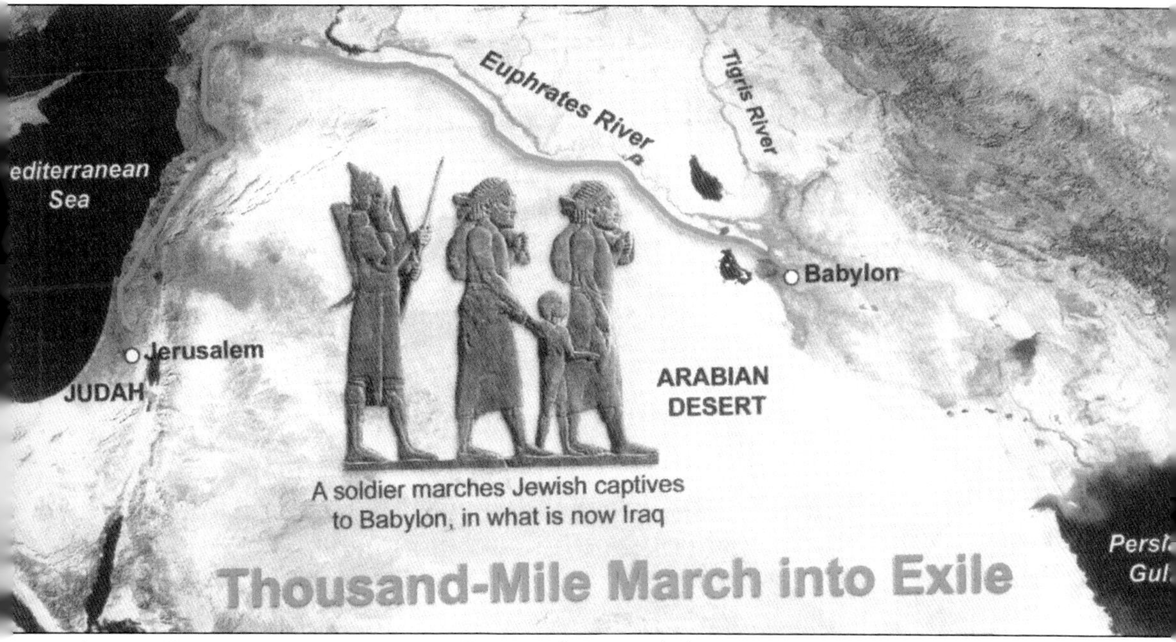

ANCIENT BABYLONIA VERSUS THE JEWISH PEOPLE. The Neo-Babylonian Empire began with Nabopolassar (ruled 626–605 BCE), who overthrew the Neo-Assyrian Empire through alliances with the Medes and others, establishing an empire that lasted 87 years (626–539 BCE). His son Nebuchadnezzar II (605–562 BCE) was its most influential ruler, expanding territories, securing control over the Levant, and playing a pivotal role in the conquest and captivity of Judah. After the Battle of Carchemish (605 BCE), Nebuchadnezzar II besieged Jerusalem for the first time in 597 BCE, when King Jehoiakim rebelled. Jehoiakim's death led to his son Jehoiachin's surrender and the exile of Judah's elite to Babylon. Zedekiah, Jehoiachin's uncle, was installed as a puppet king but rebelled, prompting a second siege in 586 BCE. This siege resulted in famine, the breach of Jerusalem, the destruction of Solomon's Temple, and the capture of Zedekiah, who was blinded and exiled. The aftermath saw Judah depopulated and governed by Babylonian officials. The Babylonian captivity lasted decades, profoundly impacting Jewish society, religion, and culture, marking the end of the First Temple period. In 539 BCE, Cyrus the Great of Persia defeated Babylon and issued an edict allowing Jews to return, beginning the Second Temple period. (Courtesy of Selim Matar.)

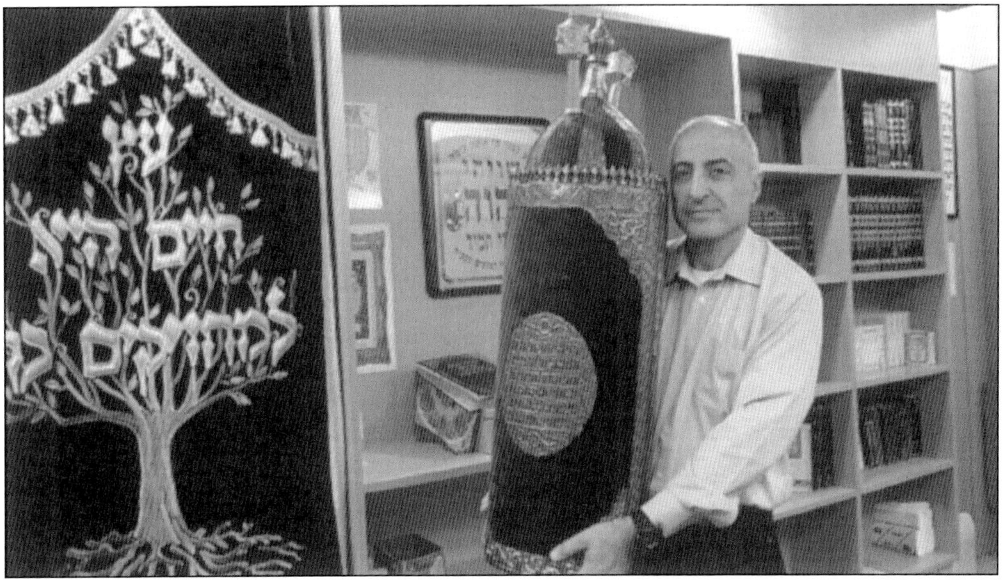

Any Lesson to Be Learned? The ancient Jewish people of Israel endured endless hardships: the brutality of many wars against them by the surrounding kingdoms, two major captivities, being killed, driven out of their homeland and away from their Holy Temple, their priests exiled and leaders imprisoned, their wealth taken away, and their lives destroyed. According to Rabbi Jonathan Sacks, the Jewish people's strength lies in their relationship with the Holy Torah. The ancient Jews took the Torah with them everywhere they had to leave. The Torah contains their history of becoming God's chosen people. As God's chosen people, the Torah shows them how to live by God's Laws and commandments, their obligation toward God, and how they should pray to him and celebrate his promise of their return to Israel. (Both, courtesy of Bishop Sarhad Jammo.)

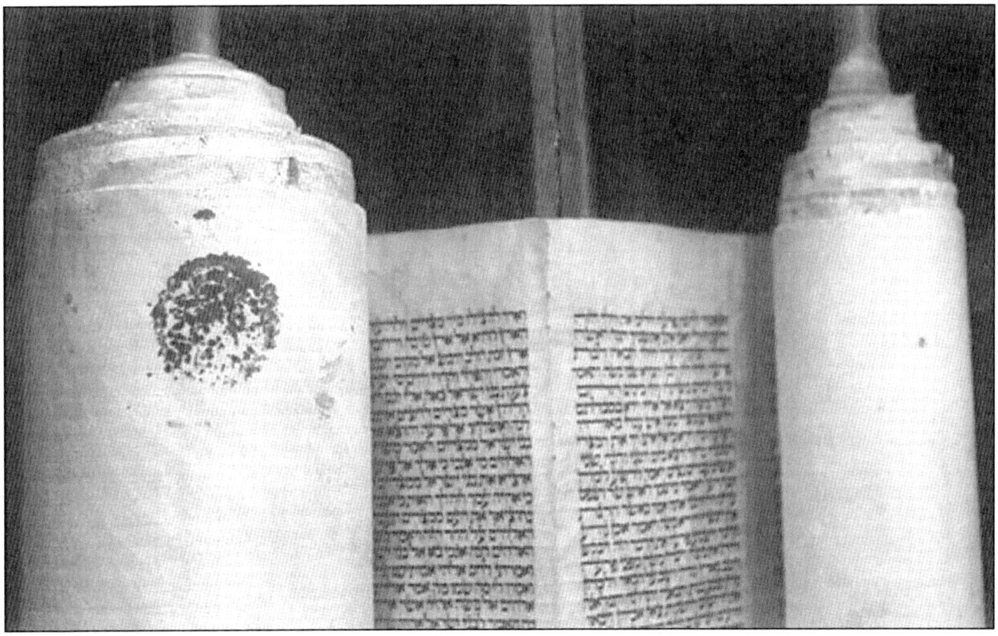

Two

Chaldeans from the Birth of Christ to the Conquest of Islam

The Chaldean Catholic Church, also historically known as the Church of the East, was founded in ancient Mesopotamia in the first century CE. Two major factors contributed to the spread of Christianity in Mesopotamia.

First, the Jewish presence in Mesopotamia increasingly flourished after the fall of Babylon in 539 BCE. Apart from Palestine, the largest Jewish population in the world lived in Mesopotamia. For nearly five centuries (242 BCE TO 226 CE), the Persian rulers granted the Mesopotamian Jews self-governing privileges called *Resh Galutha* or *Exilarchate*. They allowed a line of descendants from the House of King David to govern Jews in Mesopotamia and Iran. By the time of the birth of Jesus Christ, the Jews enjoyed a stable political climate and prosperous economic environment, especially in Babylonia.

Second, two Jewish rebellions against the Roman armies in Palestine occurred: the Jewish War (66–73 CE) and the Bar Kokhba Revolt (132–135 CE). The Romans utterly crushed both of them. As a result, the Jewish population paid a hefty price. In 70 CE, the Temple of Jerusalem was destroyed, looted, and burned down; scores of Jews were pushed into the Diaspora and scattered around the world or sold into slavery. Jews became forbidden to live in Jerusalem.

The contrast between the condition of Jews in Mesopotamia versus Palestine motivated the apostles of Jesus Christ to increase the number of missions from Jerusalem to Babylon, Edessa, Adiabene, and Persia to evangelize both Diaspora Jews and the natives of Mesopotamia, the descendants of the Babylonians, the Assyrians, and the Chaldeans. The Spirit of the Lord directed these missions because, by 120 CE, Christianity had spread out like a wildfire from the Euphrates to India. Moreover, by 224 CE, there were 24 Chaldean Church episcopal sees in Mesopotamia and Iran.

Throughout Chapters Two and Three, when using the terms "Nestorian Church," "Nestorians," or the "Church of the East," the two coauthors may have in mind mentioning the descendants of the ancient Church of the East, namely today's Chaldeans and the Assyrians. This note serves best when comments are made about the history of the Church of the East between the first and 19th centuries.

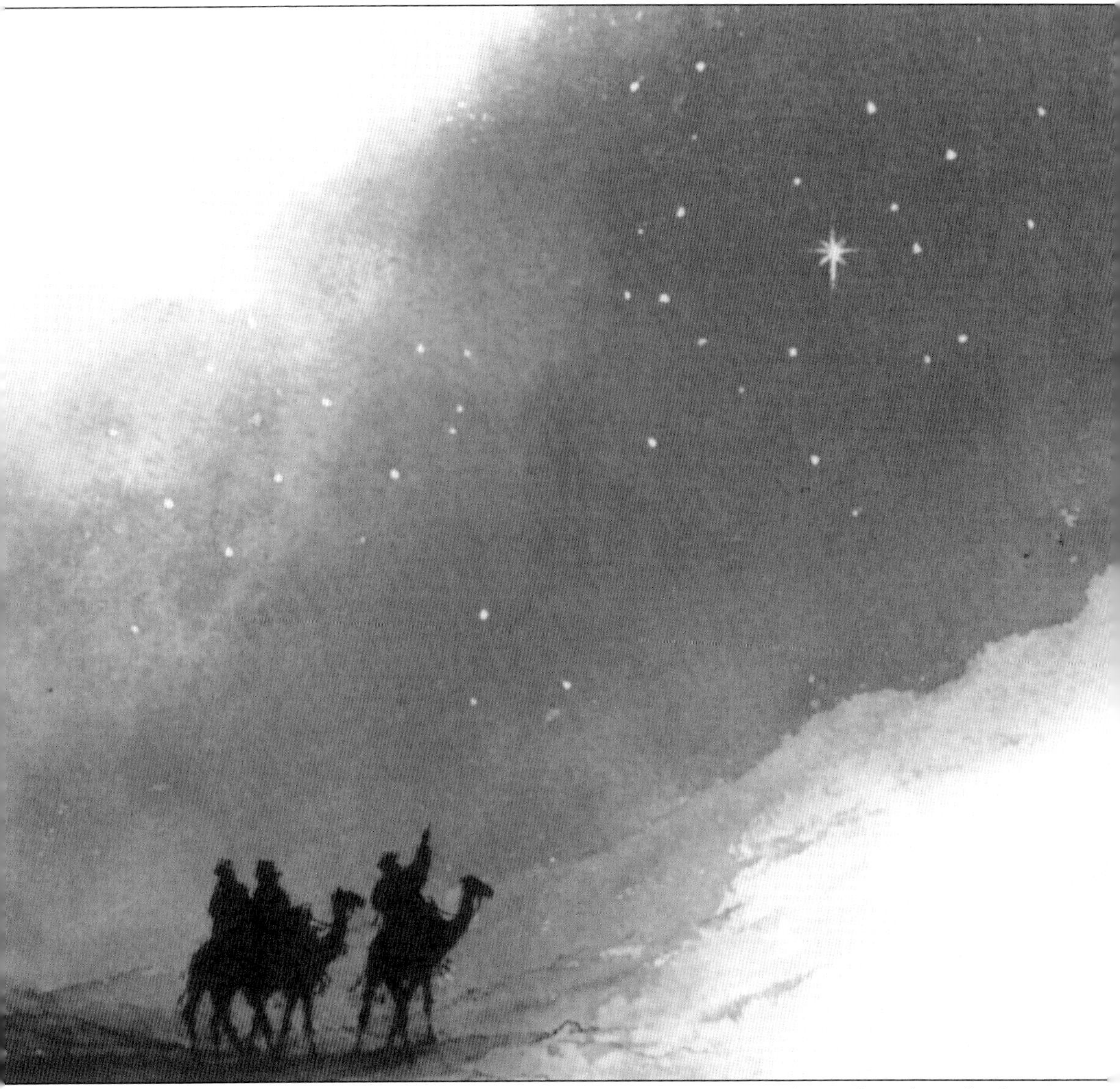

The Twelve Babylonian Wise Men. Saint Matthew's birth narrative of Jesus (Matthew 2) relates that the Jews learned from the mouth of "the Magi who came from the East" (Mesopotamia) about the birth of the Messiah. To honor the child, the Magi "bowed down and worshiped [Jesus, then] they opened their treasures and presented him with gifts of gold, frankincense, and myrrh." These Magi almost certainly journeyed from Babylon, the world epicenter of science and astronomy. They followed a miraculous guiding star from the East to Bethlehem, where they found the infant Jesus. The Chaldean Church tradition sets the number of Magi at 12, but Western Latin tradition sets their number at three, probably based on the three gifts of "gold, frankincense, and myrrh" presented to the infant Jesus. (Courtesy of Bryon Perry.)

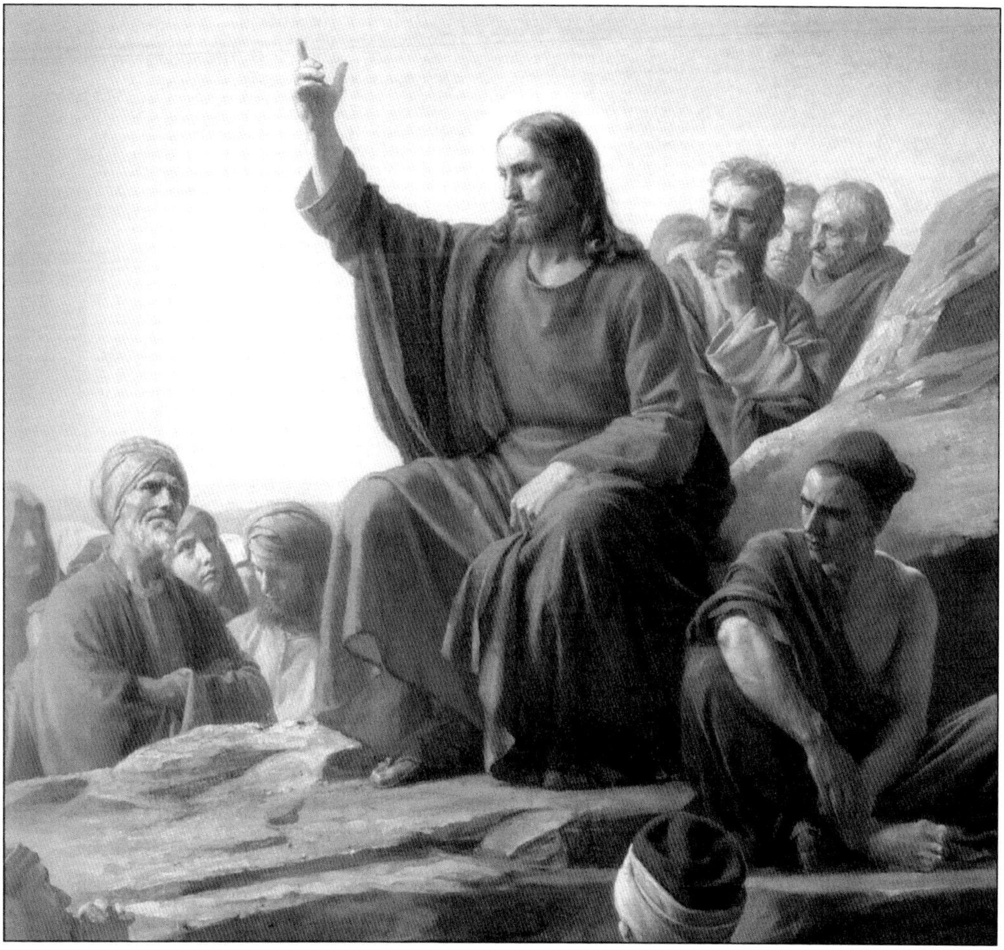

Christ's Kingdom and Divinity. One of Church of the East's most influential patriarchs, Timothy I, the Great (780–823 CE), wrote about the Magi journeying from Babylon to Bethlehem. William G. Young cites the text of Timothy in his book *Patriarch, Shah and Khaliph*, saying: "If Rome is accorded the first and the highest rank because of the Apostle Peter, how much more should Seleucia-Ctesiphon on account of Peter's Lord? If the first rank is due to [Peter] who confess Christ before all others and believe in him, then we Easterners were the ones to do so. We showed our faith openly in the persons of our Twelve Envoys (the Magi), who were guided by a star, and in the gifts which they offered to Christ. . . . Thirty years before all others, we, the Easterners, confessed Christ's kingdom and adored his divinity." (Courtesy of Bishop Bawai Soro.)

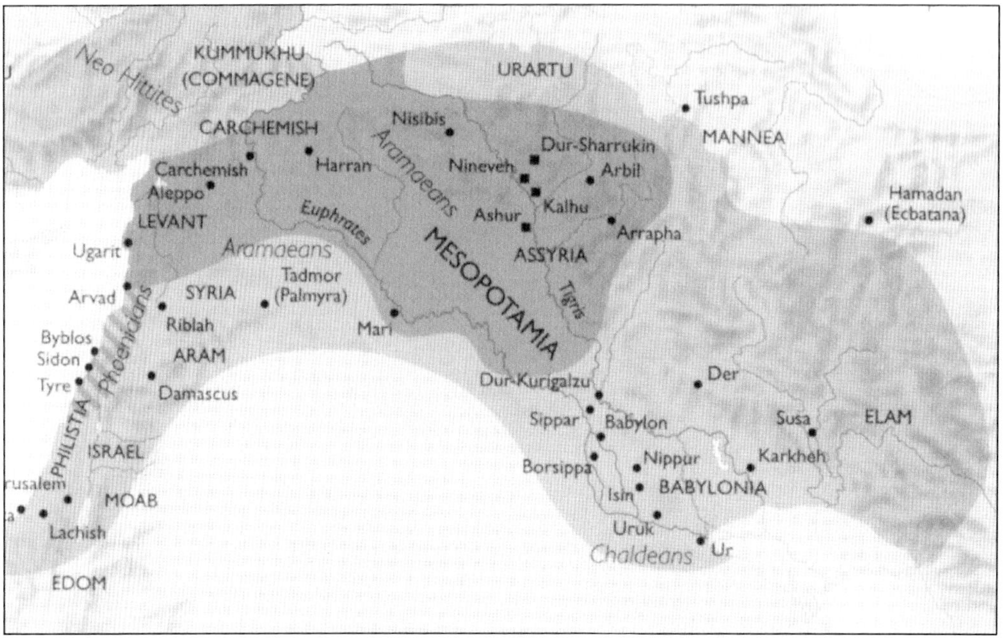

CHURCH FOUNDATION. The Chaldean Catholic Church was founded during the Apostolic Age. The book of Acts tells how the good news of the gospel was carried back to Mesopotamia by the "Parthians, the Medes, the Elamites and the inhabitants of Mesopotamia" who came to Jerusalem for the Feast of Pentecost (Acts 2:9). Then several missionaries were dispatched from Jerusalem to Mesopotamia: Saints Thomas, Thaddaeus (Jude), and Bartholomew (Nathanael) of the "Group of the Twelve," Addai of the "Group of the Seventy," and his disciple Mari. These missions established Christian communities first among Mesopotamian Jewry and then others. (Courtesy of Chaldean Catholic Diocese of Saint Thomas the Apostle.)

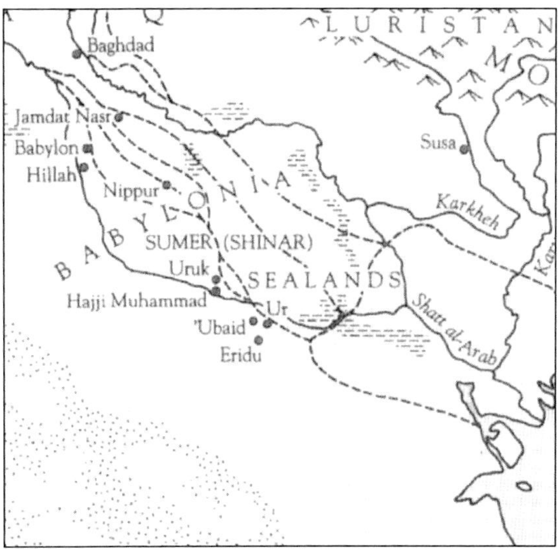

WHO'S WHO IN BABYLONIA. In the first century CE, Babylonia, part of the Parthian Empire, was a diverse cosmopolitan hub. Native Babylonians, descended from Sumerians, Akkadians, and Chaldeans, formed the majority. A thriving Jewish community grew after the sixth-century BCE Babylonian Exile. Other groups included Assyrians (post-612 BCE), Greeks (from 331 BCE), Persians (under Parthian rule), Arameans, Arabs, and Chinese and Indian immigrant workers. Babylonia excelled in astronomy, astrology, mathematics, medicine, law, literature, agriculture, and trade, maintaining its reputation as a vibrant multicultural region. (Courtesy of Chaldean Catholic Diocese of Saint Thomas the Apostle.)

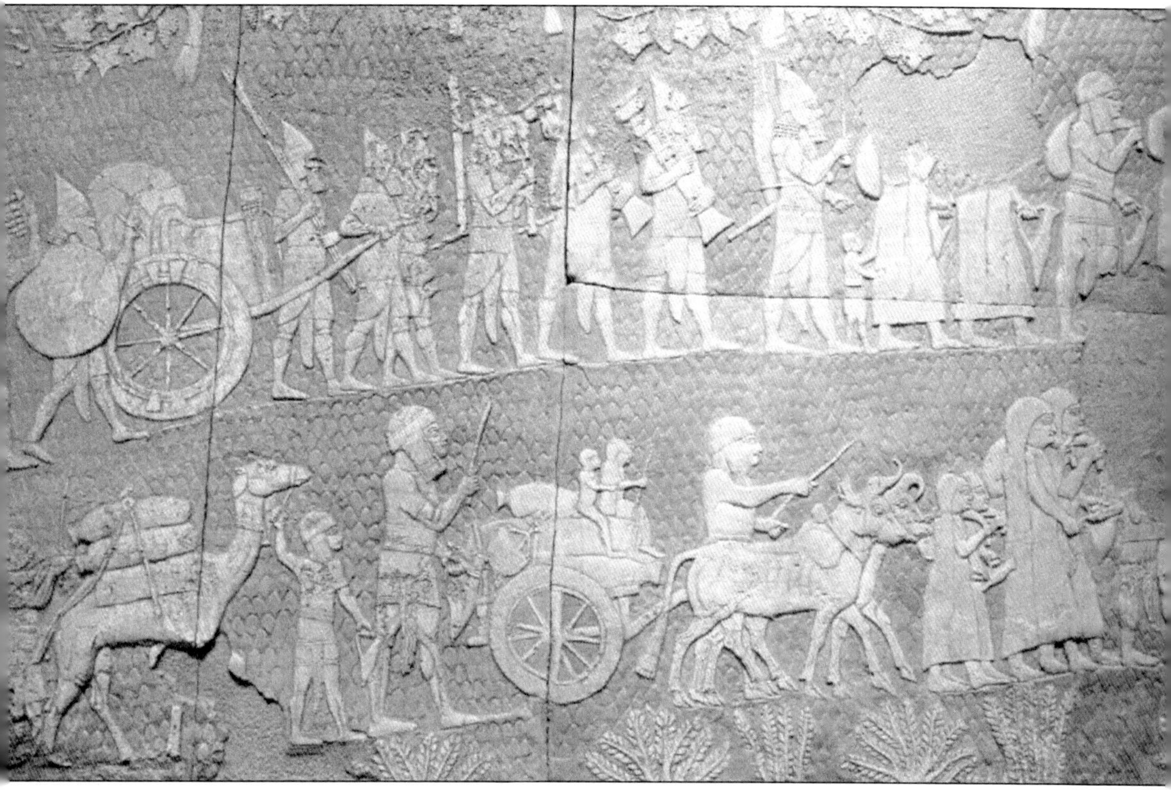

Importance of the Jews. In 539 BCE, Cyrus the Great of Persia defeated Babylon and issued an edict allowing Jews to return to their homeland Palestine (above is a depiction of Babylonia Jews returning home in the sixth century BCE). Nevertheless, many others decided to remain in Mesopotamia. These Jews eventually played a significant role in establishing the Church of the East, based on the following factors: (1) In Jerusalem, as Jews, the Apostles were persecuted and had to flee somewhere welcoming. Mesopotamia was ideal because it had the largest Jewish community that tolerated Jews. (2) The Jews of Mesopotamia turned the tragedy of the Assyrian and Babylonian exiles into triumph. They became strong allies with the Persian kings, who allowed them to self-govern, attain religious freedoms, establish four major religious academies, and build countless synagogues. (3) Before Christ, these Jews offered several Old Testament prophets who were either born or lived in Mesopotamia. The apostles who came from Jerusalem had a fertile ground because of the existing ethics and values of Jewish monotheism, which prepared Jews to accept Jesus as their messiah. (4) The apostles used the existing synagogues, their services, scriptures, prayers, and hymns to establish the Church of the East, as the most "Jewish-like" if compared to others. The Eucharistic Anaphora of Addai and Mari is a prime example, which was adapted from the Jewish "Prayer After Meal," Birkat HaMazon. (Courtesy Frédéric Soltan/Corbis via Getty Images.)

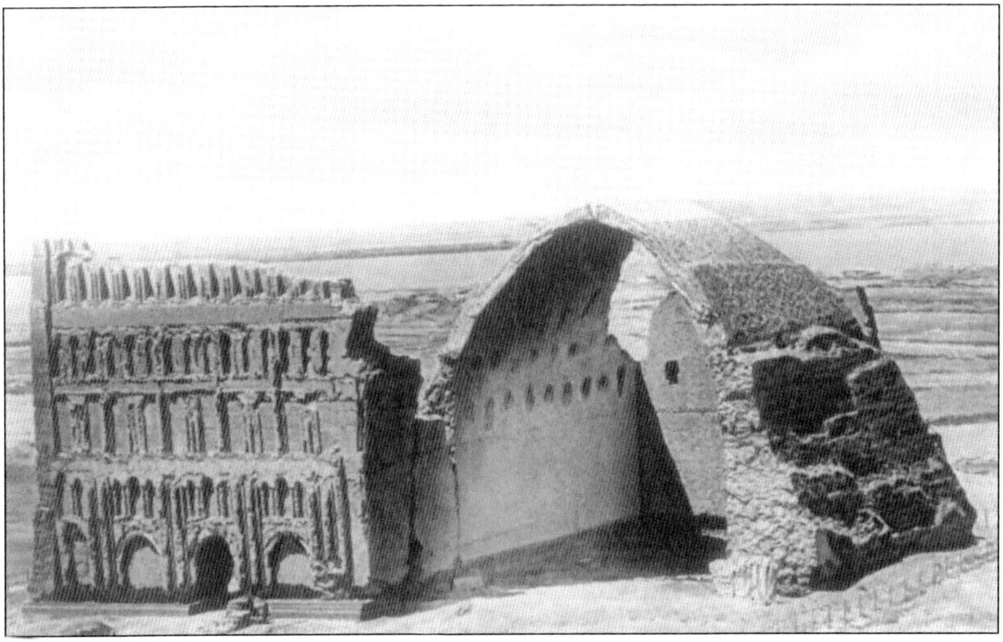

The Standing Arch of Seleucia. Papa bar Aggai (247–326 CE) became the first bishop of Seleucia-Ctesiphon in 305 CE and claimed centralized episcopal authority over the Church of the East. His goal was to organize the church and consolidate ecclesiastical power; thus he established his see as the head bishop (catholicos) of all Christians in the Sassanian Empire. Papa's actions sparked controversy, especially from the bishops of Arbil and Susa, who called a council in 315 CE to address his "innovative" approach and challenge his authority. (Courtesy of Jacob Bacall.)

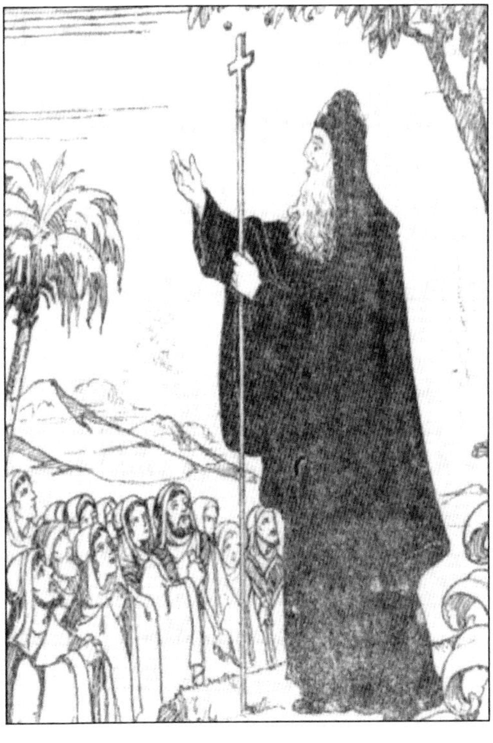

And the Winner Is . . . The events of the 315 CE synod, recorded in the *Synodicon Orientale*, reveal Papa bar Aggai's struggle for authority. Facing strong opposition, he was deposed as bishop of Seleucia-Ctesiphon and replaced by Shimun bar Sabba'e, a clergy member with royal connections. Papa appealed to the "Western Bishops" in the Roman Empire, who rejected Shimun's election and restored Papa to his position. This intervention solidified Papa's authority and marked a significant moment in East-West relations. Some scholars view Papa as the first link between Eastern and Western Christianity, while others see him as the catalyst for the Church of the East's independence. (Courtesy of Jacob Bacall.)

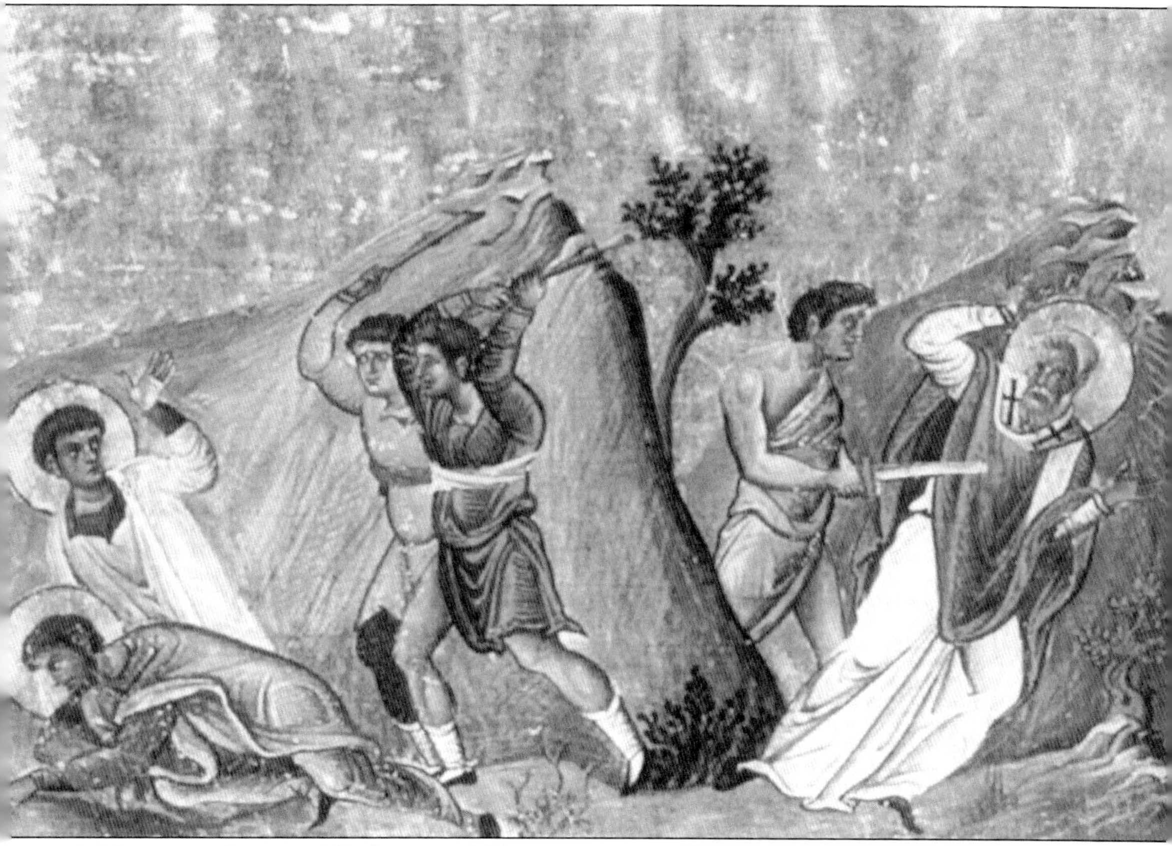

A Martyred Church. The history of Christianity in modern-day Iraq and Iran is marked by periodic persecutions, with the third and fourth centuries under Persian rule being particularly dark for the Chaldean Church. Sassanian King Ardashir I (180–242 CE) enforced Zoroastrianism as the state religion, viewing Christians as religious dissidents and potential collaborators with Rome. Emperor Shapur II (309–379 CE) intensified this persecution, especially after Rome's Emperor Constantine began to tolerate Christianity in 313 CE. In 339 CE, a decree by Shapur formalized the persecution of Christians, leading to executions, property confiscation, and church destruction. Key martyrs included Mar Shimun bar Sabba'e, the catholicos of Seleucia-Ctesiphon, executed in 344, along with numerous bishops, priests, and monks. This era forced the church into secrecy as Christians were viewed as traitors. Despite these hardships, the Chaldean Church endured, preserving its faith and traditions. (Courtesy of Father Michael Bazzi.)

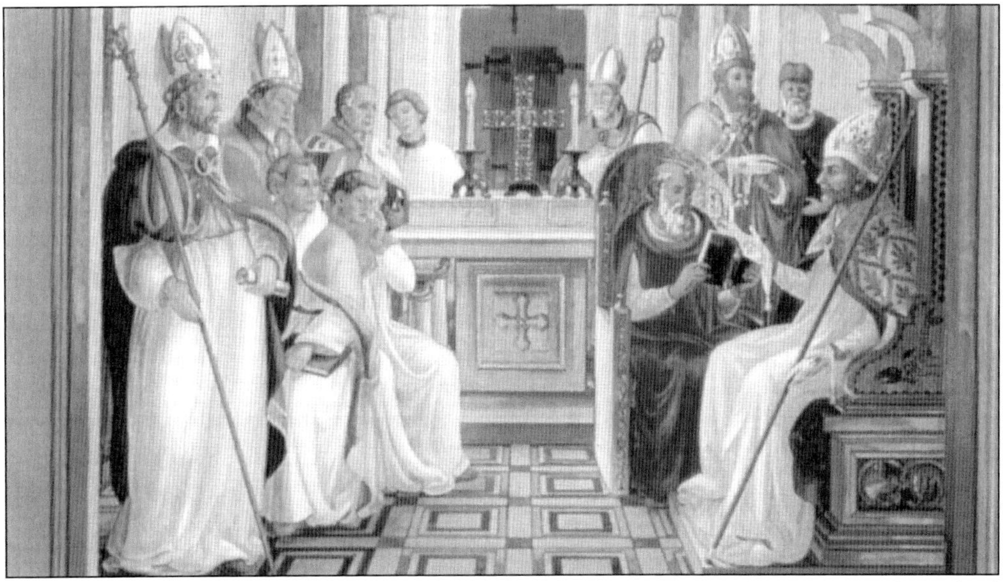

THE NESTORIAN CONTROVERSY. Nestorius, patriarch of Constantinople, emphasized a radical distinction between Christ's human and divine natures, leading to his condemnation at the Council of Ephesus in 431 CE. Though the Nestorian Controversy was mainly between the episcopal sees of Alexandria and Antioch, the Church of the East was affected because it declined to condemn Nestorius. Thus this controversy damaged the status and reputation of the Church of the East for centuries. (Courtesy of Bishop Sarhad Jammo.)

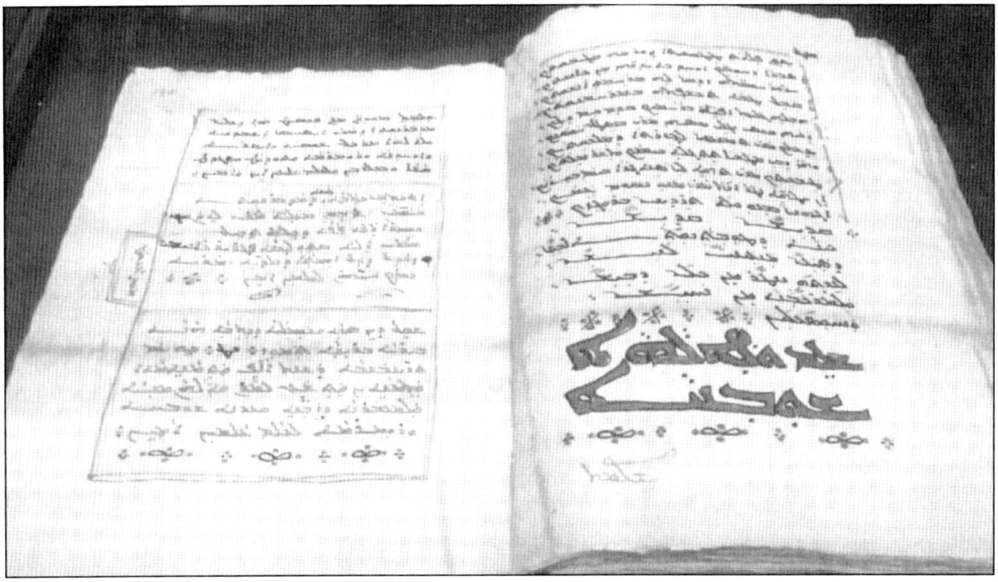

JESUS'S MOTHER TONGUE. Aramaic is a Semitic language closely related to Hebrew and Arabic. It was the language of Mesopotamia since the 10th century BCE and was widely used in trade, administration, and religion. In 539 BCE, Cyrus the Great liberated the Jews and gave them freedom to return to Jerusalem. They took Aramaic with them and made it the spoken language there, too. Jesus thought, spoke, and later preached in Aramaic. Aramaic is still spoken by Chaldeans, Assyrians, and Syriacs in Iraq, Iran, Syria, and diaspora communities. It holds a vital part in the Chaldean Church's identity and heritage. (Courtesy of Jacob Bacall.)

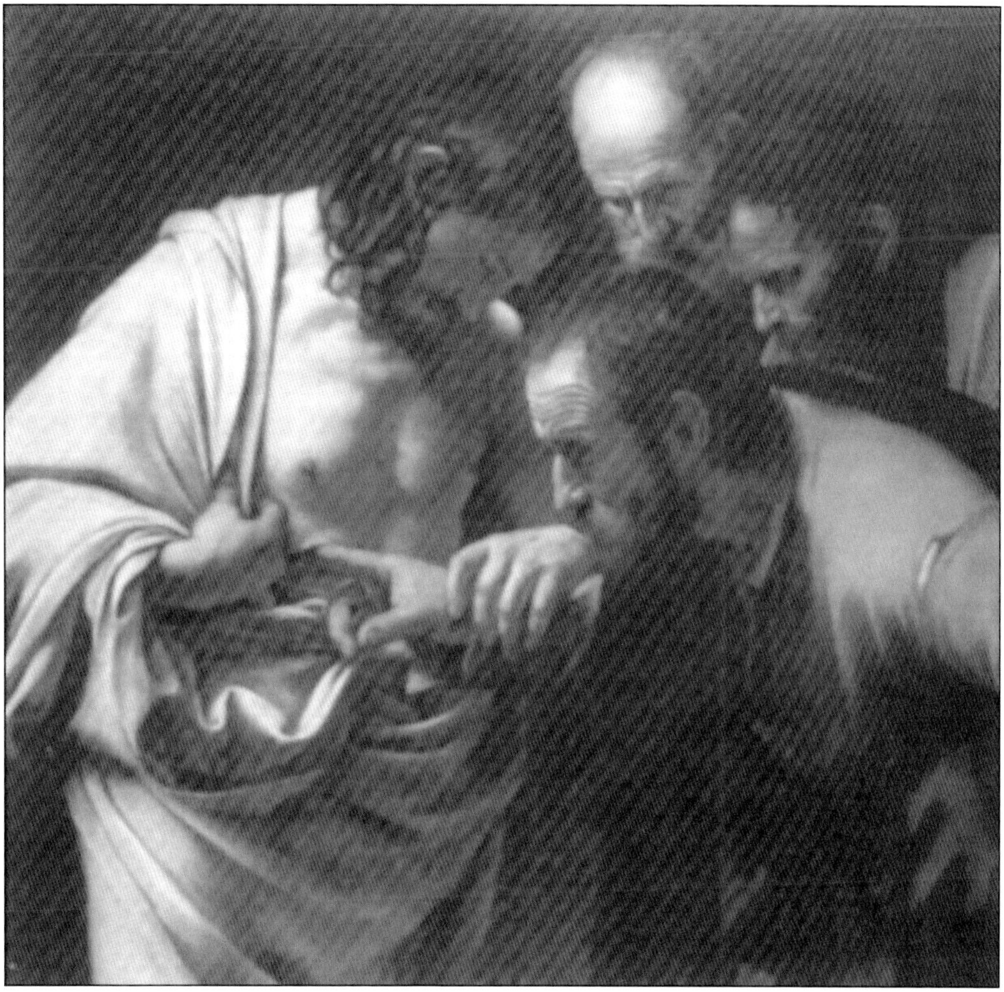

THE INCREDULITY OF SAINT THOMAS. The Saint Thomas Christians trace their origins to Saint Thomas the Apostle, who is believed to have arrived in India from Jerusalem after evangelizing in Mesopotamia in the first century CE. Initially under the jurisdiction of the Church of the East, they were overseen by metropolitans appointed by the Chaldean patriarch. The archdeacon, an indigenous Indian clergyman, acted as an intermediary between local Christians and bishops. They followed the Chaldean Rite, using Aramaic in services, and adopted the Anaphora of Addai and Mari. The Portuguese arrival in the 16th century led to the Synod of Diamper in 1599, enforcing Latinization and severing ties with the Chaldean Church in Mesopotamia. This caused divisions, with some groups reconnecting with the Assyrian Church of the East, while others aligned with the Syriac Orthodox or Roman Catholic Churches. Today, Saint Thomas Christians are divided into denominations such as the Syro-Malabar Catholic Church, Malankara Orthodox and Catholic Churches, and Jacobite Syrian Christian Church. (Courtesy of Bryon Perry.)

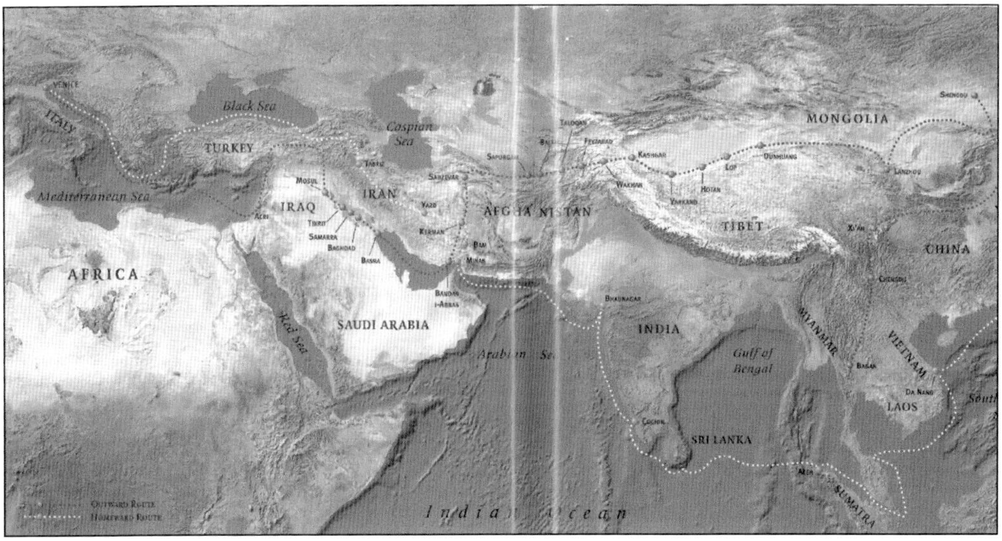

Church of the East in China. The relationship between the Church of the East and the Nestorian Christians in China is a fascinating chapter in the church's history in Asia. Marked by significant missionary activities, these missions date back to the seventh century along the trade routes of Central Asia. Patriarchs Ishoyahb II (620–644 CE) and Ishoyahb III (649–659 CE) had significant roles in this evangelization. During their tenures, missions to China were actively promoted, leading to the arrival of a mission led by a priest named Alopen. In 635 CE, Alopen reached the Tang dynasty capital of Chang'an (modern-day Xi'an) during the reign of Emperor Taizong. In 781 CE, a monument known as the Nestorian Stele was erected in Chang'an. This stele, inscribed in both Chinese and Aramaic, commemorates the arrival of Christianity in China and provides valuable insights into the early presence and activities of the Nestorian Christians in the region. Rediscovering the Nestorian Stele in the 17th century brought renewed attention to this early chapter of Christianity in the Far East. (Both, courtesy of Chaldean Catholic Diocese of Saint Thomas the Apostle.)

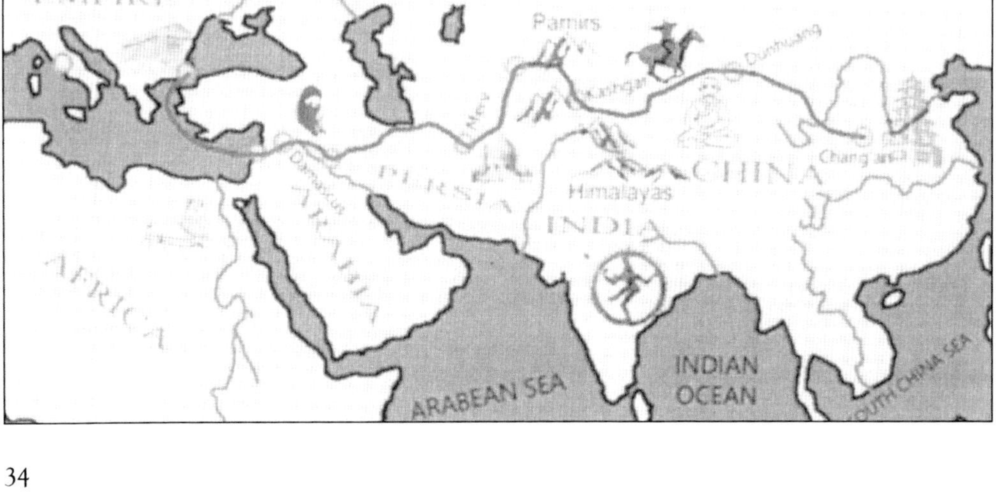

Three

Chaldeans after the Rise of Islam

Islam came to Mesopotamia approximately 1,000 years after the fall of Babylon. During the interim, Mesopotamia experienced the rule of several empires: the Achaemenid Empire (c. 539–330 BCE); the Seleucid Empire, established by Alexander the Great (312–63 BCE); the Parthian Empire (247 BCE–224 CE); and finally, the Sassanian Empire (224–651 CE). In 636 CE, the Battle of Al-Qadisiyya marked a pivotal moment when the newly established Islamic state achieved a decisive victory over the Sassanian Empire, leading to the Islamic conquest of Mesopotamia and Persia.

Chapter Three will explore how the Islamic Age influenced the history of Mesopotamia and its indigenous Chaldean and Assyrian peoples in the Church of the East from the seventh to the 21st centuries. Despite enduring rigorous periods and bloody conflicts, the Church of the East persisted. It also experienced scientific advancements and expanded to the Far East, testifying to its faithfulness and love for the Lord Jesus Christ. The following outlines significant events and key Islamic caliphates and dynasties that ruled Mesopotamia from the seventh century until the abolition of the Ottoman Empire in early 20th century:

1. The founding of Islam (610–632 CE) started after Islam's Prophet Muhammad received messages as revelation and began preaching to the Arabs in Mecca and Medina (present-day Saudi Arabia).

2. The Al-Rashidun Caliphate (632–661 CE) first ruled the early Muslim state from Medina and then moved to Kufa (present-day Iraq).

3. The Umayyad Caliphate (661–750 CE) moved the capital to Damascus and expanded the empire from Spain in the west to the Indus River in the east.

4. The Abbasid Caliphate (750–1258 CE) overthrew the Umayyads and moved the capital to Baghdad. This caliphate's power waned after the Mongol sack of Baghdad in 1258, but it continued as a spiritual authority until 1517.

5. The Mongolian, Turkoman, and Iranian Periods (1258–1534 CE) are considered Mesopotamia's "Dark Age." Control shifted to the Mongolian, Turkoman, and Iranian rulers.

6. The Ottoman Caliphate (1517–1924 CE) claimed power in Mesopotamia after defeating the Mamluk Sultanate and controlling the Muslim holy cities of Mecca and Medina. It established the empire's capital in Constantinople (present-day Istanbul) and continued ruling until Mustafa Kemal Atatürk, the founder of modern Turkey, formally abolished the Ottoman Empire in 1924.

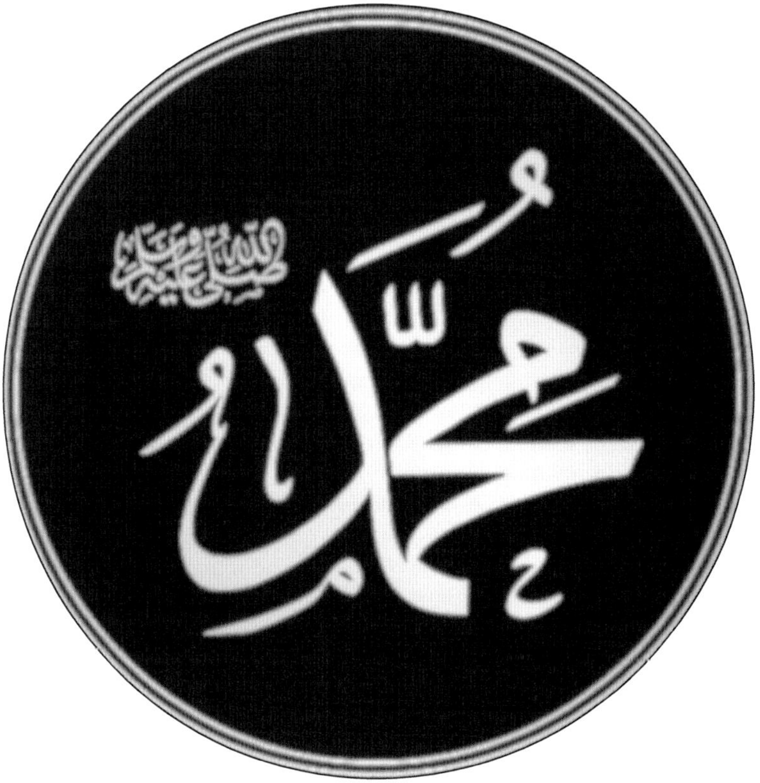

The Prophet and His "Guided" Caliphs. Islam's prophet, Muhammad, born in Mecca in 570 CE, began receiving divine revelations in 610 CE, which were later compiled into the Quran, which means in Aramaic the "reading book." His first followers included his wife, Khadijah, friend Abu Bakr, his cousin Ali, and adopted son Zayd. By 613 CE, his monotheistic message and calls for social justice faced severe opposition from the Quraysh tribe but later gained followers, especially from lower social classes and also some prominent figures. In 615 CE, Prophet Muhamad and his followers sought refuge by the Christian King of Ethiopia. In 622 CE, they migrated to Medina, marking the start of the Islamic lunar calendar (Al-Hijra) and establishing a unified Muslim community. After the death of Muhammad, in 632 CE, four successors—Abu Bakr, Umar ibn al-Khattab, Uthman ibn Affan, and Ali ibn Abi Talib—were appointed to rule from 632 to 661 CE. These leaders are collectively known as the Al-Rashidun Caliphate, or "the Rightly Guided Caliphs." During this period, Islam expanded beyond the Arabian Peninsula, to all directions, thereby transforming itself into a political entity that would evolve into a multiethnic, transnational empire. (Courtesy of Selim Matar.)

From Persecution to Peace. The Prophet Muhammad and his successors, the caliphs, granted Jews and Christians protection through *dhimmi* status, which provided limited religious freedom in exchange for loyalty to the Islamic state and payment of the *jizya* tax. The Nestorian patriarch Ishoyahb II of Gadala (628–645 CE), pictured here, was granted a "Charter of Protection" by Islam's Prophet Muhammad. (Courtesy of Patriarch Louis Sako.)

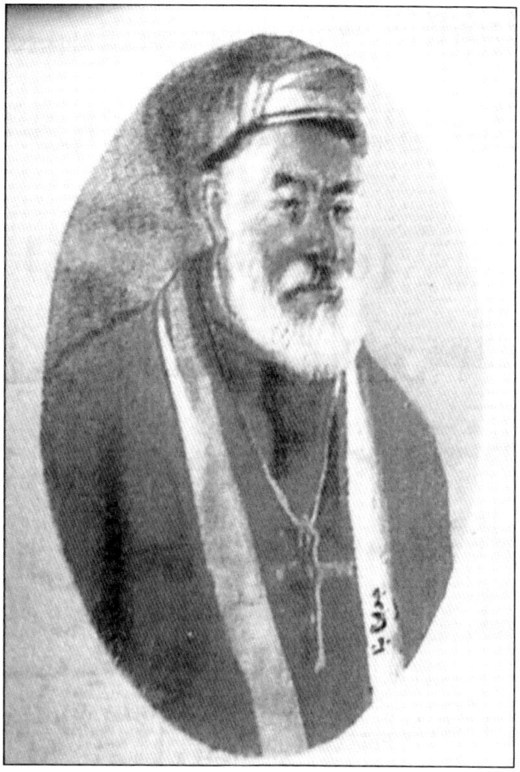

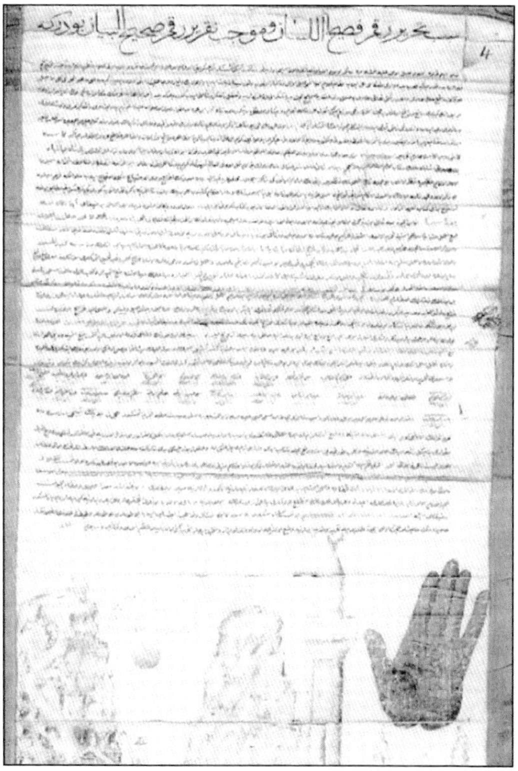

But Peace Has a Price. The Prophet of Islam, Muhammad, and his successors, the caliphs, initially granted Jews and Christians distinct forms of protection that were not afforded to other non-Muslims. This protection status, called al-dhimmi, was a legal framework that was consistently applied throughout the Rashidun, Umayyad, and Abbasid Caliphates and later with some modification by the Ottoman Empire. While the implementation of dhimmi status varied under different caliphs, its fundamental principles remained constant: granting Jews and Christians protection and limited freedom of worship in exchange for their loyalty to the Islamic State and the excessive payments of the jizya tax. Pictured here is the Covenant of the Prophet Mohammad with Christians. (Courtesy of Dr. Mohammed M. Adhami.)

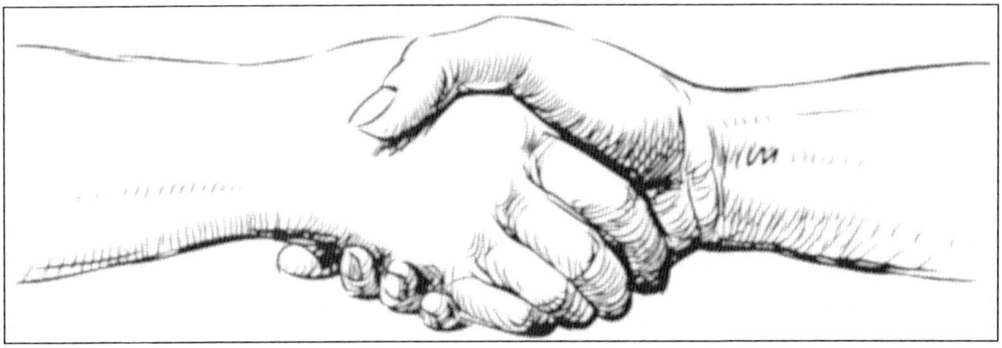

Charter of Protection: Its Effects. These covenants and charters were protection that was premised on the idea that the Islamic state allowed Christians and Jews, who are the "People of the Book" (the Bible), to coexist within the Islamic state if they paid the jizya (a tax levied on non-Muslims) and adhered to specific regulations, including accepting a subordinate social and economic status. The protection was a package deal; some things were good, others were bad, and a few were ugly. (Courtesy of Dr. Mohammed M. Adhami.)

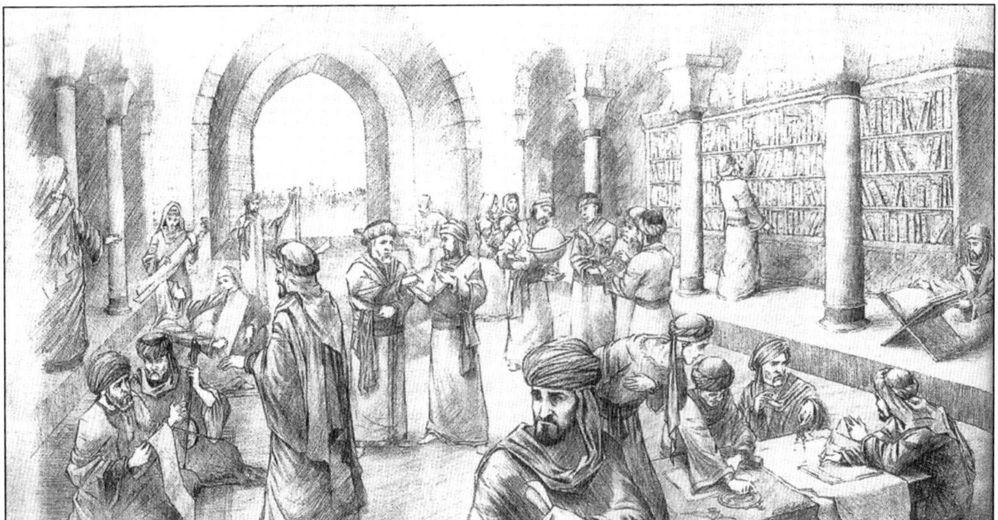

The Good. Under the dhimmi status during the Rashidun Caliphate, Jews and Christians enjoyed freedom of worship, followed their spiritual practices, and maintained their places of worship without fear of persecution. Church leaders had legal autonomy over their followers. The Islamic state exempted them from military service and protected these communities, preventing violence against them and fostering coexistence. In return, Nestorian Christians contributed significantly to Islam. They excelled in medicine, with families like the Bukhtishu serving as court doctors, and played a key role in the translation movement, preserving ancient Greek knowledge to the Arab Muslims. They also contributed to education, interfaith dialogue, and the arts. (Courtesy of AramcoWorld.)

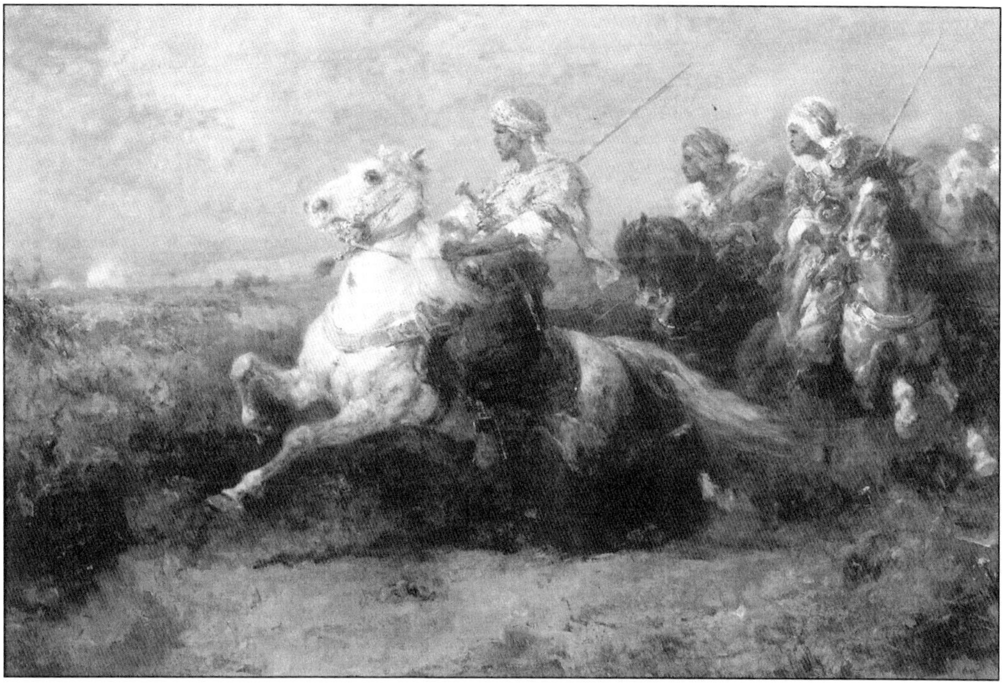

THE BAD. The so-called "protection" agreements led to severe consequences for Christians and Jews. While dhimmi status offered some protections, it came with heavy taxes. The *zakat*, a mandatory almsgiving, was one of the Five Pillars of Islam, set at a fixed rate of 2.5 percent of a Muslim's accumulated wealth annually. In contrast, the jizya was much higher for non-Muslims, starting at 10 percent, but it eventually could be raised to 50 percent, often devastating Christian families and communities. These taxes, along with numerous restrictions on religious and social freedoms, gradually became an unbearable burden, thus reducing Christian and Jewish populations in Persia and Mesopotamia as they began converting to Islam as a remedy. (Courtesy of Selim Matar.)

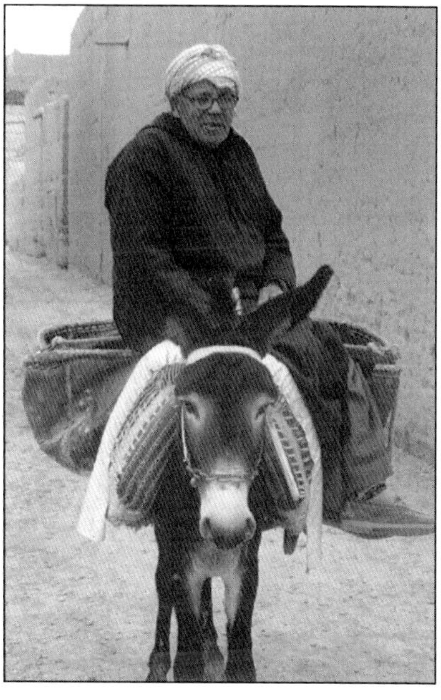

AND THE UGLY. When Islam entered Mesopotamia in the early seventh century, the population was around six million. Christians (mainly "Nestorians" and "Jacobite" were over 50 percent) and Jews (150,000) faced severe restrictions in exchange for protection. Christians were prohibited from displaying crosses, holding processions, or building churches and were treated as lower-class citizens. They had to wear clothing with distinctive colors, could not ride horses (only donkeys, sideways, as a sign of humiliation), and were Jizya-taxed heavily. Today, after 1,400 years, Iraq's Jewish community has completely vanished, and Christians now constitute less than 0.5% of the 46 million Iraqis. (Courtesy of Jann Huizenga via iStock.)

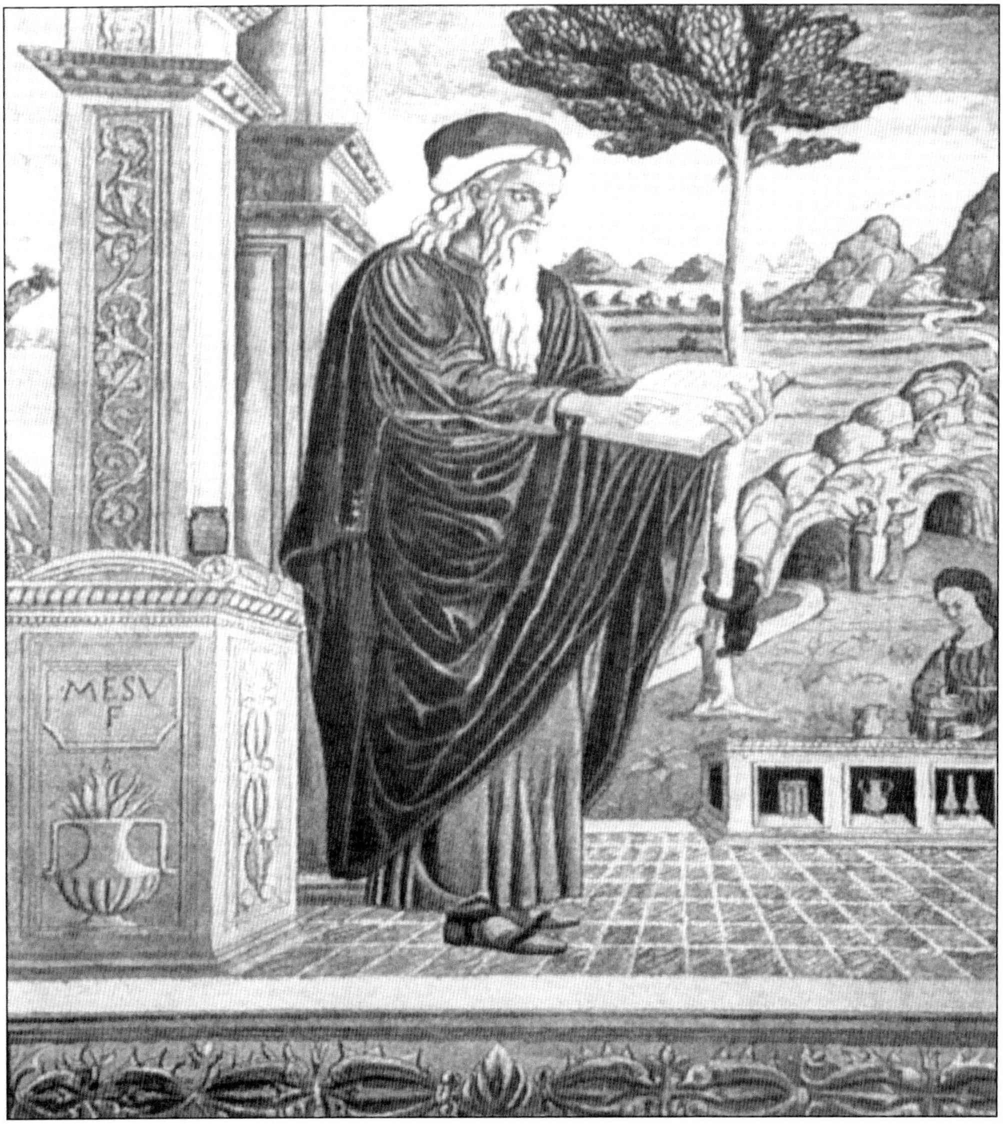

THE GOLDEN AGE OF ISLAM. The Abbasid Caliphate (750–1258) took a pragmatic approach toward Christians, granting them dhimmi status with both privileges and limitations. Due to their intellectual and medical contributions, Christians were included in civic roles. Christian scholars like Hunayn ibn Ishaq played a key part in translating Greek texts into Arabic, enriching the Islamic Golden Age. The Bayt Al-Hikmah (House of Wisdom) in Baghdad became a center of intellectual collaboration, fostering advancements in mathematics, astronomy, medicine, and philosophy during this period. (Courtesy of Patriarch Louis Sako.)

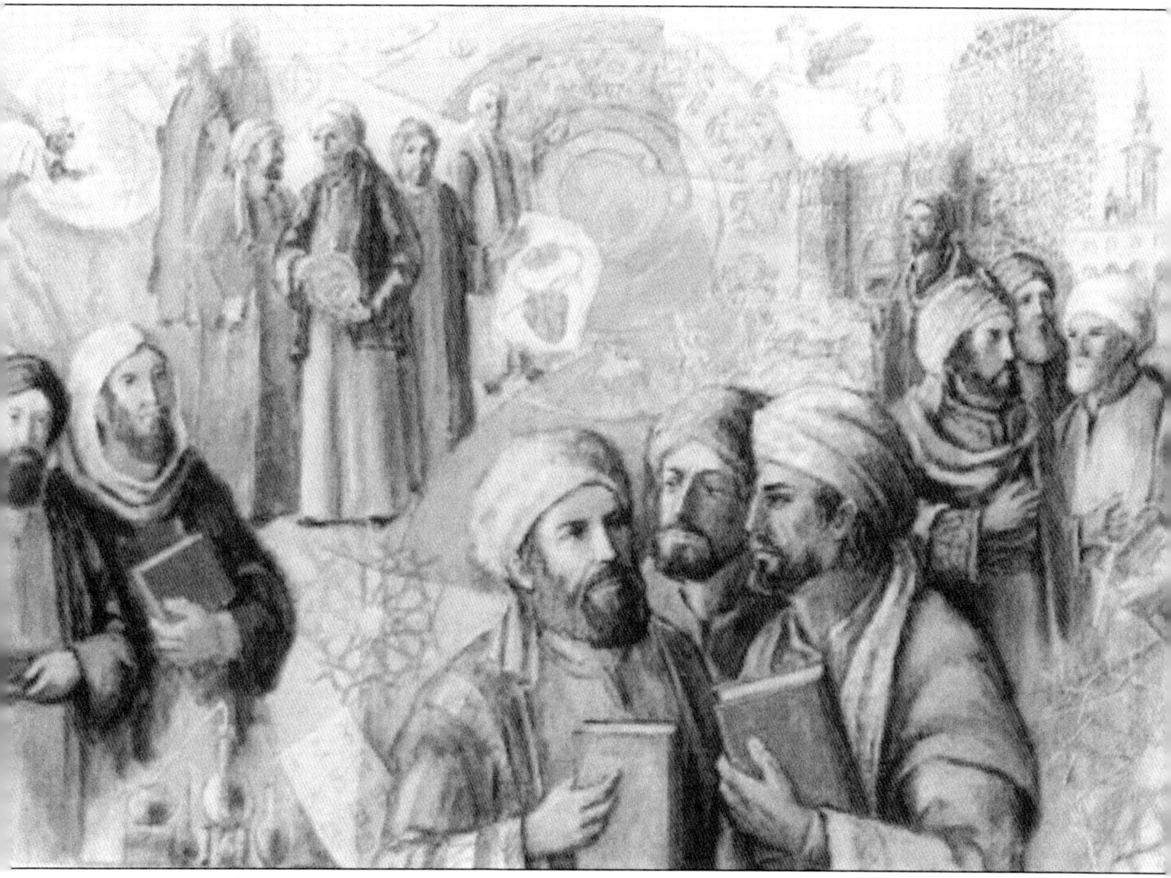

A Good Soul. Hunayn ibn Ishaq was a prominent ninth-century Nestorian physician and translator during the Islamic Golden Age. Caliph Al-Ma'mun paid him 500 dinars monthly and gold equal to the weight of translated books. Hunayn translated key scientific and philosophical texts from Greek and Syriac into Arabic, including the works of Galen, Hippocrates, Plato, and Aristotle, impacting medicine, philosophy, and science. Once, Hunayn refused to poison an enemy of his caliph. When he was threatened with death, he declared, "I have skills only in what is beneficial and have studied nothing else. My religion commands me to do good and my profession orders me to heal." (Courtesy of Dr. Mohammed M. Adhami.)

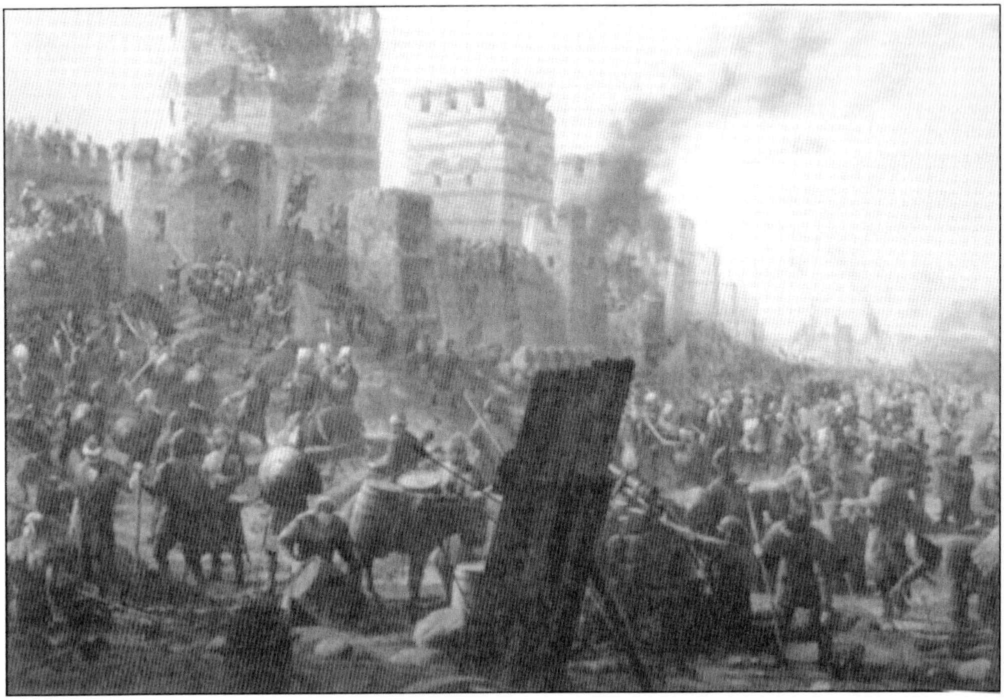

THE RED AND BLACK RIVER. After their invasion in the 13th century, the Mongols initially granted Christians in Mesopotamia religious freedom. After Ghazan Khan's (1295–1304 CE) conversion to Islam, Christian privileges were revoked, properties were seized, and forced conversions to Islam ensued. Subsequent Mongol rulers, especially Timur Lang (1370–1405 CE), began mass killings, destruction of churches, and dismantling of Christian communities. A folkloric chant in history books captures this turmoil as follows: "The Tigris ran black with ink, and red with blood anew, as Mongol fury cast both knowledge and life to its turbulent view." By the end, Christianity in Mesopotamia was nearly eradicated, yet faith and fidelity to Christ always survived. (Courtesy of Dr. Mohammed M. Adhami.)

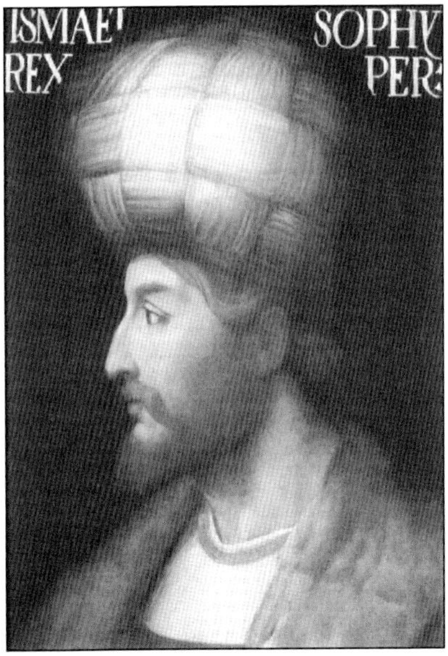

MORE STORMS AHEAD. During the 14th and 15th centuries, two Turkoman factions, the Black Sheep and the White Sheep, ruled over Western Iran and Mesopotamia. The Safavid dynasty succeeded them, ruling from 1501 to 1736. All three of these groups subjected Christians more often than not to periods of persecution. Under Safavid rule, furthermore, the pressure to convert to Islam increased tremendously, leading to a gradual but consistent decrease in the Christian population in Mesopotamia. (Courtesy of Dr. Mohammed M. Adhami.)

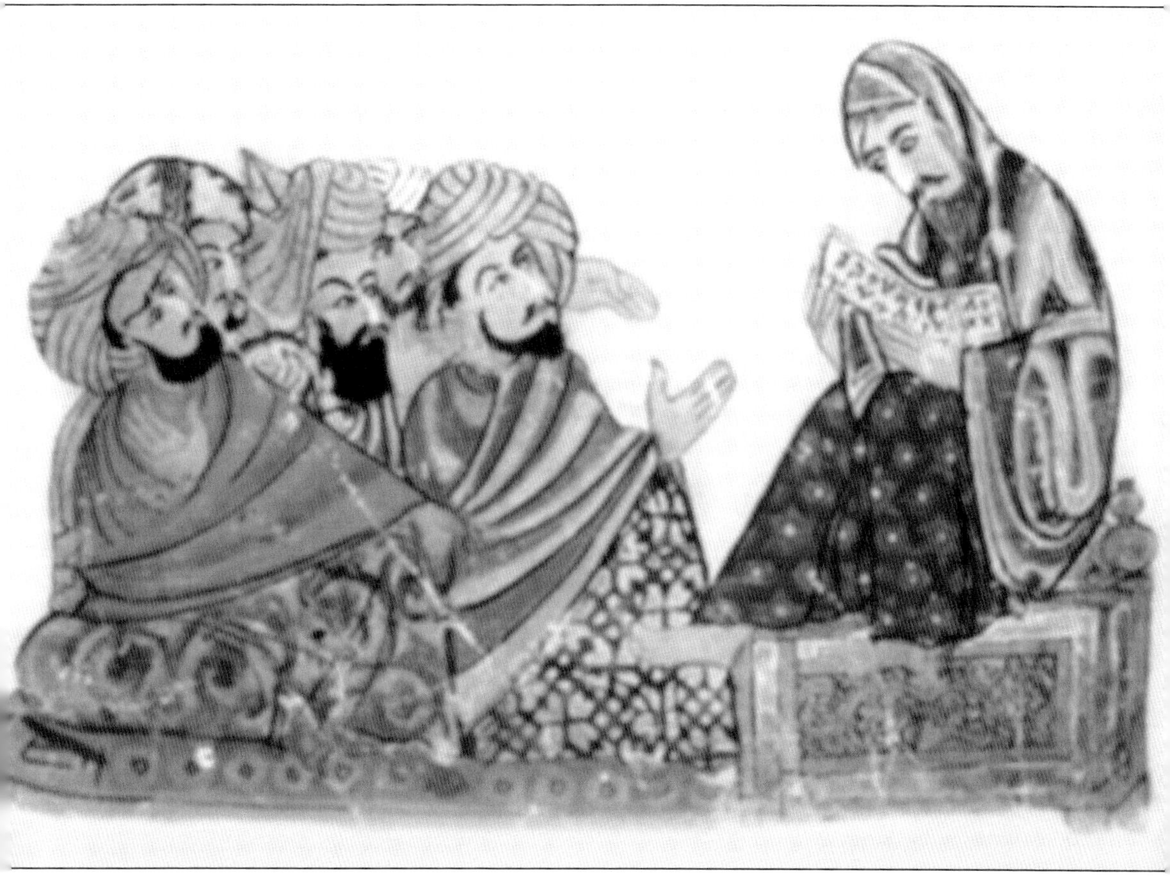

Linking Civilizations Together. In the third century, the Church of the East's scholars translated ancient Greek philosophical and scientific texts into Syriac, and later into Arabic, in the Christian schools of Edessa, Nisibis, and Jundishapur. In the eighth century, the same movement began at Bayt al-Hikmah and the School of Baghdad, advancing medicine, mathematics, and philosophy. From the eighth to the 15th centuries, Muslims ruled Spain. There, Greek philosophy and sciences were reintroduced to Western scholars like Thomas Aquinas, who led the European Renaissance in the 13th century. Thanks to the Church of the East fathers, Greek, Muslim, and European civilizations were linked together. By bringing ancient knowledge to Spain, they ignited Western civilization. Here a Christian monk mentors Muslim students. (Courtesy of Dr. Mohammed M. Adhami.)

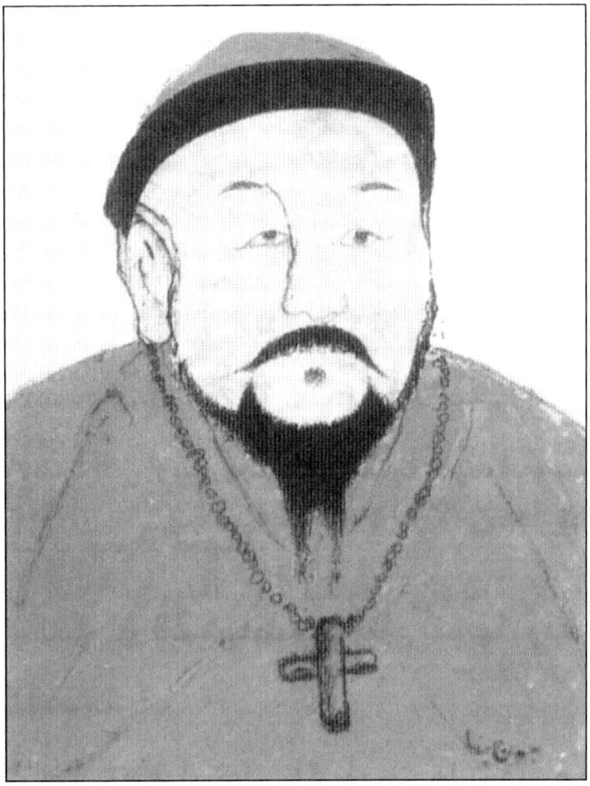

LEFT FOR DESPAIR. After the devastating Mongolian invasion and the Turkoman and Iranian rules, the Church of the East faced profound despair. Christian communities were decimated and ecclesiastical structures weakened. Clergy and laity confronted upheaval, forced conversions, and oppressive policies. Yet they remained motivated to preserve their faith, culture, and identity against all these odds. The Nestorians began to look to the West for protection and alliances. This was their Christian "common sense." They strived for solidarity, always exercising the Christian virtue of hope. (Courtesy of Patriarch Louis Sako.)

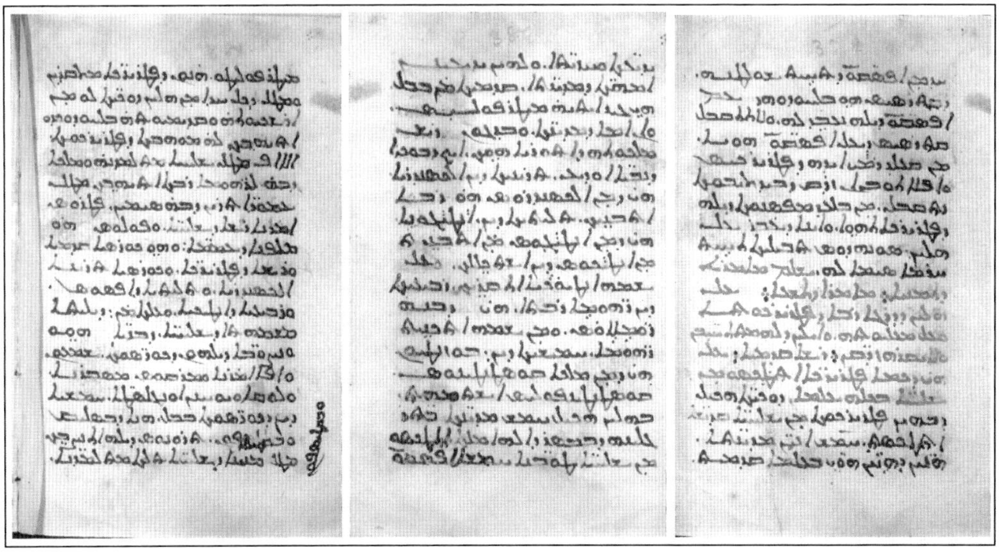

LIGHT AT THE END OF THE TUNNEL. Metropolitan Abdisho of Soba, a uniquely excellent 14th-century Nestorian theologian, linguist, and canonist, wrote his renowned *Nomocanon*. In this theological and canonical work, Abdisho set the foundation for the Church of the East's unity with Rome by arguing in favor of the modern concept of ecumenism. Abdisho advocated for the primacy of Saint Peter as the "Head of the Apostles" and the central standing of the city of Rome as the "First See and the Head of All the Patriarchates," preceding Alexandria, Ephesus, Antioch, and Babylon in preeminence. (Courtesy of Bishop Bawai Soro.)

The Martyr of Union. Known for his deep spirituality and leadership qualities, Youhanan Sulaqa was a Chaldean monk from the Rabban Hormizd Monastery in Alqosh, Mosul, Iraq. Nearly 300 years after the devastating Mongolian destruction of Mesopotamian Christianity, Sulaqa was elected patriarch in 1552 to unite the Church by restoring communion with Rome. In 1553, Sulaqa was consecrated as patriarch by Pope Julius III in Rome, thus initiating a Catholic lineage of patriarchs in Mesopotamia. These efforts faced strong opposition, leading to Sulaqa's execution in 1555, making him a martyr for unity. (Courtesy of Patriarch Louis Sako.)

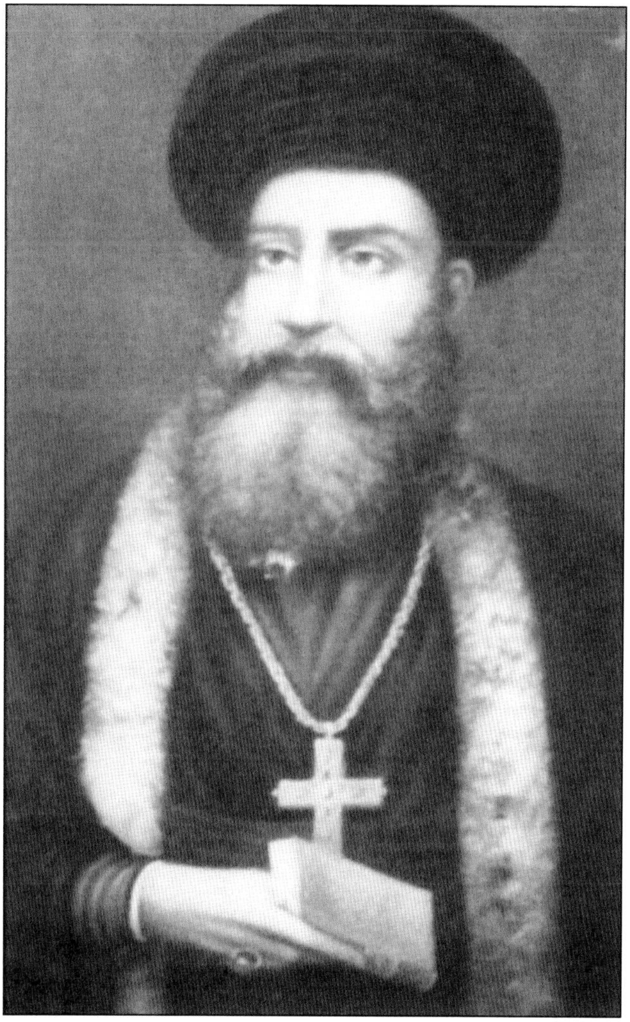

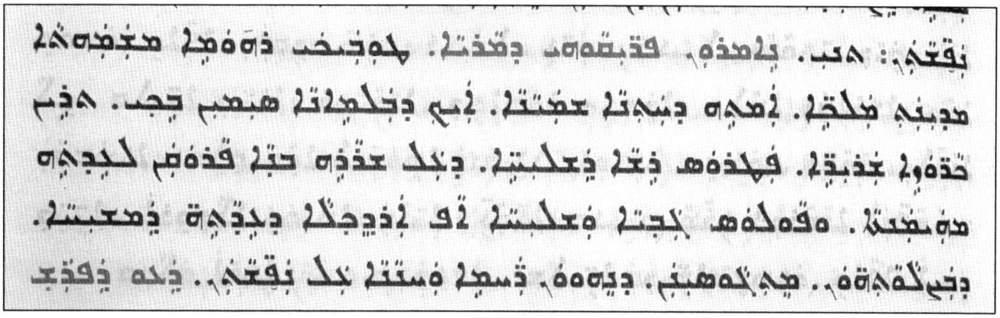

Sulaqa's Guiding Light. Two elements inspired Youhanan Sulaqa's path to Church unity: church fathers and the liturgy. Abdisho of Soba, the Church of the East's last major theologian, wrote his legendary *Nomocanon*, where the status of Rome and its bishops (the popes) is clearly emphasized. Regarding the liturgy, a seventh-century hymn chanted during the Feast of Ss. Peter and Paul expresses these thoughts: "Blessed are you, O Rome, renowned city of kings, handmaid of the heavenly Bridegroom, for the two true preachers are laid up in you . . . Peter, the head of the apostles . . . and Paul the elect." (Courtesy of Bishop Bawai Soro.)

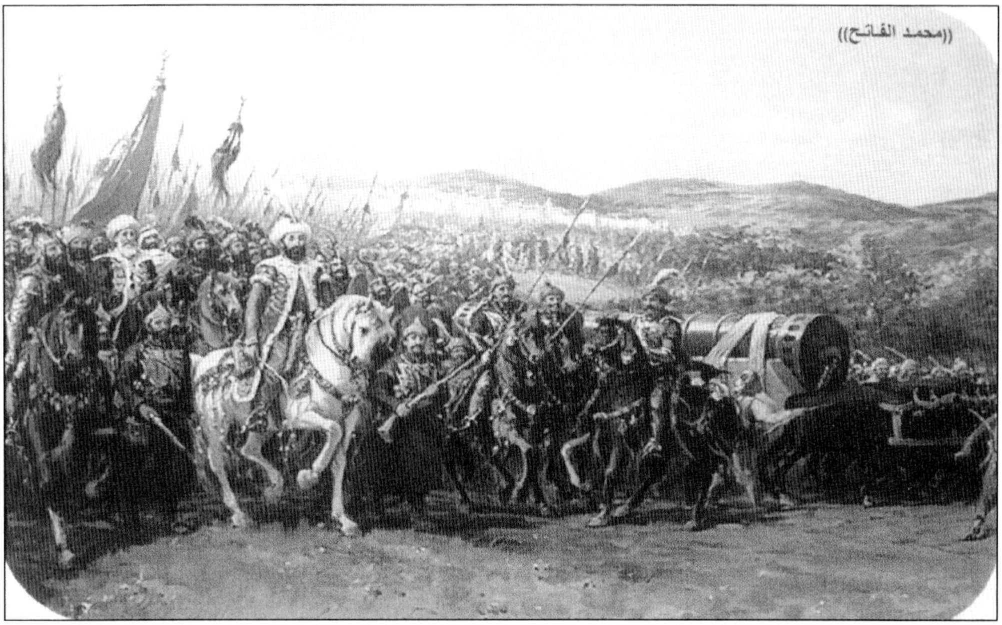

The Ottoman Empire: Its Impact. The Ottomans reconquered Baghdad and much of Mesopotamia in 1534 CE. Christians initially experienced some tolerance under the millet system. However, they often faced discrimination, heavy taxation, and persecution. Though they preserved their faith and identity, they lost monastic life, educational institutions, and population. The 400-year Ottoman period marked a dark age of decline in Mesopotamia lasting until 1918, when the British captured Baghdad. (Courtesy of Selim Matar.)

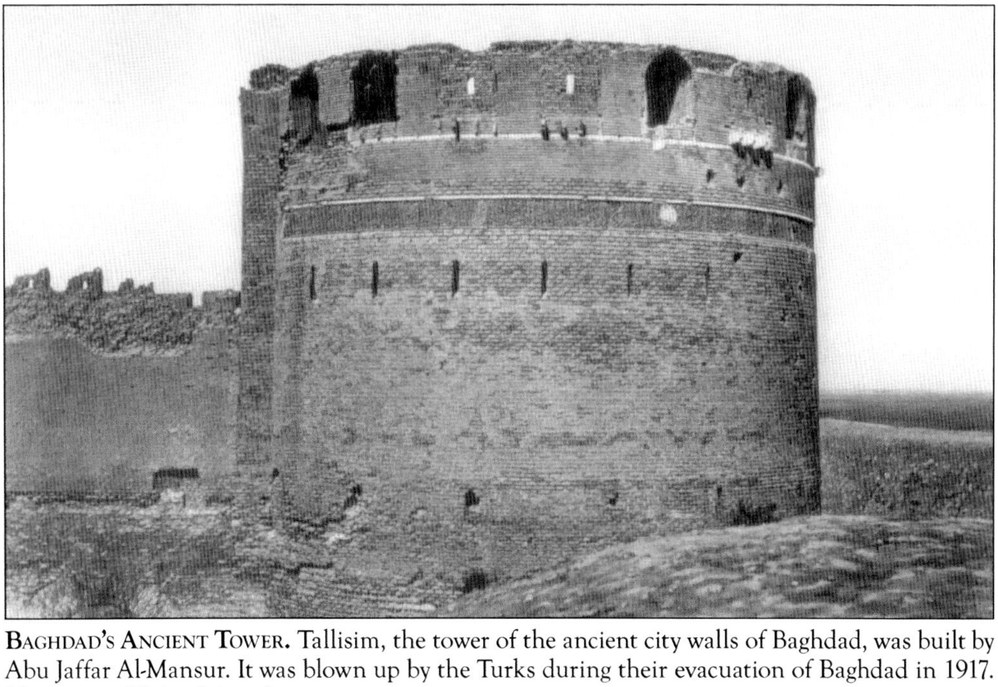

Baghdad's Ancient Tower. Tallisim, the tower of the ancient city walls of Baghdad, was built by Abu Jaffar Al-Mansur. It was blown up by the Turks during their evacuation of Baghdad in 1917. (Courtesy of Selim Matar.)

Four

Modern History of the Chaldeans

The situation of the Chaldeans in Iraq has been burdened with immense challenges and tragic events, stretching from World War I to the present day. This period began with the Sayfo Massacres, where around 1.5 million Christians (Armenians, Chaldeans, Assyrians, Syriacs, Greeks, and others) were slaughtered in Turkey by the Ottoman Empire. Over the centuries, the government of Iraq has been far less kind to the Christians. This atrocity profoundly affected the Christian communities in the broader Mesopotamian region, including the Chaldeans, by fostering an atmosphere of persecution and fear. These initial blows were devastating enough, but their echoes resonated through the decades, culminating horrifically with ISIS's campaign of terror in the early 21st century, when hundreds of Christians were once again subjected to killing and torture along with mass displacement.

The persistent cycle of violence and instability has caused irrevocable change in the demographic landscape of Iraq's Christian population. Over this period, more than 80 percent of Christians have left Iraq, seeking refuge and stability in Western countries. This exodus has significantly weakened the once-thriving Church of Mesopotamia, leading to a dramatic erosion of cultural and religious heritage that adds to the poignancy of Christians' plight.

The challenges facing the Chaldean community in particular have not been limited to external threats. Recent Iraqi governments have shown volatile tendencies toward Christians and, specifically, towards the Chaldean community. A recent controversy has put the Chaldean church leadership in jeopardy: a 2013 presidential decree recognizing Patriarch-Cardinal Louis Raphael Sako as the head of the Chaldean Church, who oversees Chaldean church properties and affairs in Iraq, was withdrawn. This startling move not only undermines the status and authority of the Chaldean patriarch but also threatens the management and ownership of the church's properties, thereby destabilizing their communal coherence and resilience.

The plight of Christians in Iraq is alarming, as their very existence in their homeland is threatened by ongoing volatility and political instability. The sense of insecurity continues to drive many to consider leaving Iraq, hoping for better prospects in Western countries. This steady drain of the Christian population could lead to the near-total disappearance of what has been a vital religious and cultural community in Iraq for millennia. It is hoped and prayed that all Iraqis, Muslim and Christian, will yearn for a life of freedom and stability in their country so that once again, Iraq becomes a cradle of a new civilization of fraternal love and prosperity.

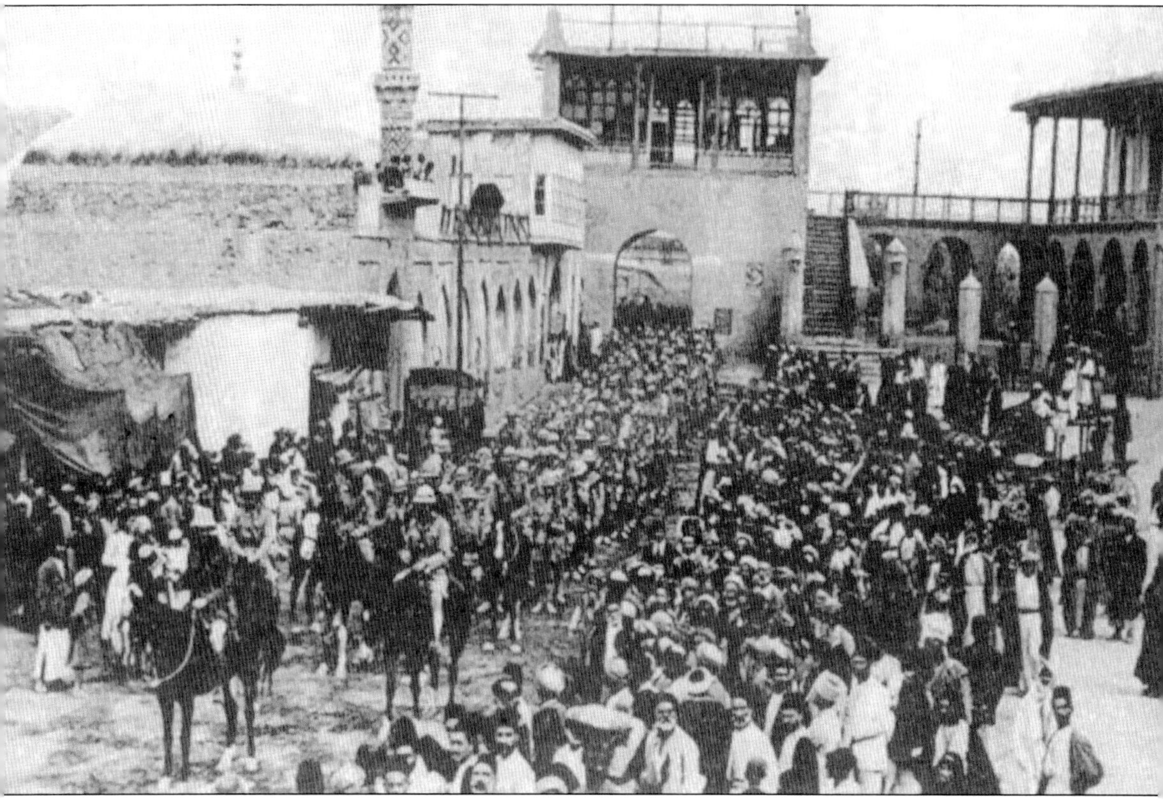

British Occupation of Iraq. Great Britain occupied Iraq during World War I and gained a League of Nations mandate to govern it in 1920. Britain's colonial interests were evident in its earlier efforts to establish relations with Assyrians, aiming to counter Islamic influence in the oil-rich region. Many Assyrian Christians, along with other minorities, were recruited into the British levies to support the British occupation of Iraq. This strategy was part of Britain's "divide and conquer" approach in the new Iraq. However, British authority faced resistance, while Christians in post–World War I Iraq experienced increased subjugation. (Courtesy of Dr. Mohammed M. Adhami.)

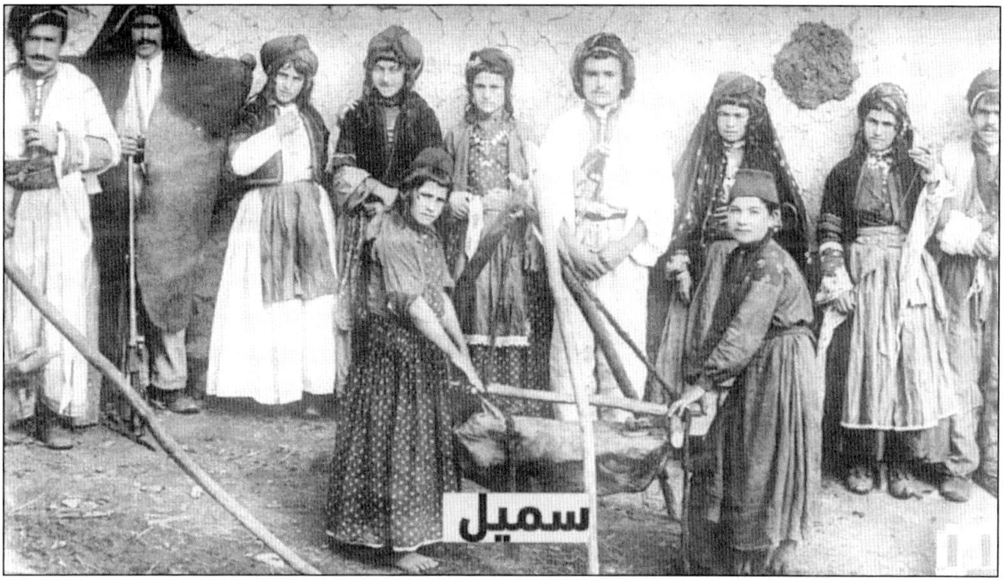

MASSACRES OF SEMELE AND SURIA. The Semele Massacre took place in August 1933 in Semele, Mosul, Iraq. It was perpetrated by the Iraqi general Bakr Sidqi against the Assyrian Christians. British sources claim several hundred Assyrians were killed, while Assyrian eyewitnesses assert that 3,000 innocent men, women, and children were slaughtered. On September 16, 1969, the Albu Ajeel tribe massacred elderly people and children in the Chaldean village of Suria, resulting in the deaths of 39 innocent Chaldean men, women, and children. Such events symbolize significant ethnic and religious suppression by the young inexperienced Iraqi State. (Both, courtesy of Amer Bader Hassoun.)

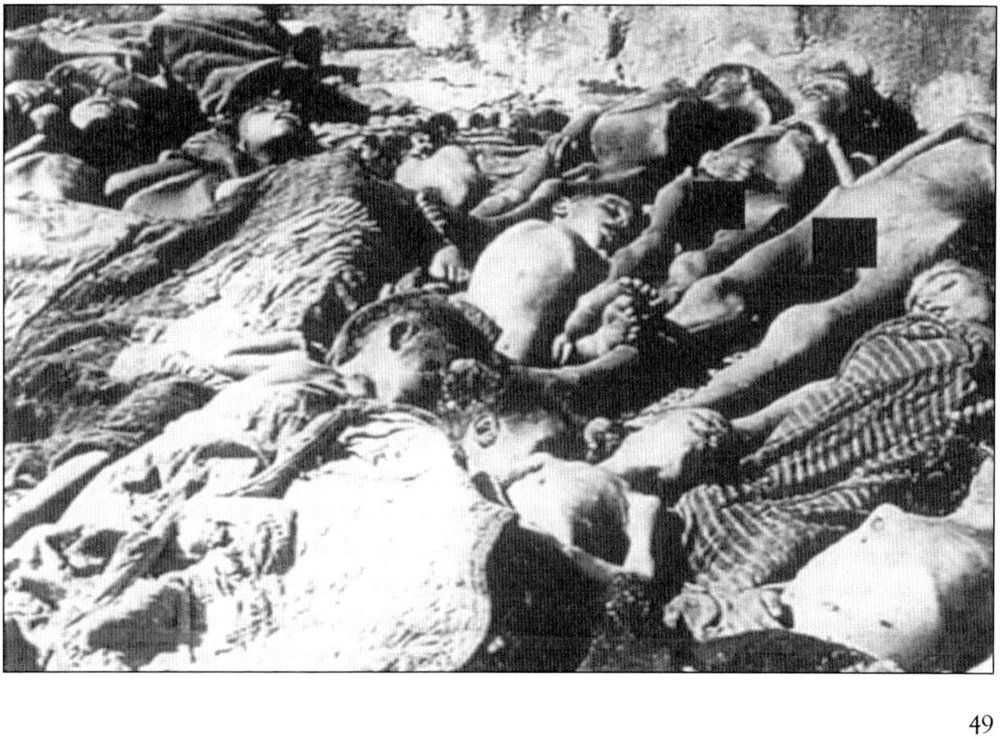

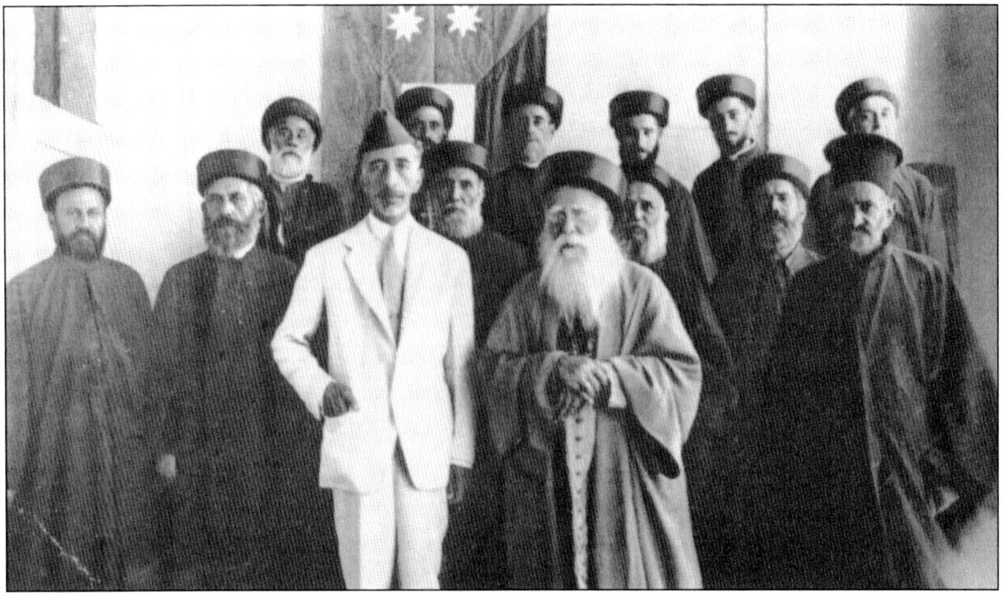

THE BOND OF THE KING AND PATRIARCH. King Faisal I of Iraq and Chaldean patriarch Emmanuel II Thomas enjoyed a very close relationship of respect and admiration for each other. King Faisal I reigned from 1921 to 1933 and initially sought an inclusive national identity, unifying various ethnic and religious groups. However, tensions rose with the Assyrians. This led to the 1933 Semele Massacre, where thousands of Assyrian Christians were killed, highlighting deep-seated divisions. King Faisal II, reigning from 1939 to 1958, faced increased Arab nationalism, marginalizing non-Arab communities. Despite efforts at inclusivity, historical grievances persisted, and his assassination in the 1958 coup further destabilized Iraq's sociopolitical landscape. This photo was taken on June 16, 1931, at Mar Oraha Monastery. (Courtesy of Najm Al-Mashriq.)

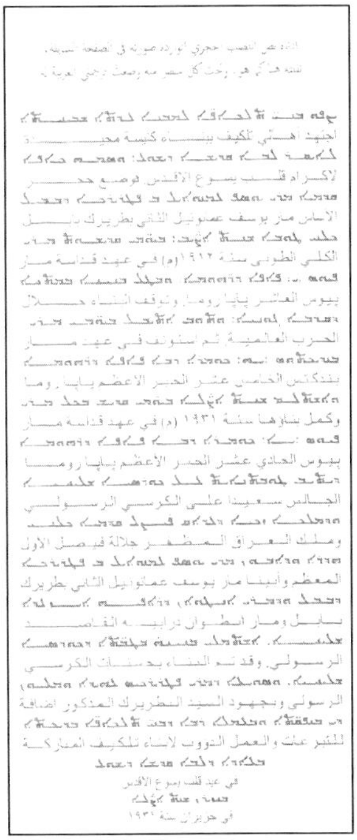

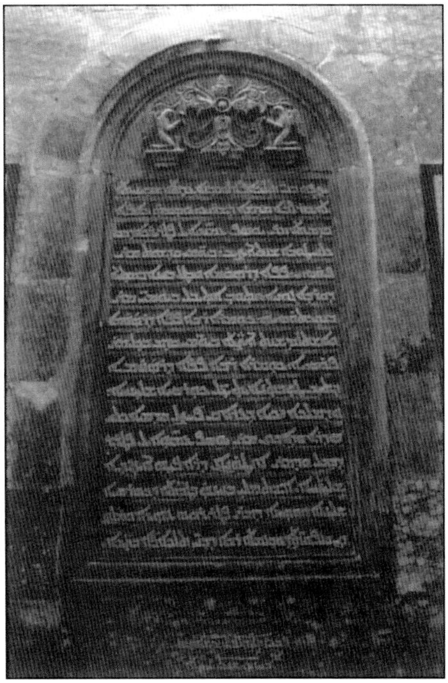

SET IN STONE. A stone monument was installed on the southern wall of Sacred Heart Church in Telkaif, Iraq, marking its construction date as shown in the photo. (Both, courtesy of Khairy Foumia.)

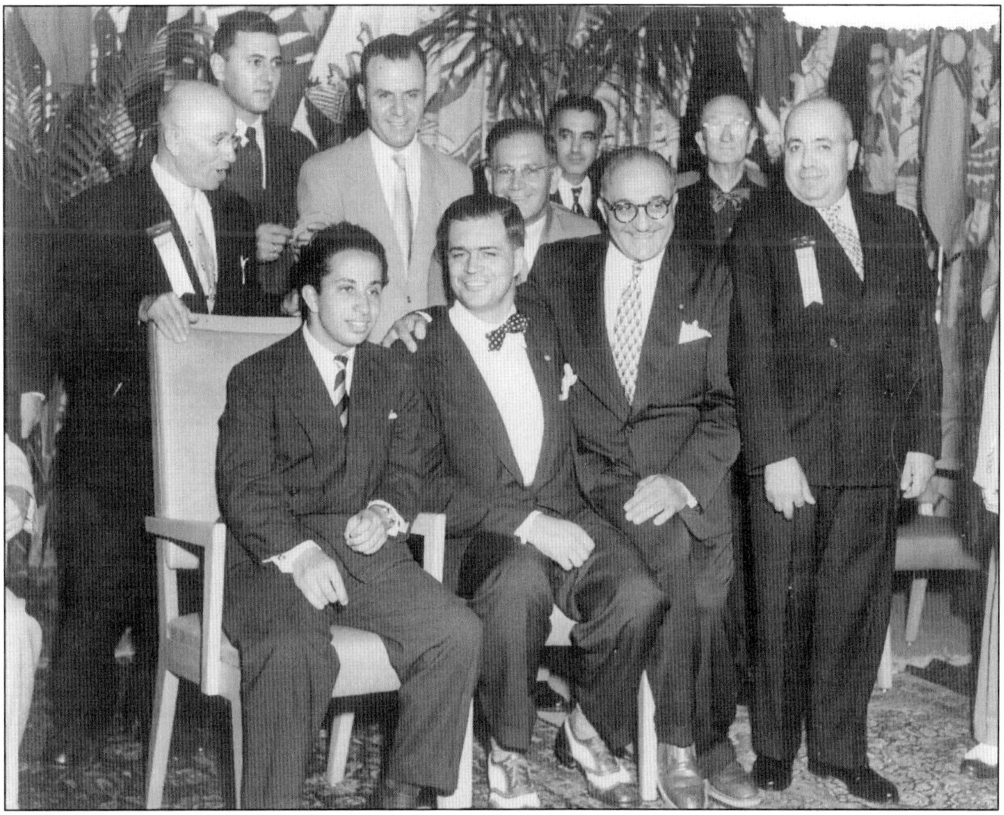

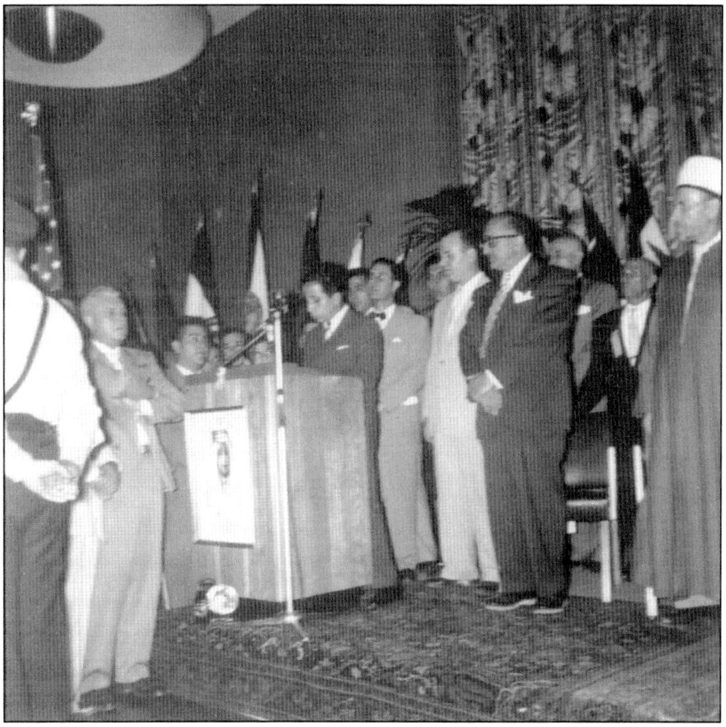

From Here Passed the Great King of Iraq. The Iraqi community of Detroit hosts a reception in honor of His Majesty King Faisal II Al-Hashimi of Iraq and His Royal Highness Prince Abdullah, regent of Iraq. The king stayed at the historic Dearborn Inn on Oakwood Boulevard in Dearborn. Their visit to the United States of America spanned from August 12 to September 8, 1952. (Both, courtesy of Eddie Bacall.)

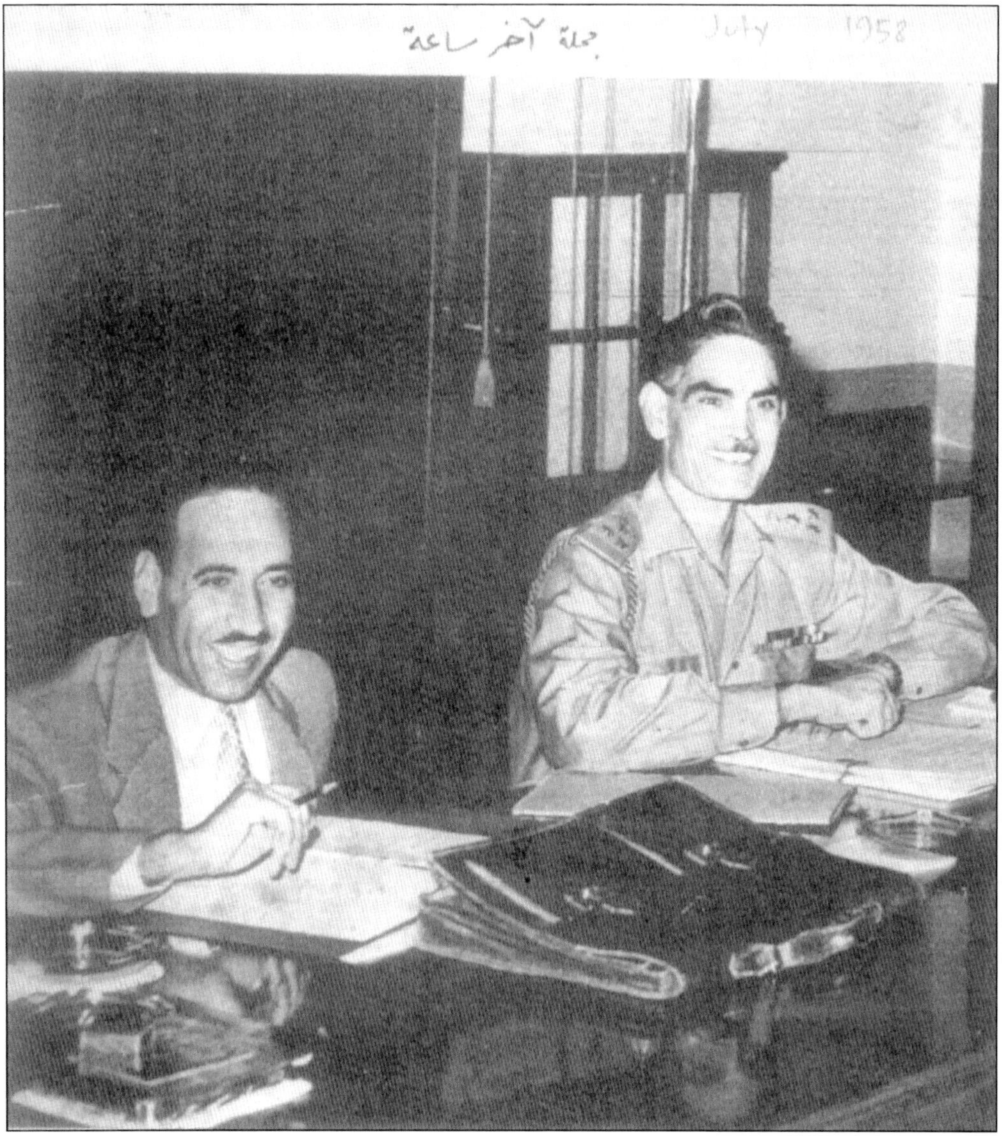

The End of the Iraqi Kingdom. Gen. Abdul Karim Qassim led the 1958 coup that overthrew King Faisal II, establishing the Republic of Iraq. Qassim promoted Iraqi nationalism and inclusivity for minorities like the Chaldeans and Assyrians, but underlying ethnic and religious tensions persisted. His regime's instability led to his overthrow in 1963, leaving many issues unresolved. Pres. Abdul-Salam Muhammad Arif, who succeeded Qassim, prioritized Arab nationalism and unity, marginalizing non-Arab communities in Iraq. His less inclusive policies strained relationships with Iraqi Christians, culminating in their diminished political status. Arif died in 1966. (Courtesy of Morey Gergis.)

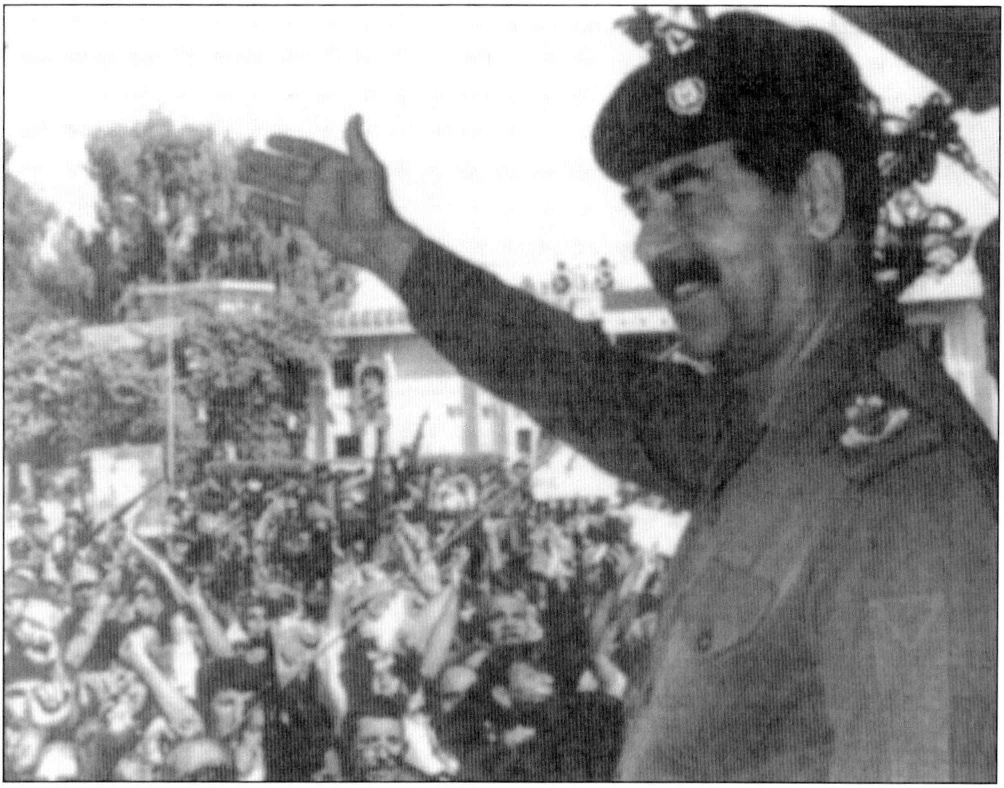

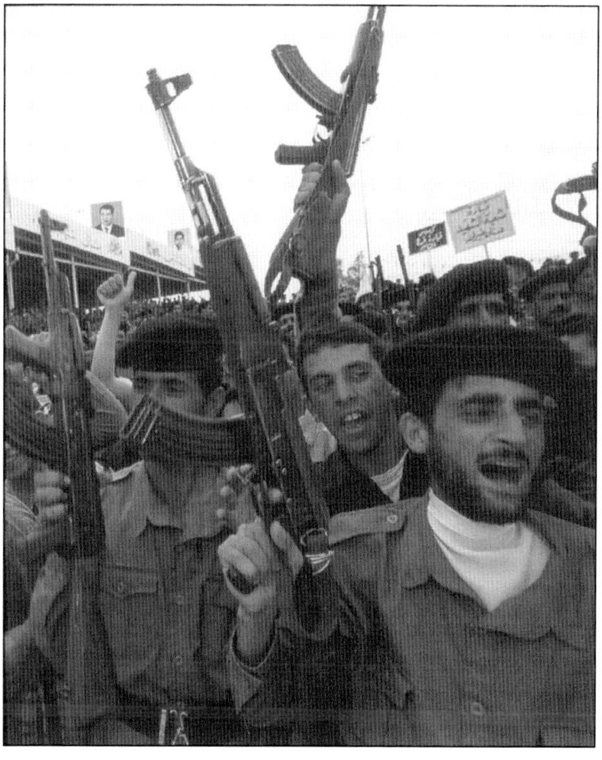

Saddam's Iraq. Saddam Hussein rose to power in 1968 and became president in 1979, ruling Iraq authoritatively and impacting all religious minorities, including the Chaldeans and Assyrians. While Saddam's regime was ruthless, especially through its Arabization policies, the Chaldeans and Assyrians had some leeway. Although they were allowed to practice Christianity, they experienced systematic marginalization, a lack of political representation, and forced Arabization. The Iran-Iraq War and subsequent conflicts exacerbated these hardships, leading to significant emigration of Christians. Saddam's policies consistently undermined the rights and existence of Iraq's Christian minorities, contributing to their ongoing vulnerability until his capture in 2003. (Both, courtesy of the *Chaldean News*.)

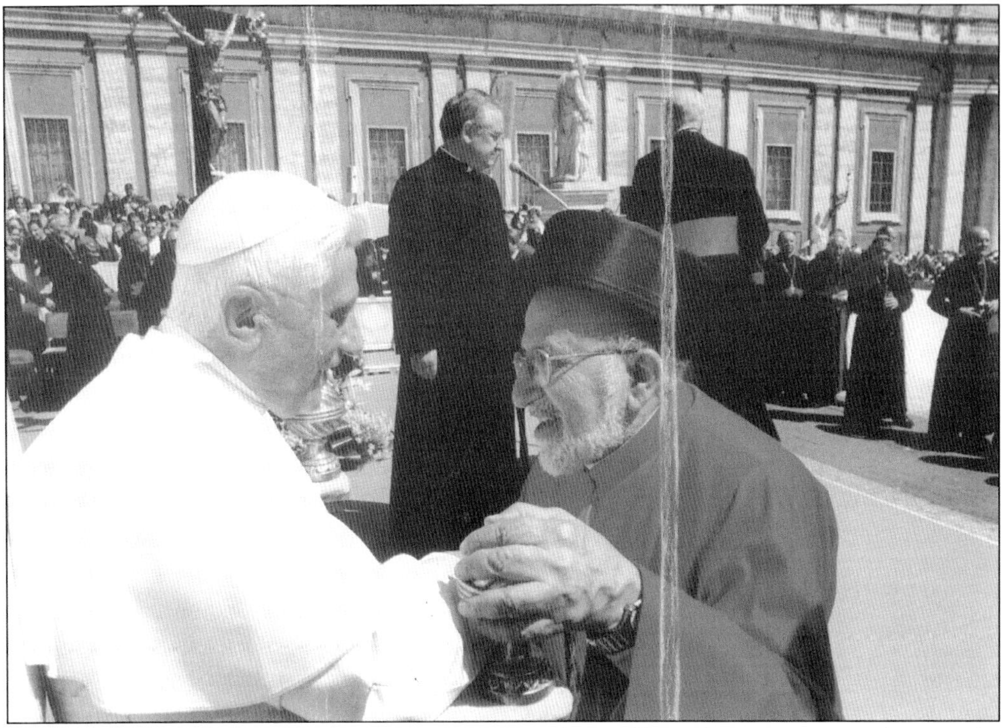

The Fatherly Patriarch. Cardinal-Patriarch Emanuel III Delly was born in 1927. He became the Chaldean patriarch of Babylon in 2003 and a cardinal in 2007. His tenure was marked by war, violence, and political upheaval, events that severely affected Iraqi Christians. Yet he remained a beacon of hope for all Iraqis during this time, advocating for peace, national unity, and tolerance while striving to protect the Christians with fatherly care. Despite immense pressure, he worked tirelessly to maintain the Chaldean Church's rich heritage and status in Iraq. He resigned in 2012 and passed away in 2014. (Courtesy of Jacob Bacall.)

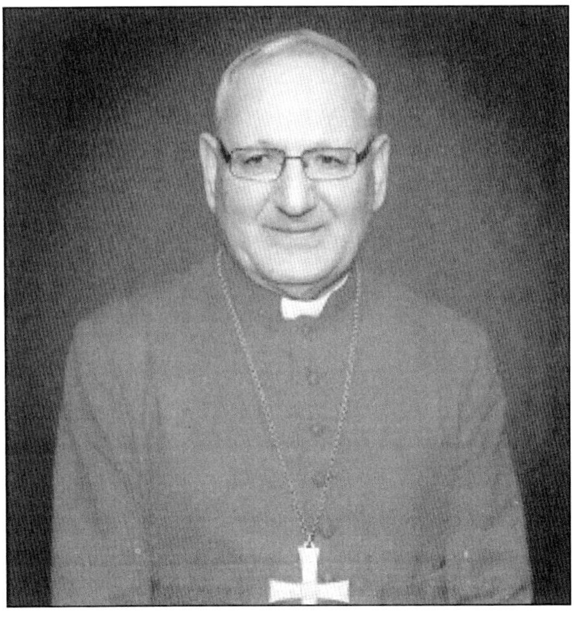

The Lionheart Patriarch. Born in 1948, Cardinal-Patriarch Louis Raphael Sako became the patriarch of Babylon in 2013 and a cardinal in 2018. His tenure is marked by addressing the status of Chaldean clergy displaced by war, reforming the Chaldean liturgy, and a sincere interreligious dialogue with Muslims. Resembling the Lion of Babylon, he has shown relentless dedication to Christians during the ISIS crisis, safeguarding the Chaldean Church from Iraqi officials attempting to seize control of church properties and influencing Christians' parliamentary representation. In 2021, Cardinal-Patriarch Sako invited Pope Francis for a historic visit to Iraq. (Courtesy of Bishop Bawai Soro.)

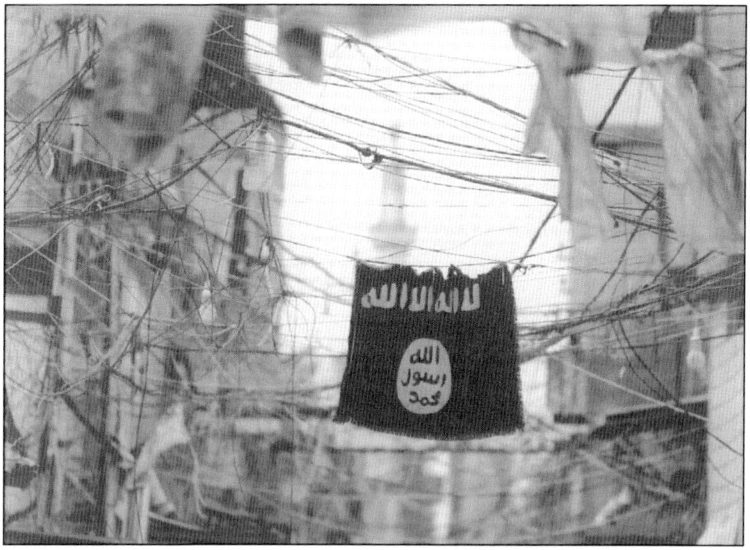

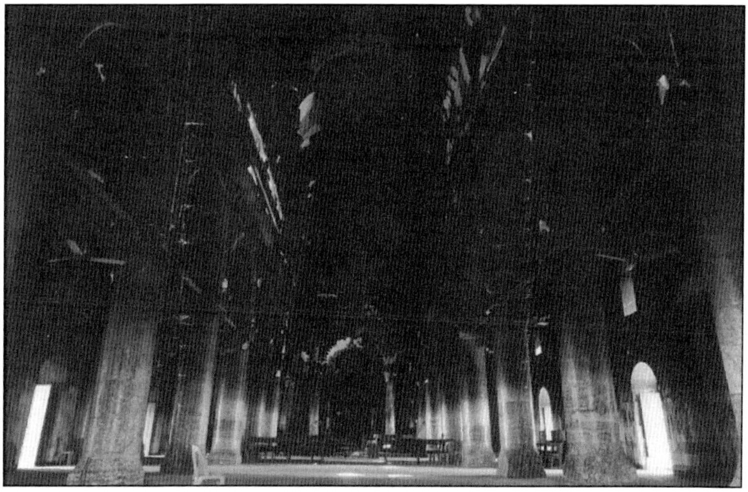

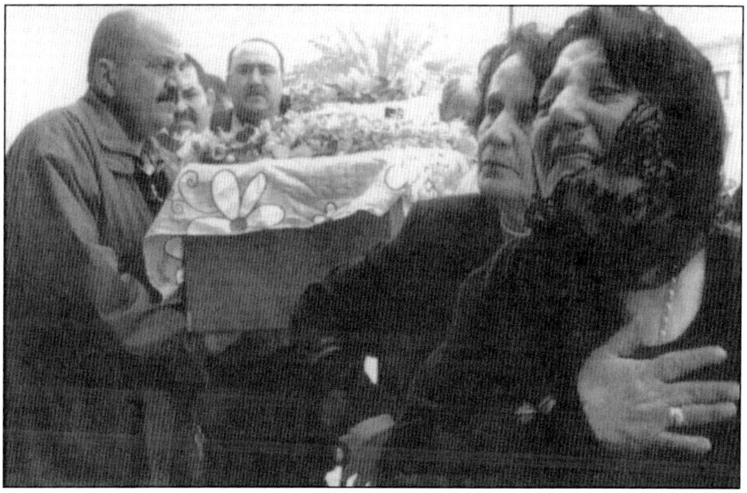

Isis (2014–2017). The rise of ISIS (the Islamic State in Iraq and ash-Sham) brought unprecedented horror to Iraq and its citizens starting in 2014. The group's extreme interpretation of Islamic law led to widespread atrocities, mainly targeting the Shi'a, Christians and Yezidis. ISIS overran key cities like Mosul, forcing thousands of Chaldeans, Syriacs, and Assyrians to flee their ancestral homes and villages. ISIS issued an ultimatum: Christians must either convert to Islam or leave within 48 hours or be killed. (All, courtesy of the *Chaldean News*.)

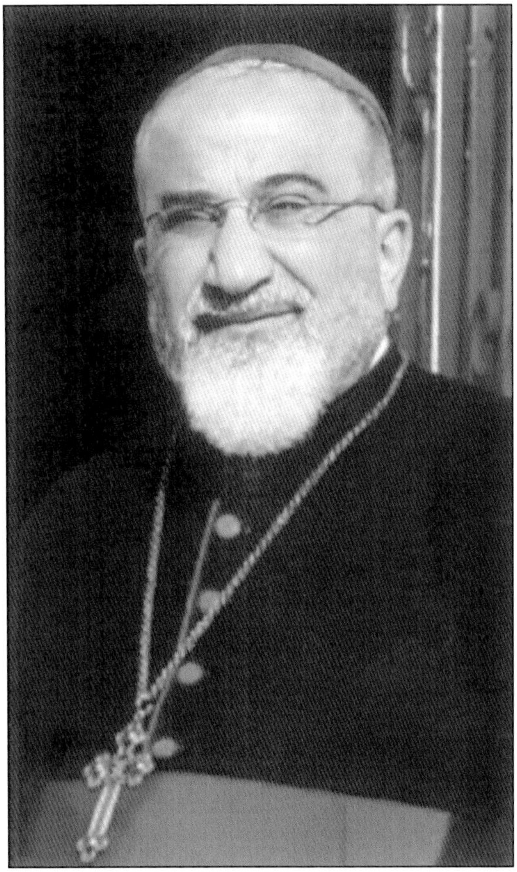

The Demise of Christians in Iraq. After ISIS gained control of Mosul, churches and Christian establishments were targeted. Among the most notable Chaldean martyrs were Archbishop Paulos Faraj Rahho (left), Father Ragheed Ganni (below), and his three deacons, and Sr. Cecil Moshi Hanna. The lasting devastation left the Christians of Iraq in a state of helplessness, as they continue to face ongoing struggles to rebuild and survive with an uncertain and challenging future ahead. (Both, courtesy of Najm Al-Mashriq.)

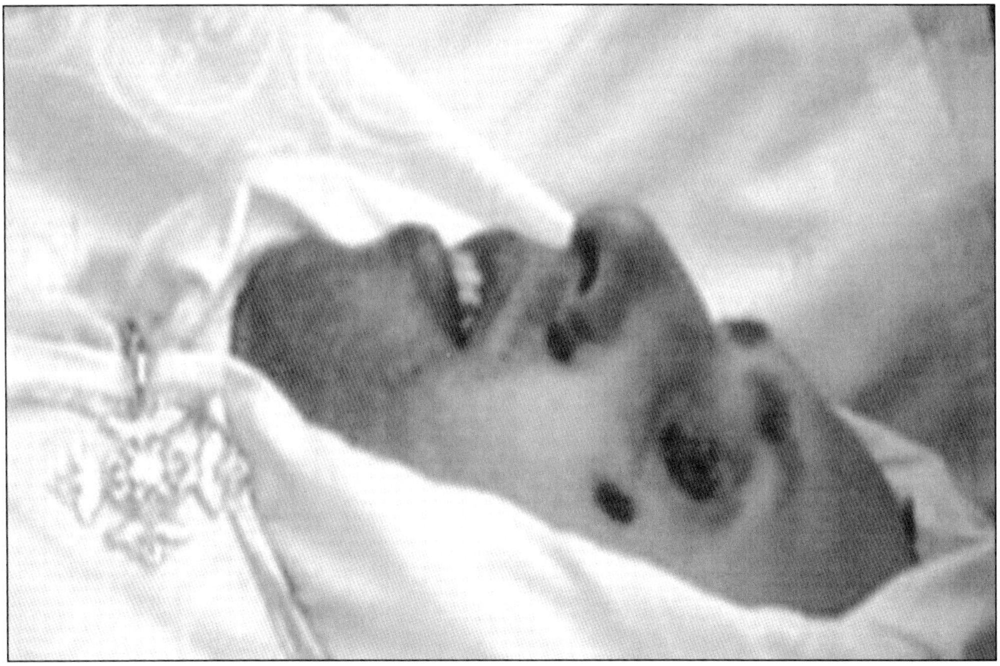

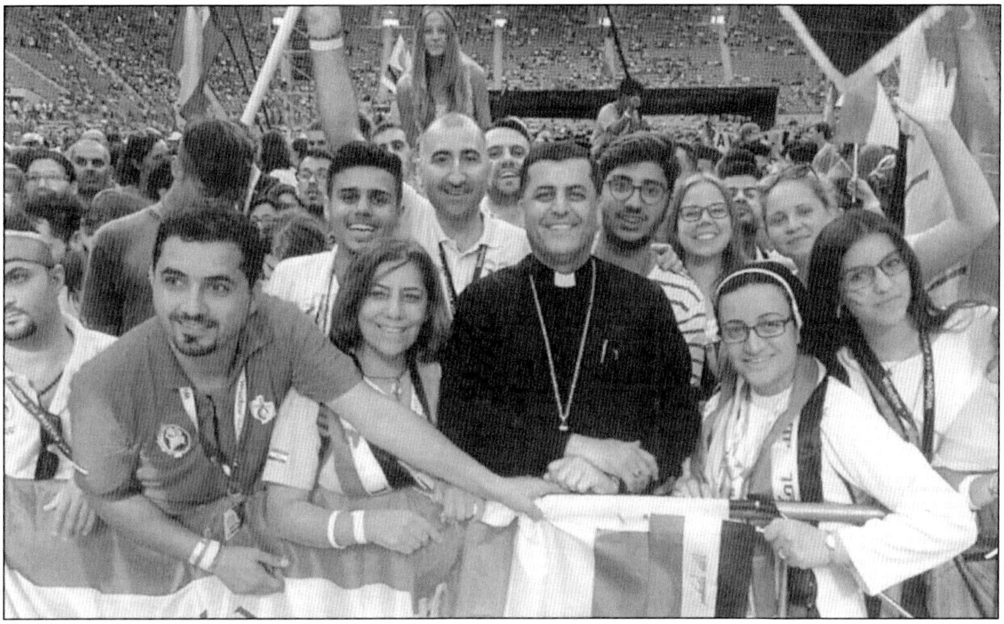

HOPE FOR THE FUTURE. Chaldean youth play a crucial role in preserving and advancing the rich heritage of the worldwide Chaldean community by embracing their cultural roots and advocating for their Catholic faith and family values. For decades, the Chaldean patriarchate and several eparchies have devoted efforts to education, activism, and community building for the youth, paving the way for a brighter future where Chaldeans worldwide can thrive without fear of persecution or torture. Such a plan will empower Chaldean youth to carry forward their centuries-old traditions and faith into the third millennium and beyond. The Chaldean Church has many youth programs all over the world that reveal the great zeal and passion of young people who represent the future of the church. Aside from the various weekly gatherings and Bible study groups, youth conventions are organized where hundreds gather to worship together and join in community with one another to learn about their identity as Chaldeans and their faith in Jesus Christ. Pictured here are Iraqi youth in Poland for World Youth Day in 2016 and the Saint Peter Eparchy Youth Convention in 2024. (Above, courtesy of Bishop Basillios Yaldo; below, courtesy of Father Simon Esshaki.)

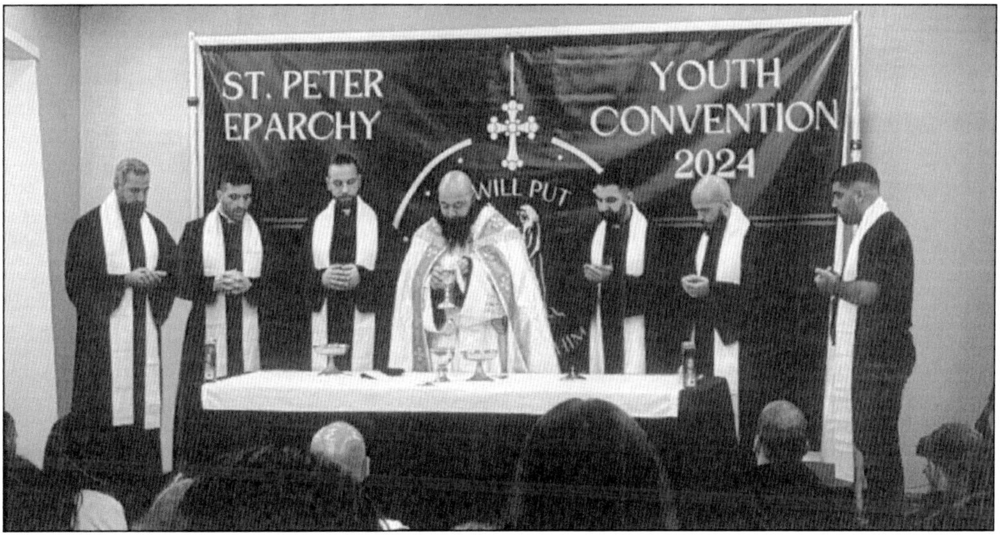

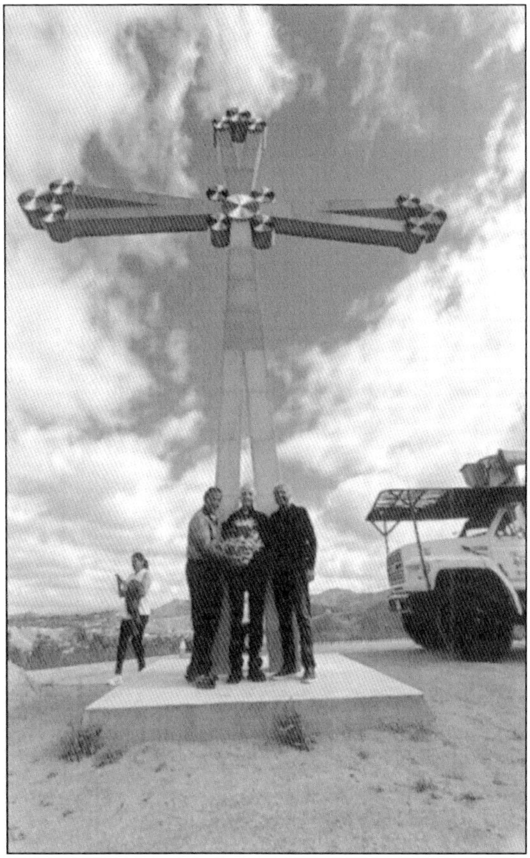

The Chaldean Holy Cross of San Diego. On December 14, 2023, a remarkable Holy Cross monument was inaugurated with the presence of Chaldean hierarchy, clergy, and faithful. The event was streamed live from the site of the monument in Jamul, California, on social media. This project was solely financed, built, and managed by Samad and Evone Attisha. A team of family members and friends was involved in the planning and executing of this project. They equally deserve prayers and recognition for their amazing contributions. The Christian faithful are tremendously attracted to the sign of the Holy Cross because this sacred symbol represents the Lord Jesus Christ himself. While the Holy Cross reveals to those who approach it prayerfully the suffering of Jesus and his sacrifice for the sake of the salvation of the world, the Holy Cross also embodies the biggest hope humanity has, namely, the promise of the resurrection from the dead and the life everlasting in the Kingdom of God, which the Lord Jesus promised those who believe in him, who love him, and who obey him. (Both, courtesy of Jacob Bacall.)

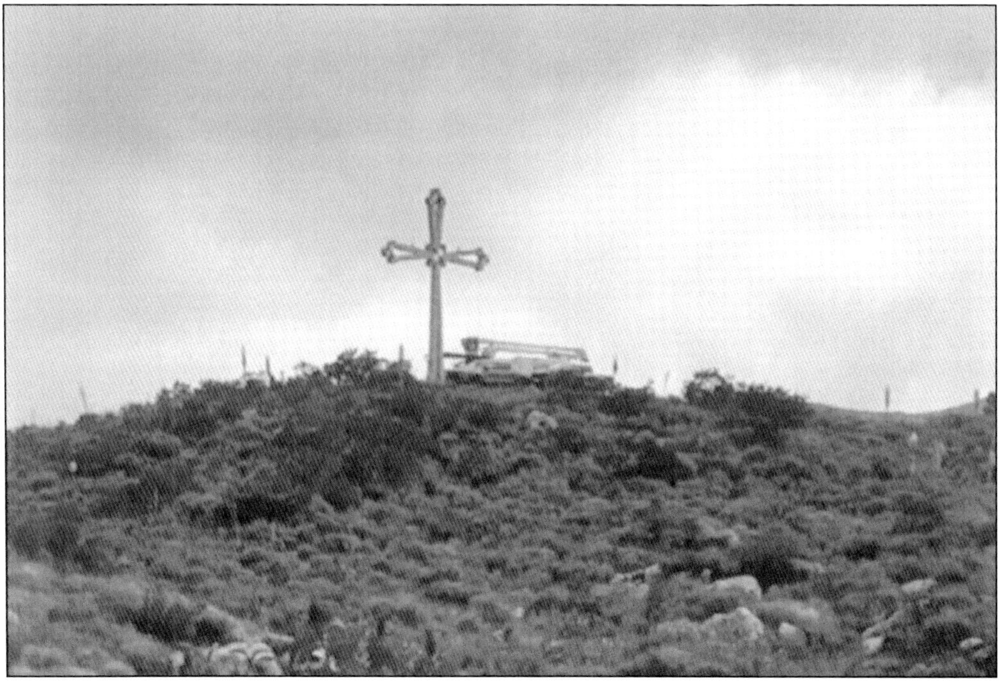

Five

Chaldean Catholic Diocese of Saint Thomas the Apostle in Eastern United States

The Chaldeans are a Catholic ethnic group primarily originating from Iraq. Their mother language is Aramaic (Surath, also known as Chaldean), the language of ancient Babylon and the language spoken by Jesus Christ. Classical Aramaic was heavily used in church masses.

In the Chaldean liturgy, Chaldeans belong to the Chaldean Rite of the Roman Catholic Church. They are in full communion with Rome and have their own patriarch, although the pope is recognized as the head of the church. Chaldeans were converted to Christianity by Saint Thomas the Apostle and his disciples, Bishop Addai and Bishop Mari.

The vast majority of early Chaldeans in the United States originated from the village of Telkeppe (Telkaif in Arabic) and were later followed by those from other northern villages of Iraq such as Alkosh, Aradan, Tesqopa, Baqofa, Zakho, and Batnaya. Chaldeans began immigrating to the United States in the early decades of the 20th century. Many settled in Detroit, Michigan, attracted by Ford Motor Company's famous (and unprecedented) pay rate of $5 per day. Other factors, such as the proximity to the Canadian border and the presence of Syrian Arabic-speaking communities, also played a role. After the fall of Saddam Hussein in 2003, the greater Detroit metropolitan area became the new capital of Chaldeans in the world. The latest survey by the Chaldean Chamber of Commerce estimates the population at 200,000 people.

"The major institutions of the Chaldean community are family and church. It is important to point out that Chaldeans have a strong commitment to home and family," said Mary Sengstock in her book *Chaldeans in Michigan*.

The Chaldean community welcomed its first priest, Rev. Toma (Thomas) Bidawid, at Michigan Central Station on February 24, 1947. Less than a year after his arrival, a church was purchased to serve about 80 Chaldean families and was named Mother of God. In 1982, Pope John Paul II established the Eparchy of Saint Thomas the Apostle. A few years later, it was elevated to the Diocese of Saint Thomas the Apostle, based in Southfield, Michigan, to serve the approximately 30,000 Chaldeans in the area. Twenty years later, in May 2002, an apostolic decree divided the diocese into two: the Diocese of Saint Peter covering the western part of the United States and Saint Thomas for the eastern part.

In addition to family and church, Chaldeans value both business and education. They initially became entrepreneurs in retail, food, and real estate. Today, American-born Chaldeans are increasingly pursuing professional careers in law, medicine, engineering, and accounting; both males and females attend college and graduate school. Chaldeans are historically known for their merchant mentality and the instinct of a barterer.

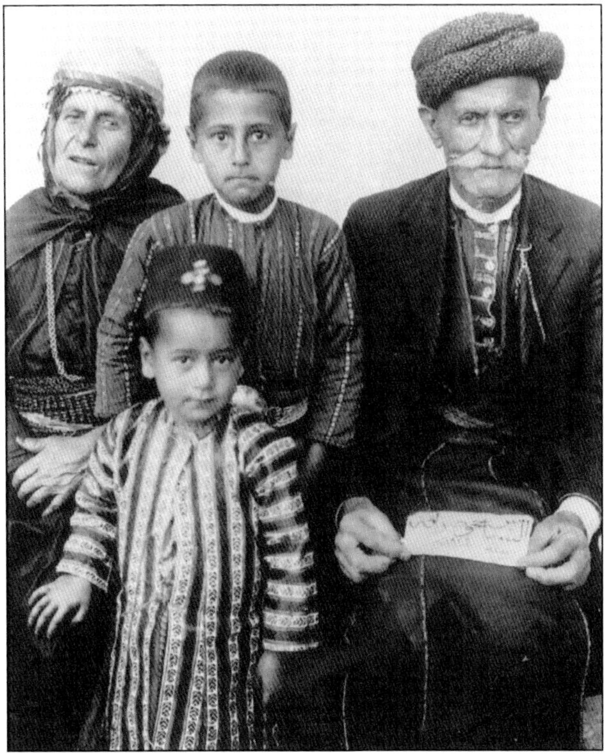

OUR ORIGIN, OUR ROOTS. Life in the village was simple. Each family had a plot of land outside the village to grow basic crops like wheat, barley, lentil, cantaloupes, and a specific type of cucumber, *tarouz*. "The people of Telkaif are adventurous people who have spread throughout Iraq, where they worked on ships and as waiters in hotels. They are also successful immigrants in North and South America," said Harry Charles Luke in his 1924 book, *Mosul and Its Minorities*. Extended family members lived together under their father's roof as one household. Youngsters were surrounded by grandparents, uncles, aunts, and cousins. Then and now, Chaldean parents emphasized the values of morality, integrity, hard work, ethics, and strong family ties. (Left, courtesy of Anmar Sarafa; below, courtesy of Eddie Bacall.)

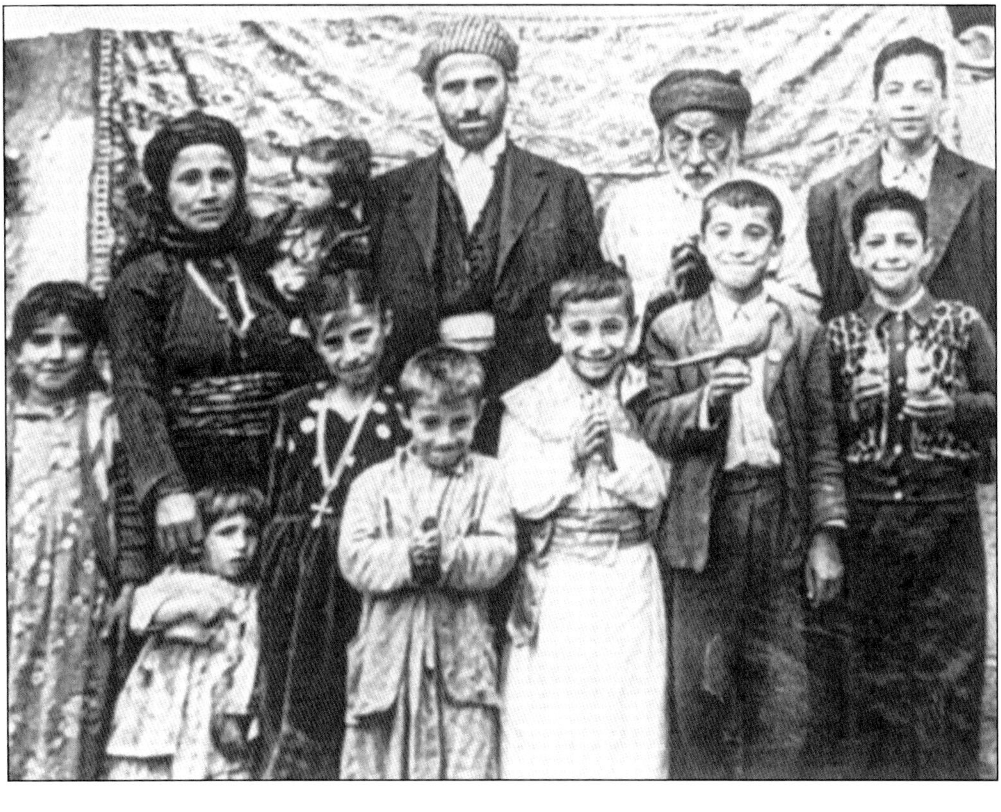

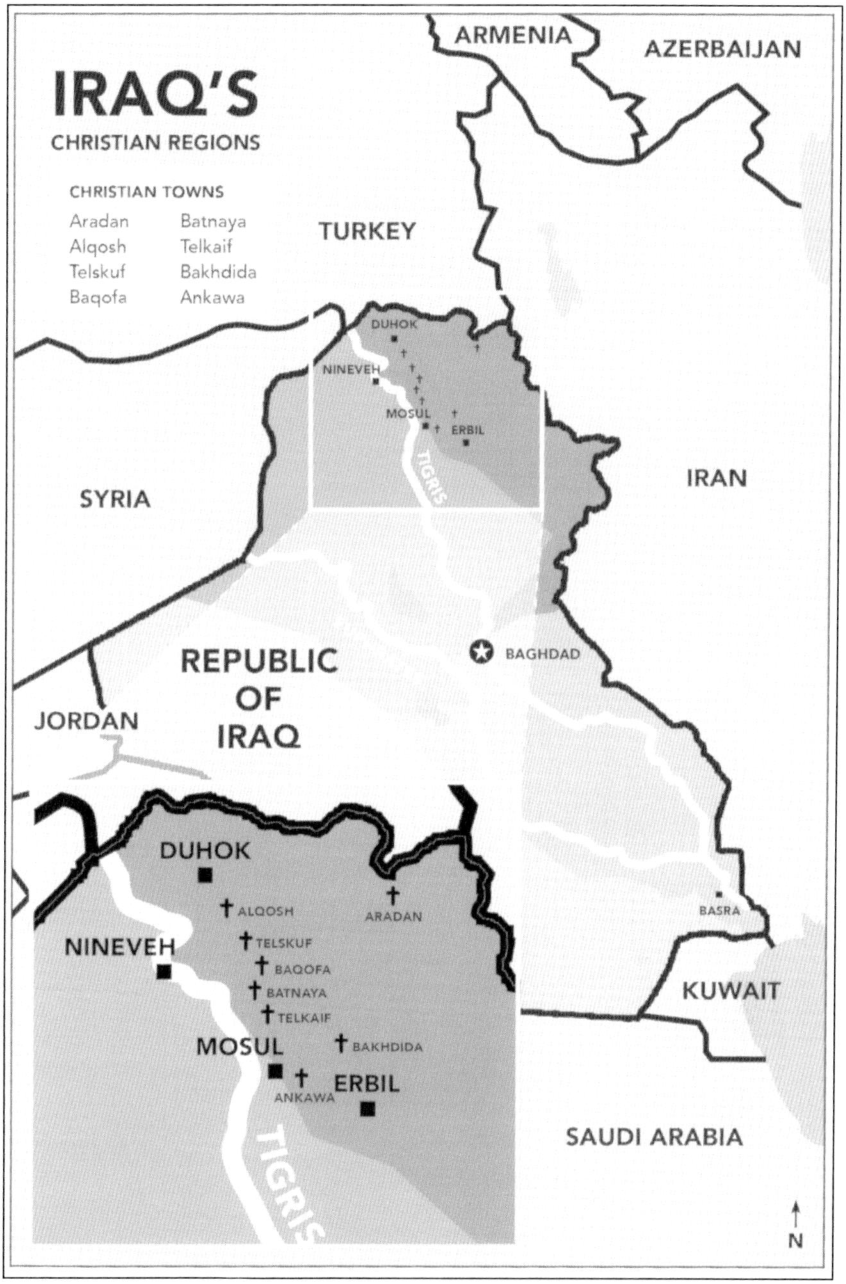

THE CHRISTIANS OF MESOPOTAMIA. For more than 6,000 years, Chaldeans have lived in the traditional geographic land of Mesopotamia, known today as the nation of Iraq. Mesopotamia is the place of origin of all Chaldeans in the world, including those in nearby Turkey, Iran, Syria, Lebanon, and Egypt. "The early Christians of Mesopotamia were Jews who worshiped in synagogues and read the Hebrew Bible as their Holy Book," wrote Dr. Suha Rassam in her book *Christianity in Iraq*. Christians have been consistently marginalized in war-torn Iraq, which has taken a dramatic turn towards fundamentalism. Today, Chaldeans are scattered all over the world as a result of the ethnic cleansing of Christians and other non-Muslim minorities. Nonetheless, their roots remain deep in Iraq. (Art by Alex Lumelsky.)

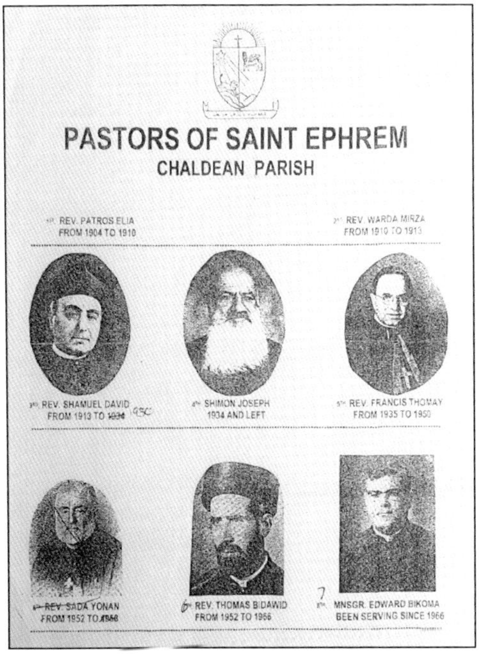

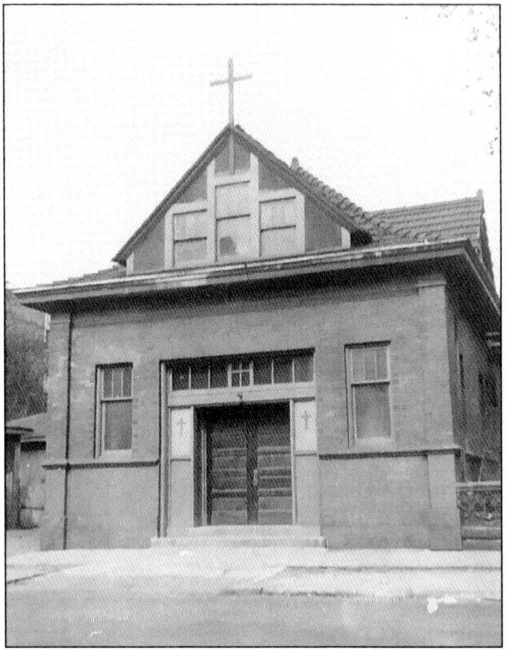

FIRST CHALDEAN CHURCH IN AMERICA. In 1904, the fledgling community of about 25 Assyrian and Chaldean families who immigrated to Chicago, along with their priest, Father Patros Elia from Urmia, Iran, foresaw history in selecting an especially noted patron saint. They designated their precious church under the patronage of Saint Ephrem, a fourth-century Eastern Church father famous for his hymnology praising the Mother of God and for his defense of her Immaculate Conception. In 1920, Pope Benedict XV declared Saint Ephrem a doctor of the Catholic Church, and in 2007, Pope Benedict XVI praised the saint, saying, "His hymns and writings are unparalleled, written in rare skill in their praise of God." Pictured here are the first pastors of Saint Ephrem, its first location, and its second location at 2537 West Bryn Mawr Avenue in Chicago. (All, courtesy of Father Hermiz Haddad.)

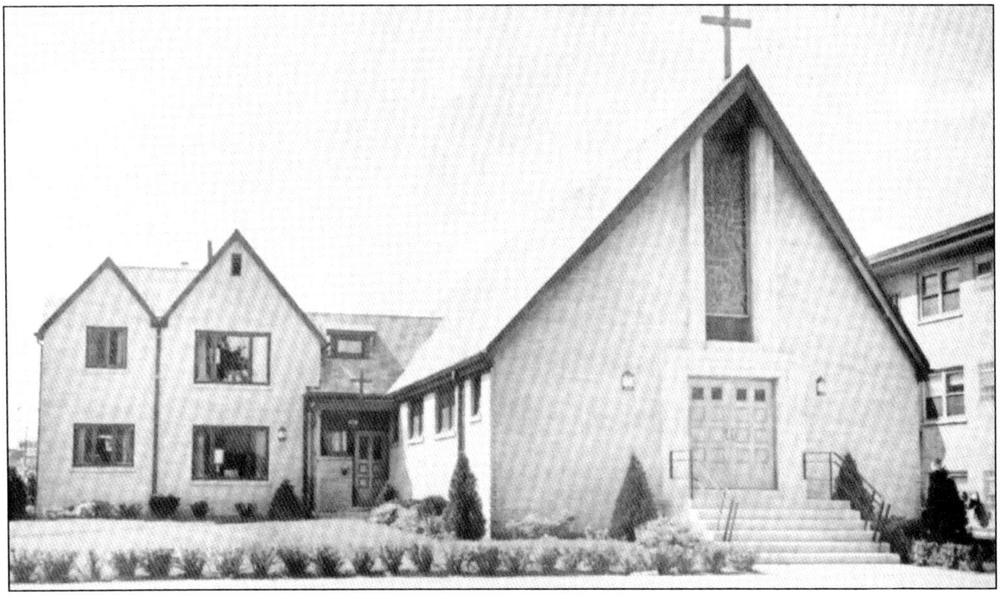

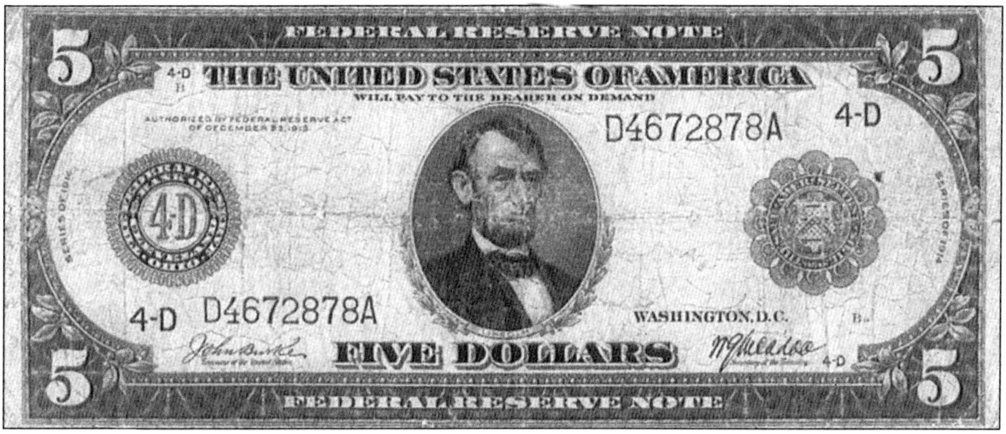

The $5 Day. As the automobile industry continued to grow in Detroit, immigrants, including Chaldeans, came in great numbers to take advantage of Henry Ford's $5-a-day pay rate by working at the Ford Highland Park assembly plant. John Joseph was the first known Chaldean to receive that unprecedented salary at Ford's state-of-the-art facility, which included the industry's first moving assembly line in 1913. A May 2, 1915, article in the *Sunday Chronicle* tells of Joseph's perilous journey from young peddler in Mesopotamia to the Ford factory and finding his own unique "Garden of Eden where even Adam could not have had a happier existence." Even Chaldeans who did not work for Ford benefited from the businesses that were generated by the influx of population. (Both, courtesy of Bryon Perry.)

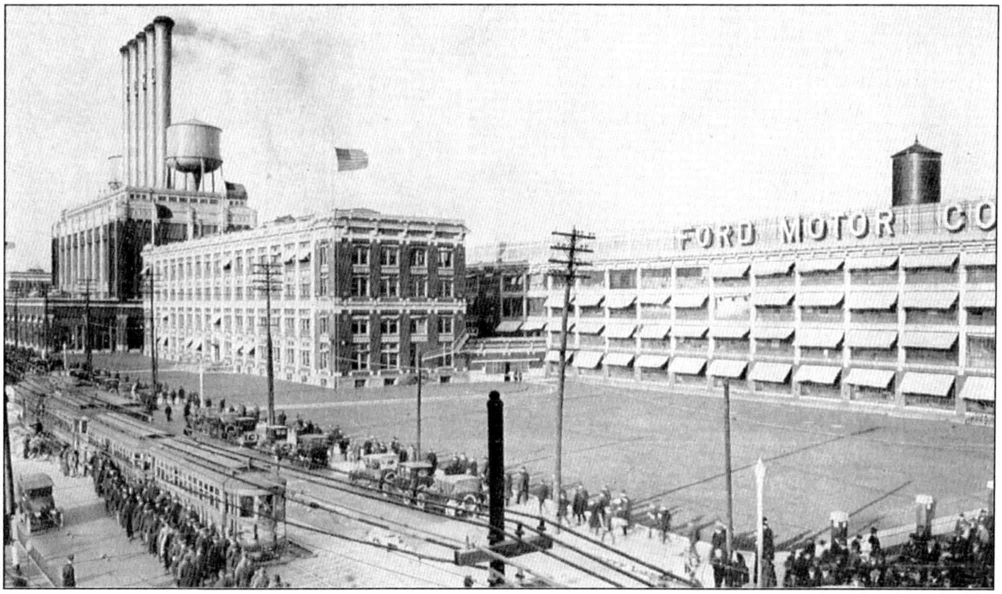

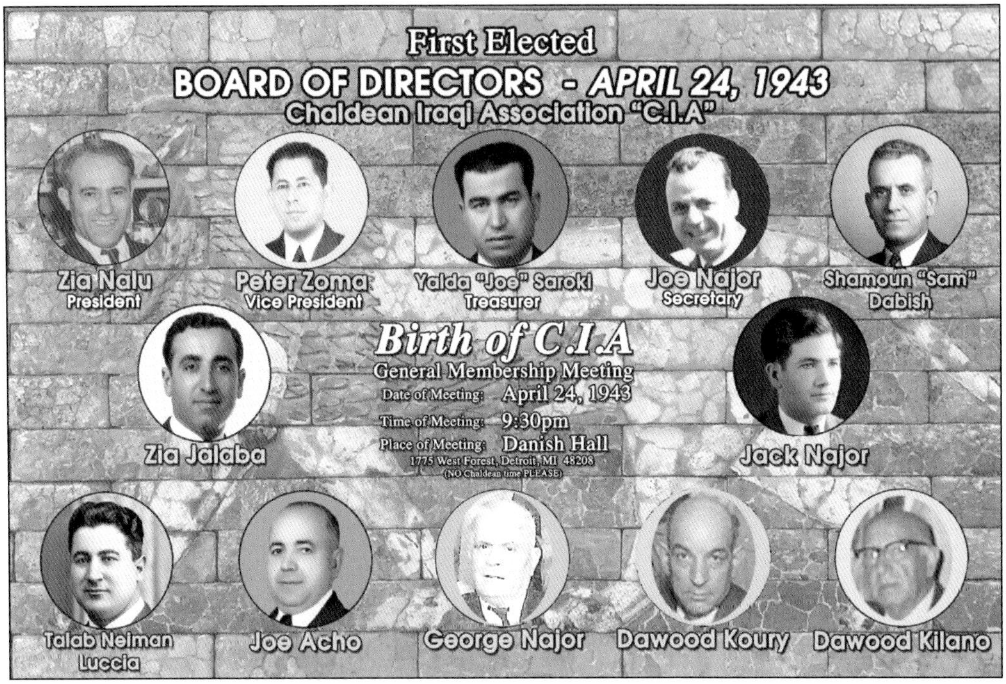

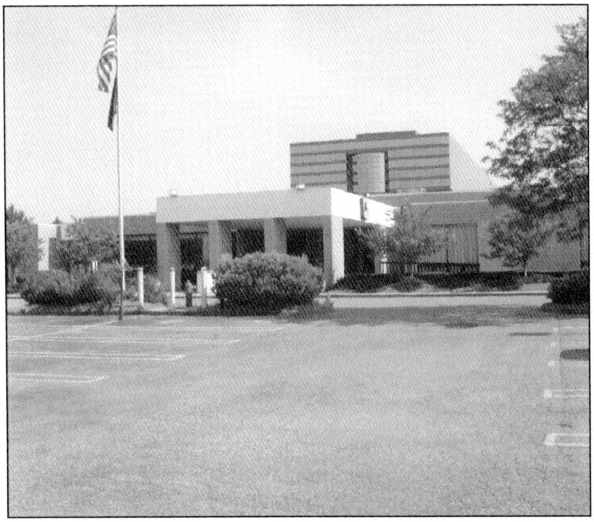

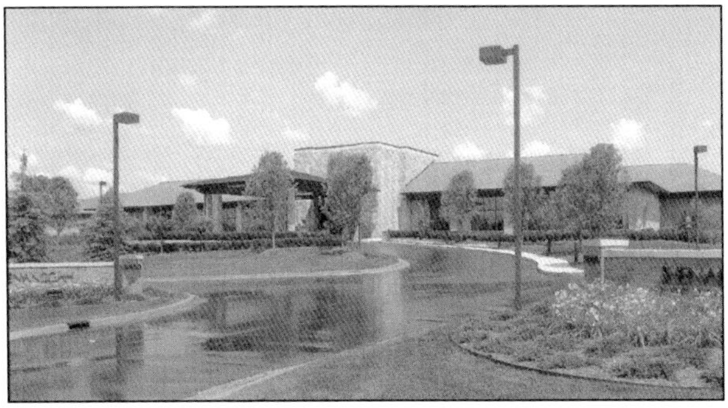

OUR STORY. The Chaldean Iraqi Association (CIA), known now as Chaldean Iraqi American Association of Michigan (CIAAM), was formed by a small group of immigrants. They were good-hearted individuals who strived to build a solid foundation for their community. CIAAM takes the lead as the mother of all organizations, serving the community since 1943. CIAAM has owned two facilities. The first, Southfield Manor in Southfield, Michigan, pictured in the middle, was constructed in 1981. The second, Shenandoah Country Club in West Bloomfield, Michigan, pictured below, was purchased in 1989 and completely rebuilt in 2002. It is cherished as a gathering spot for friends and family, hosting many weddings and other events, as well as educational programs that preserve Chaldean history, identity, and culture, all accompanied by authentic, delicious traditional dishes representing all three regions of Iraqi cuisine. (All, courtesy of Jacob Bacall.)

PROMISE MADE, PROMISE KEPT. Cardinal Edward Mooney (1882–1958) agreed to meet a group of CIA members consisting of Yalda "Joe" Saroki, Jack Najor, Sam Dabish, and CIA president Zia Nalu. Cardinal Mooney, the archbishop of Detroit, listened to their request to bring a Chaldean Rite priest to Detroit. After multiple conversations and a second face-to-face meeting on January 5, 1946, Cardinal Mooney said, "I will write to Rome, and Rome will write to the Chaldean patriarch in Iraq to nominate a priest to serve your Chaldean community in Detroit." Cardinal Mooney's official approval came on March 9, 1948, to establish the first Chaldean parish under the name Mother of God Church. Cardinal Edward Mooney is pictured here. (Courtesy of Sam Dabish.)

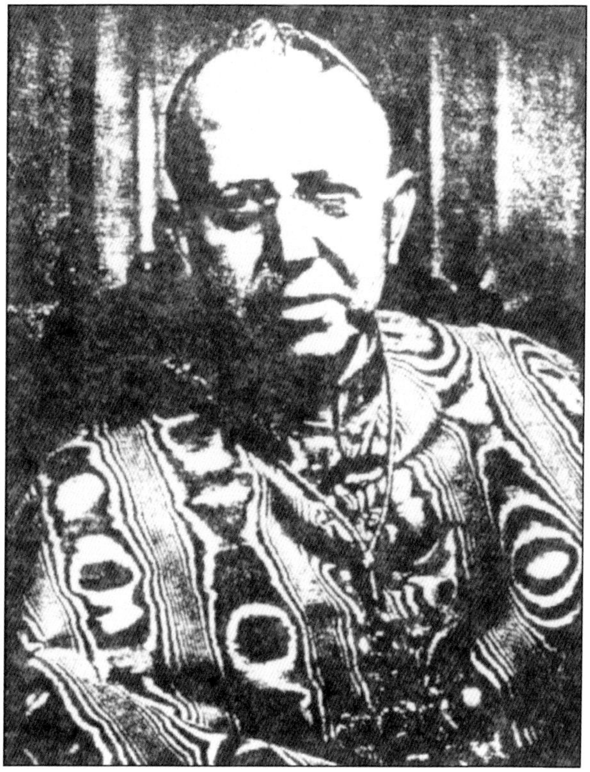

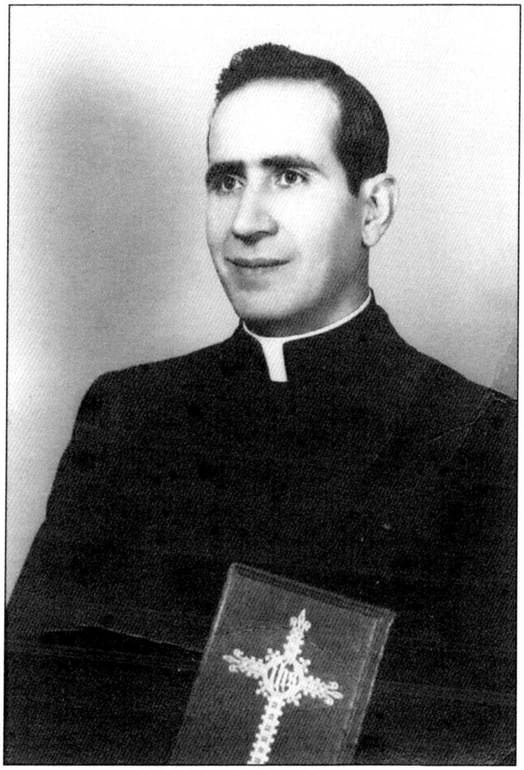

YOUR PRAYERS HAVE BEEN ANSWERED. Father Toma (Thomas) Bidawid, born in Ballo, Turkey, in 1910, was ordained in Mosul in 1935. Arriving in Detroit in 1947, he held the first Chaldean Rite mass in Aramaic at Mar Maron Catholic Church. As founder and first pastor of Mother of God Church, he served Detroit's Chaldean community until 1952. Later, he became bishop of Ahwaz, Iran, and represented the Chaldean patriarch in Cairo, where he passed away in 1971. (Courtesy of Samira Essa.)

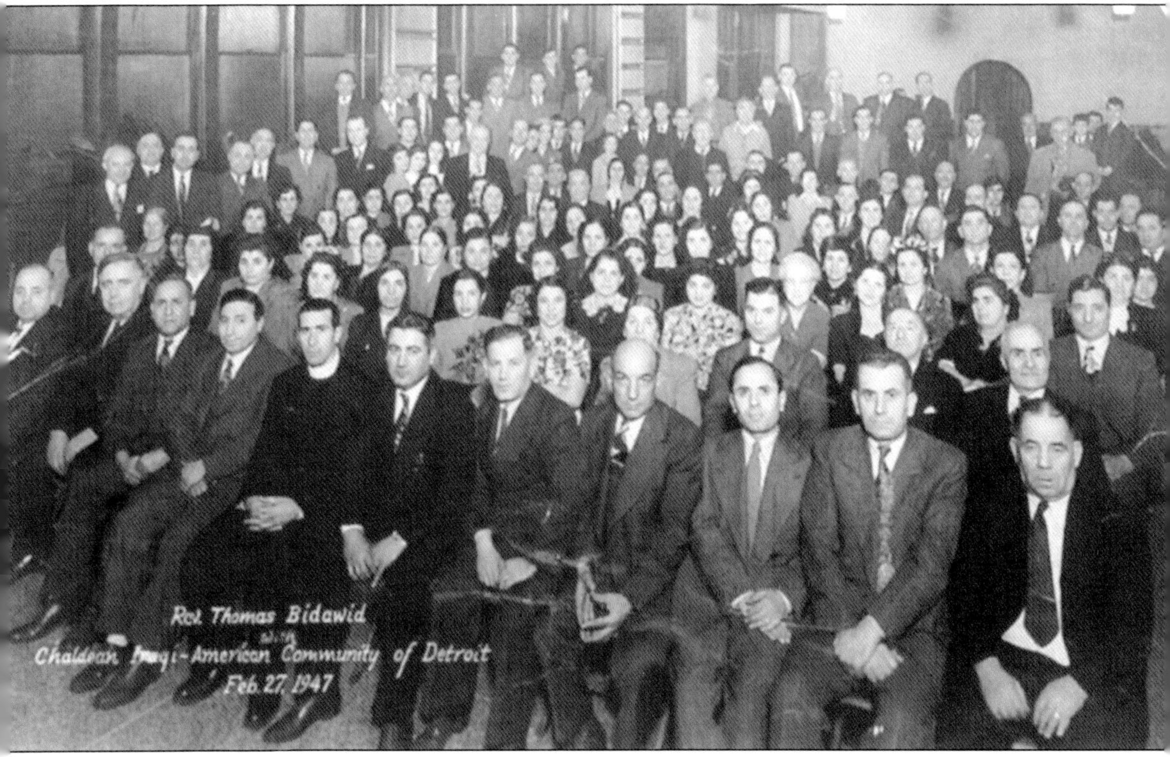

One Small Step, One Giant Leap. Since the first Chaldean arrived in Detroit around 1912, the community lacked its own priest for over 30 years. They attended mass at nearby Latin Rite Catholic parishes and sent their children to associated schools. For special events like weddings and funerals, many turned to the Maronite Rite Saint Maron Church in Detroit, which served the Lebanese community with similar language and rituals. A significant milestone occurred on February 27, 1947, at Danish Hall in Detroit, celebrating the arrival of the first Chaldean Rite priest, Father Toma Bidawid. This event, resembling a wedding ceremony, marked a pivotal moment in the community's history, paving the way for its growth in the United States and beyond. The strong church foundation established then continues to influence Chaldean immigrants today, evident in the community's ongoing expansion. The centrality of the Chaldean Rite is crucial in maintaining Chaldean identity; its absence in places like Mexico led to a loss of that identity and prompted migration to the United States. Father Bidawid's arrival was a monumental step for Detroit's Chaldean community with lasting significance for Chaldeans worldwide. (Courtesy of Mary Ann Jalaba Yono.)

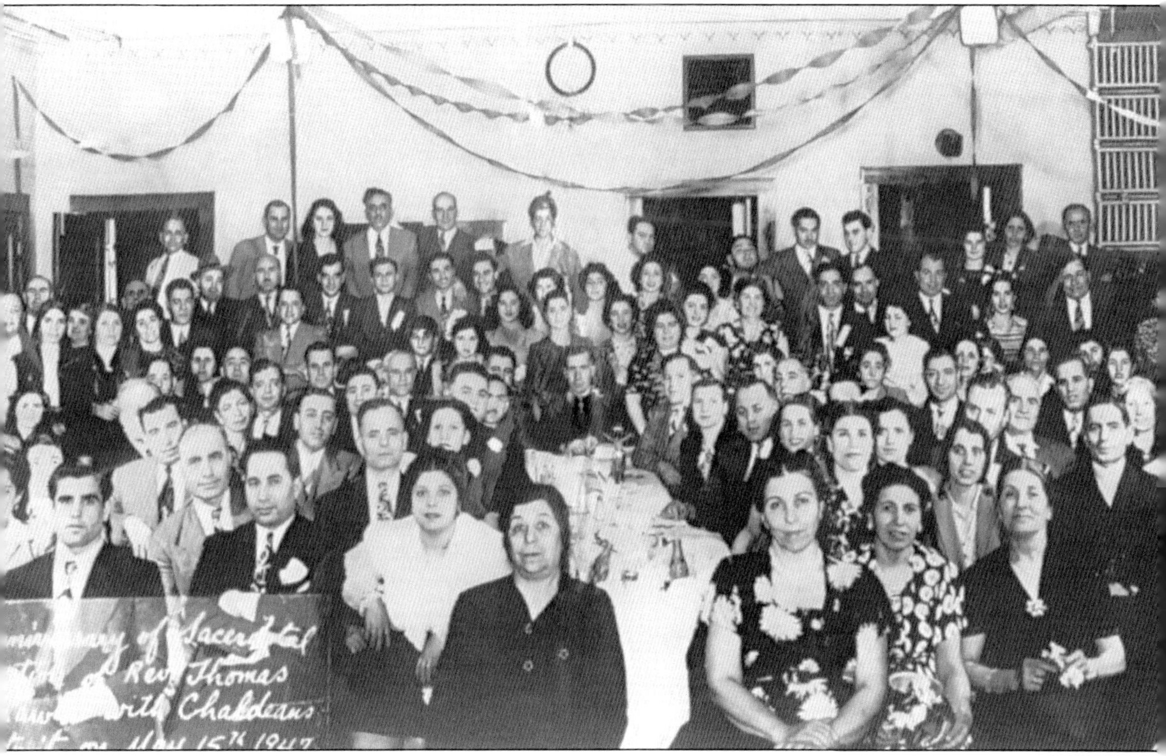

On the Cover. The arrival of the first priest played a unifying role for the community, making crucial decisions about faith, notably adopting Aramaic (Chaldean dialect) for the liturgy, which strengthened their sense of belonging. Less than a week after Father Bidawid's arrival, he held his first mass on March 2, 1947, officiating the first Chaldean Rite baptism in the United States for Emmanuel Paul Abbo, son of Peter and Katrina (Habba) Abbo, with Don Cassa as godfather. Within three months, on May 15, 1947, the community celebrated Father Bidawid's 12th priesthood anniversary at the Danish Hall in Detroit, as they lacked their own church. Sam Dabish, in his 1975 book *The History of the Iraqi Community in America*, described the event as "extremely splendid and well-organized," highlighting the generosity and chivalry of the Iraqi people. He noted that several guests and priests delivered congratulatory speeches, and special thanks were given to the Chaldean ladies who organized the event and prepared the food, desserts, and refreshments. Father Bidawid is seated at the center of the table. (Courtesy of Margaret Gabbara Atto, Chaldean Cultural Center.)

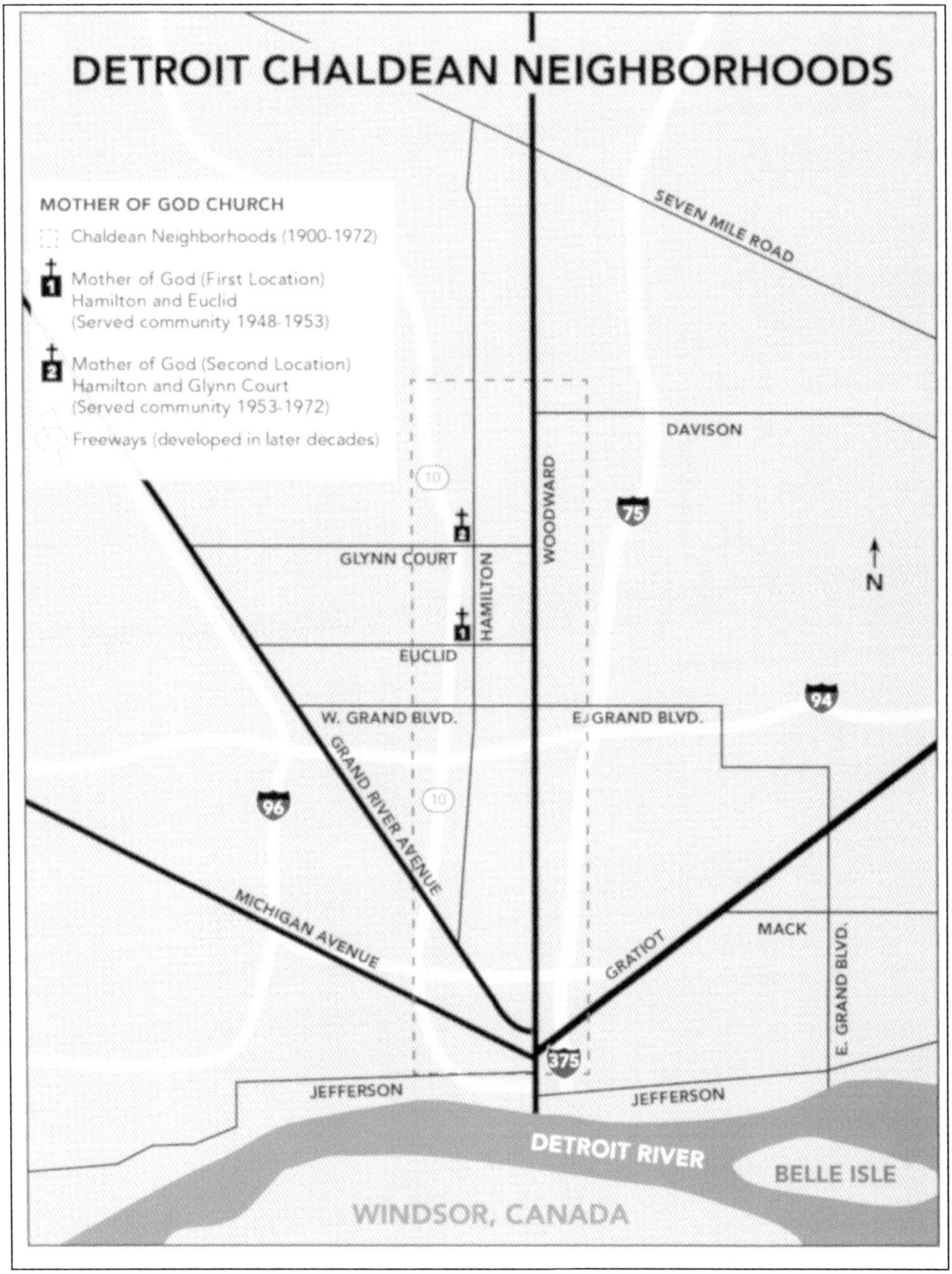

The Streets Where They Lived. The earliest Chaldean immigrants lived on Detroit's Eastside in the vicinity of East Jefferson Avenue and East Grand Boulevard. The excitement of new job opportunities meant new immigrants chose to follow their relatives and cousins where they could work, have a social life, freely express their faith, and send their children to good schools. The practicality of being within walking distance to work, church, and a community center was the deciding factor in choosing Detroit as a new home. Currently, no Chaldeans remain in the area. In the 1950s and 1960s and until the mid-1970s, most Chaldeans lived in the West Central and Northwest areas of the city and the suburbs northwest of the city. Today, Chaldean households are spread out in Wayne, Oakland, Macomb, and Washtenaw Counties. (Art by Alex Lumelsky.)

FIRST MOTHER OF GOD CHURCH (1948–1953). Mother of God was the first Chaldean church in Michigan. A former Protestant church on Hamilton Avenue and Euclid Street in Detroit was purchased, and keys were handed over on January 15, 1948, for the price of $50,000. It was renovated for use as a Chaldean Rite church and blessed and dedicated by the auxiliary bishop of Detroit, Allen Babcock, on August 15, 1948. The small Chaldean community, about 80 families at the time, finally had a sacred place of worship. The establishment of Mother of God Chaldean Catholic Church marked the real foundation of Chaldeans in the United States. This church is no longer standing; it was demolished in 1953 due to eminent domain laws to build the current John C. Lodge Freeway (M-10). Pictured at Mother of God from left to right are Dawood Kory, Zia Nalu, Father Toma Reis, Tobia Kory (Kas Gorgis), and Sam Dabish. (Courtesy of Sam Dabish.)

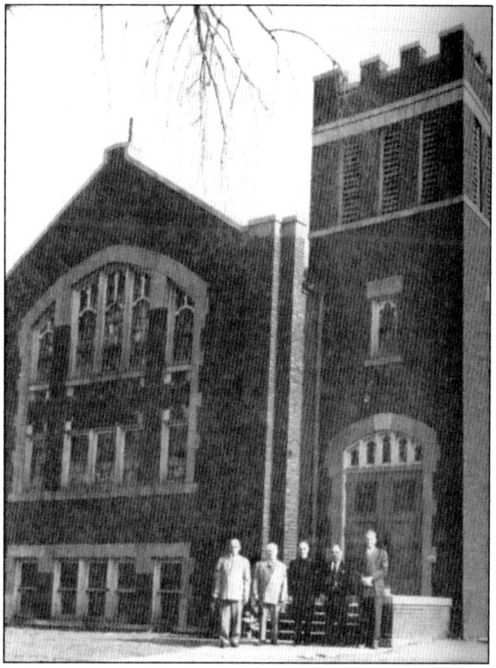

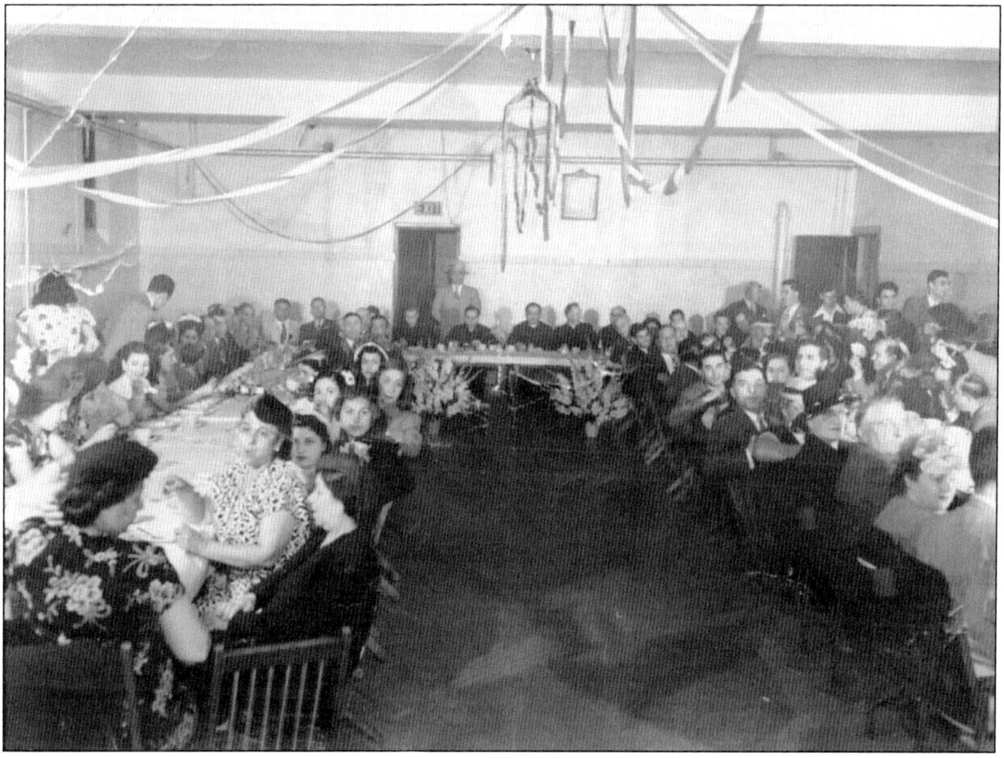

HAPPY EASTER. On March 28, 1948, the newly renovated Mother of God opened its doors for the very first time to the Chaldean community. The celebration on Easter Sunday was jam-packed with different faiths that joined in support. This image was taken in the basement. (Courtesy of Salim Kas-Shamoun.)

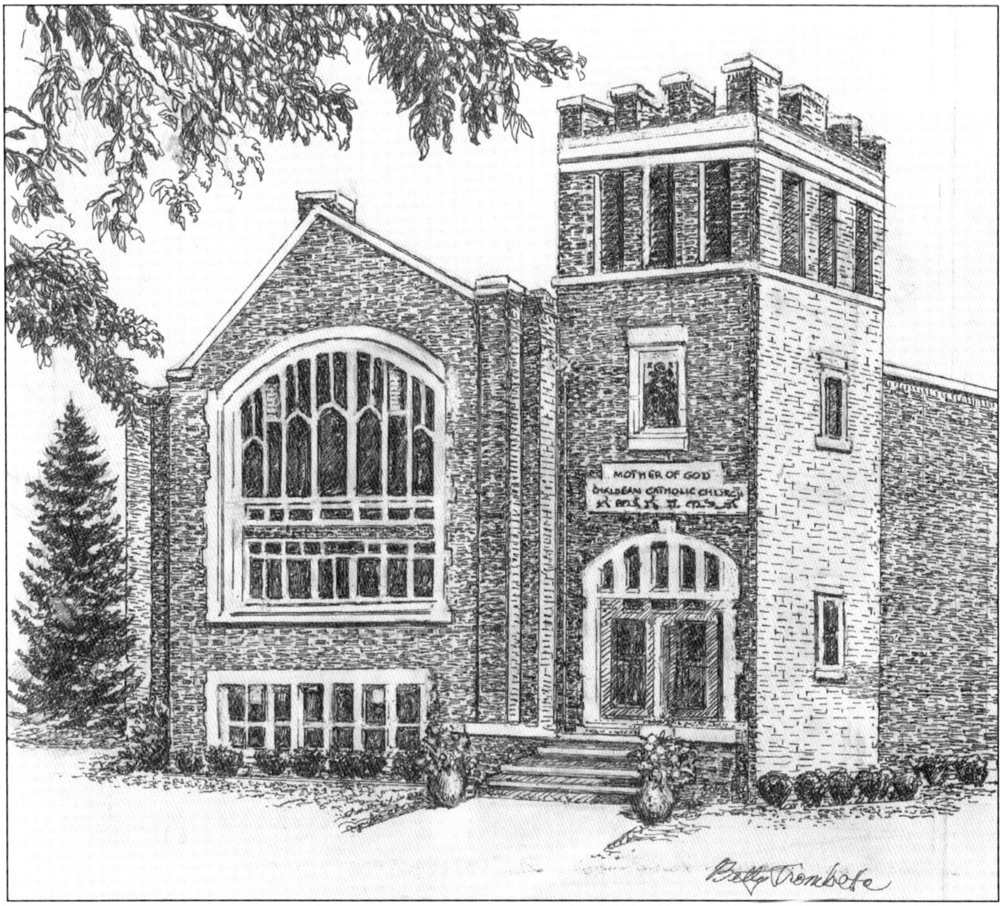

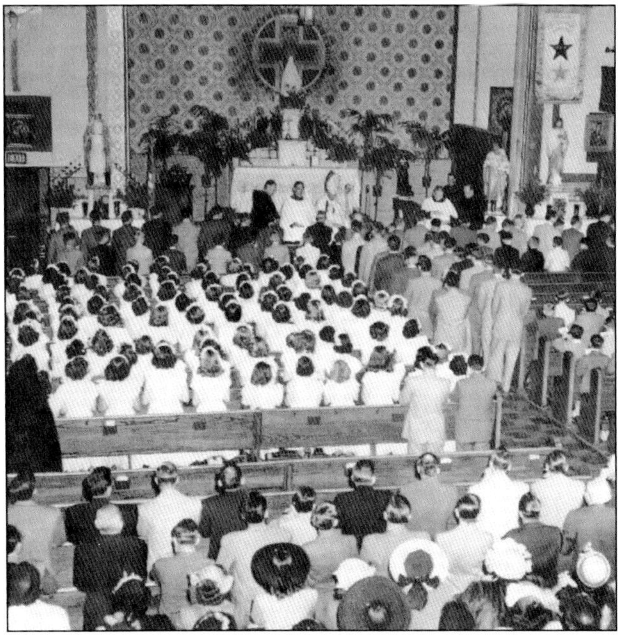

WHY "MOTHER OF GOD?" The official founding date of the parish is listed as March 9, 1948. Later that year, on August 15, Father Toma Bidawid named the church Mother of God, a title most interesting in light of the rite's former Nestorian ties. The single most important point on which Nestorians diverged from the Roman Church was its rejection of the Virgin Mary's right to the title Mother of God. The Chaldean parish name is, therefore, a symbol of its unity with Rome. Pictured here are a rendering of the first Mother of God Church (below) and an image taken inside on the First Communion Day. (Above, courtesy of Jacob Bacall; left, courtesy of the *Chaldean News*.)

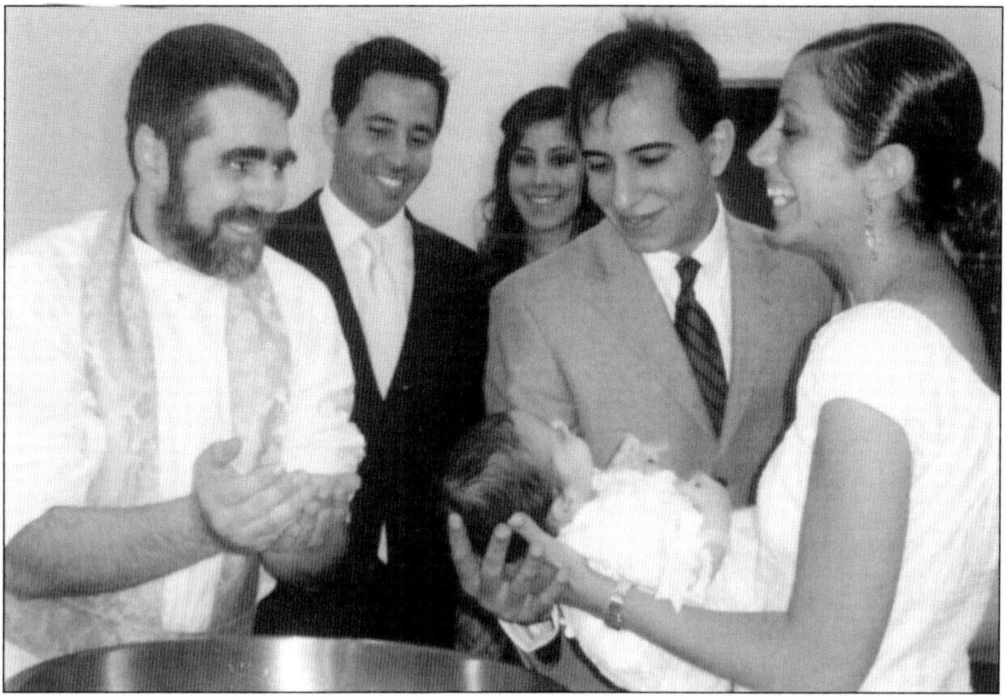

CATHOLIC YOU ARE! Baptism is one of the major ceremonies practiced by Christians all over the world, traditionally performed within the first few weeks of birth. Chaldean Rite children are baptized by pure water, a symbol of blessing and fertility, and become "confirmed" (Catholic). Parents choose the godfather and godmother, which is considered a great honor that should never be refused. It creates a lifelong bond that only grows stronger into adulthood. One Chaldean tradition is the observance of January 6 for baptisms. This is the traditional date of Christ's baptism, and it is considered a blessing to be baptized on January 6. Traditional Chaldean baptisms are pictured. (Above, courtesy of Bryon Perry; below, courtesy of Jacob Bacall.)

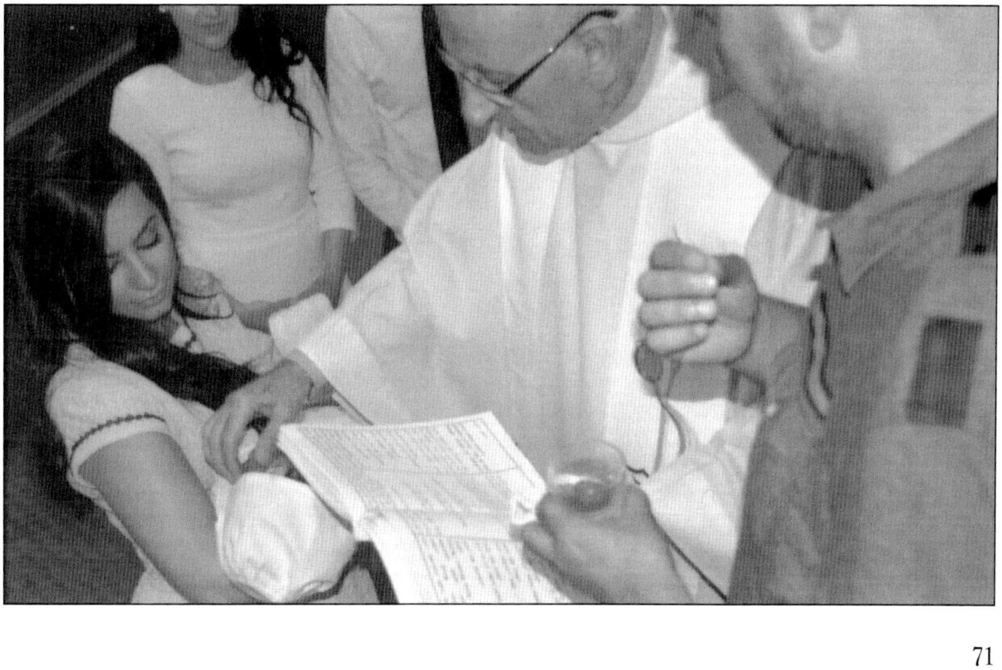

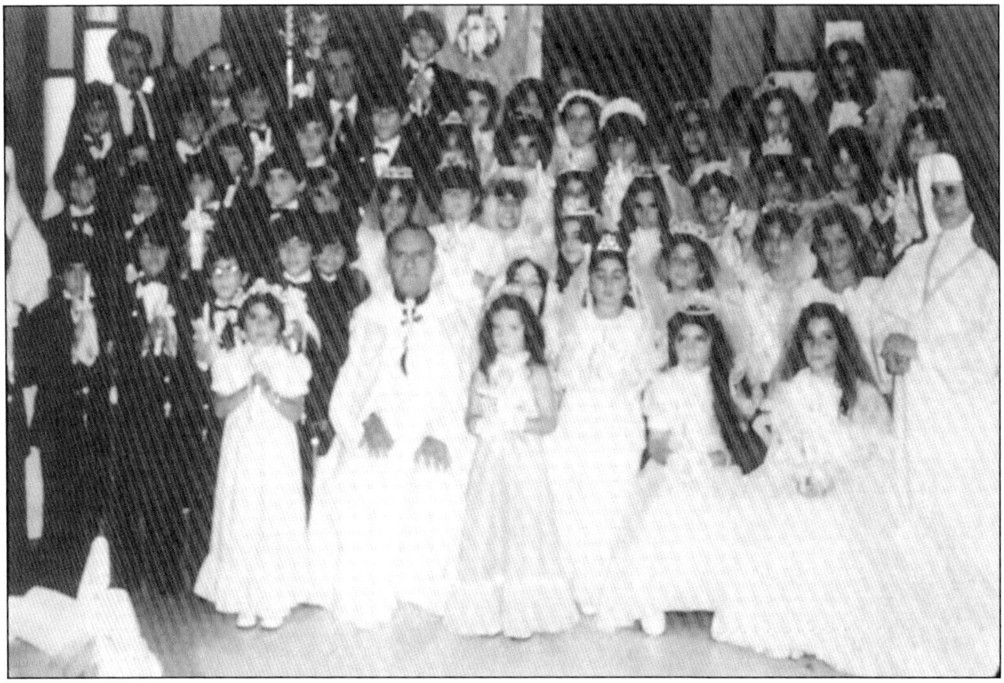

SHOU-HA TA BABA (GLORY BE TO THE FATHER). Receiving First Communion in the Catholic Church symbolizes the Last Supper of Jesus and his disciples. In preparation for First Communion, children between eight and 12 years of age attend classes at church several times a week. Families often arrange for two or more Chaldean siblings or cousins to celebrate together and host a party similar to a wedding reception, with the children dressed as miniature brides and grooms. Communion is part of every mass at a Chaldean Rite church. (Above, courtesy of Bryon Perry; below, courtesy of John Khami.)

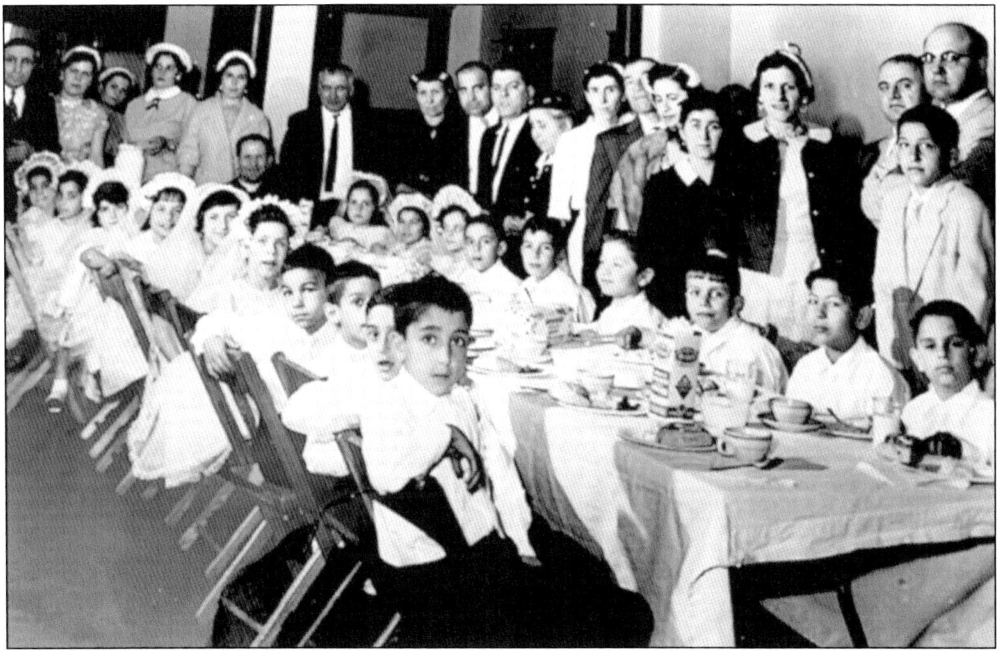

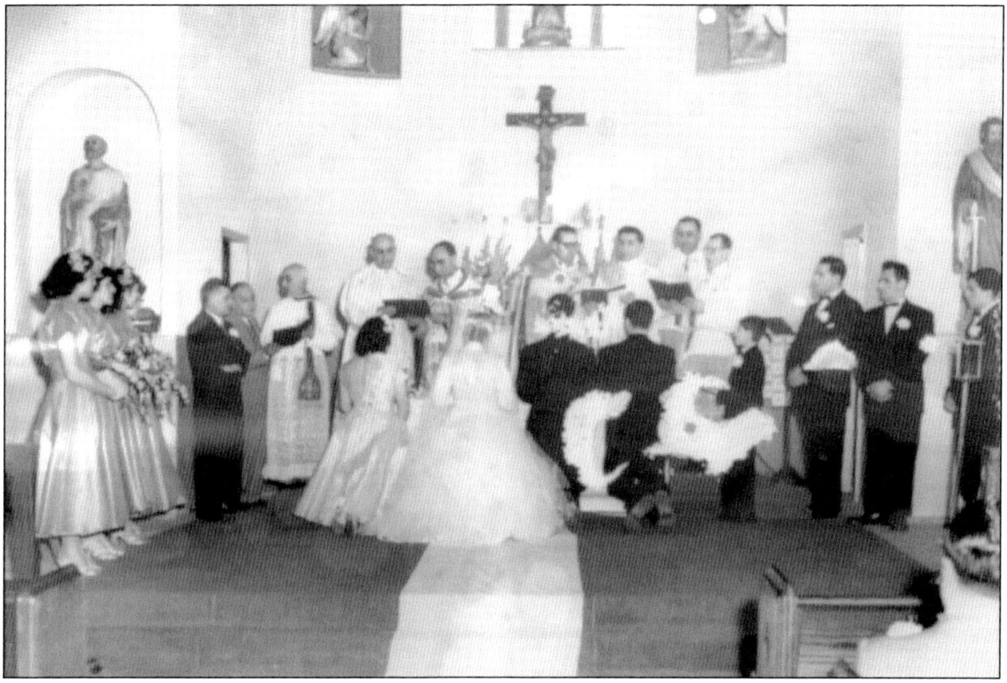

IN SICKNESS AND IN HEALTH. Weddings, or *borakha*, are central to Chaldean tradition. Historically, marriages were arranged for social or economic reasons, prioritizing family reputation and coming from the same native village. Today, Chaldeans choose partners based on personal compatibility, blending tradition with modernity. Chaldean weddings still feature Arabic music, the *khuga* dance, and the groom's family covering costs. The first Chaldean wedding in Detroit was officiated by Father Toma Bidawid in 1948. Traditional ceremonies remain a cherished part of the community's heritage. (Above, courtesy of Anmar Sarafa; below, courtesy of Mark J. Bacall.)

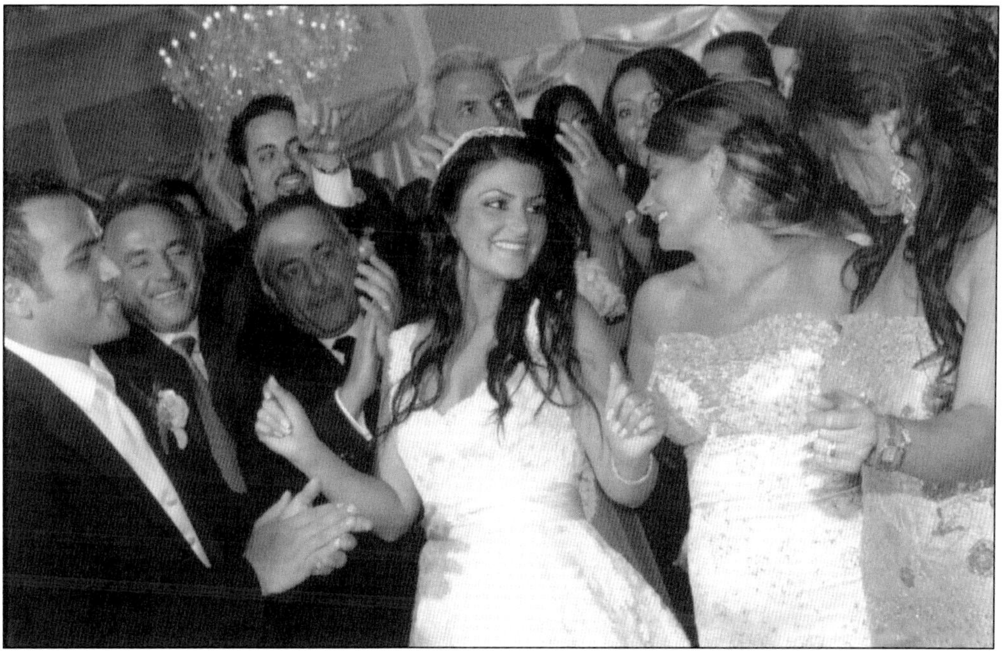

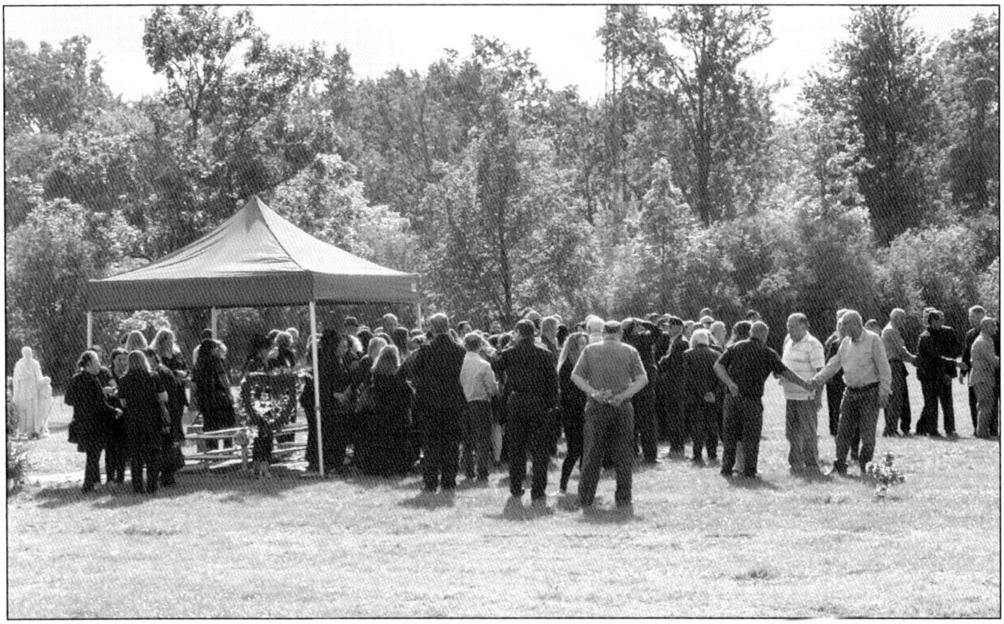

"Dust Thou Art, and unto Dust Thou Return." Funerals are known as *ta'ziyah* (pronounced tah-zee-yah), derived from the Chaldean word meaning "consolation." In Iraq, when someone loses a family member or faces a tragedy, it is customary for relatives, friends, and even neighbors to rush to their aid by preparing meals, sharing bags of rice or, in older times, offering a slaughtered sheep for a communal meal to comfort the bereaved. The mourning ceremony typically includes a procession of family, friends, and close relatives to the cemetery. (Both, courtesy of Jacob Bacall.)

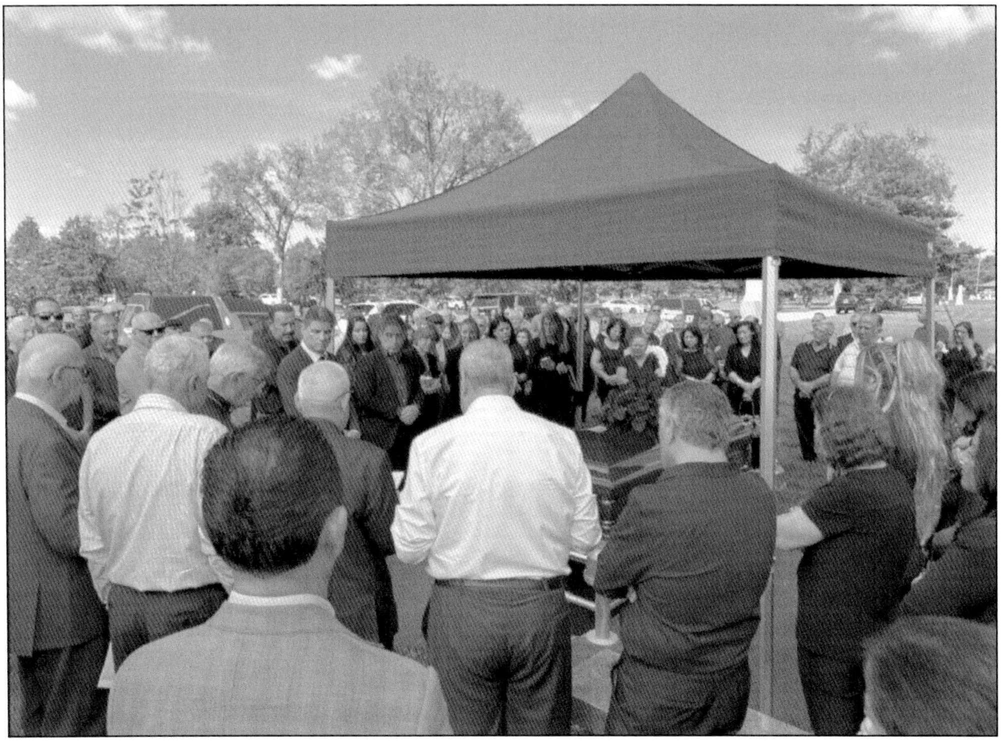

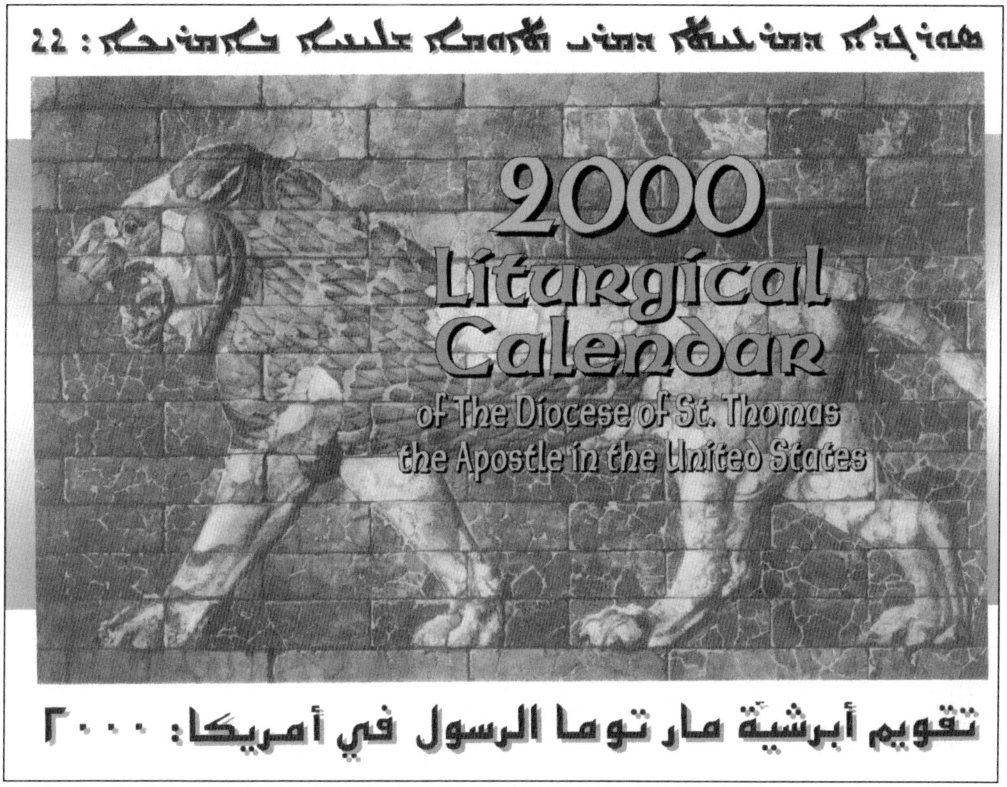

Get Your Calendar. There are multiple rites in the Catholic Church, each having its own unique liturgical traditions and practices. Among many differences of the Chaldean Rite is the order of the mass, liturgical language, music, vestments, rituals, customs, and calendar. The Chaldean liturgical calendar has differences in the timing and observance of feasts. Chaldean Catholics fast on most Fridays and for the three-day pre-Lenten observance of *Ba'utha*. (Both, courtesy of Jacob Bacall.)

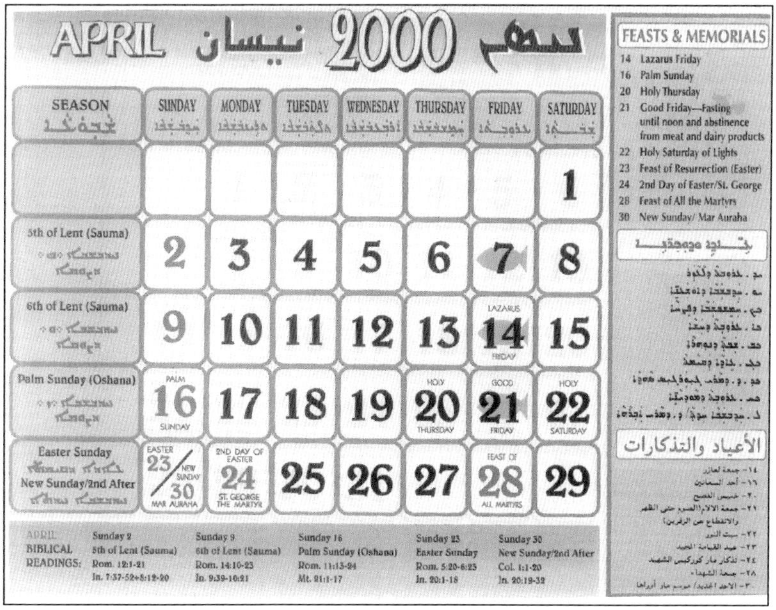

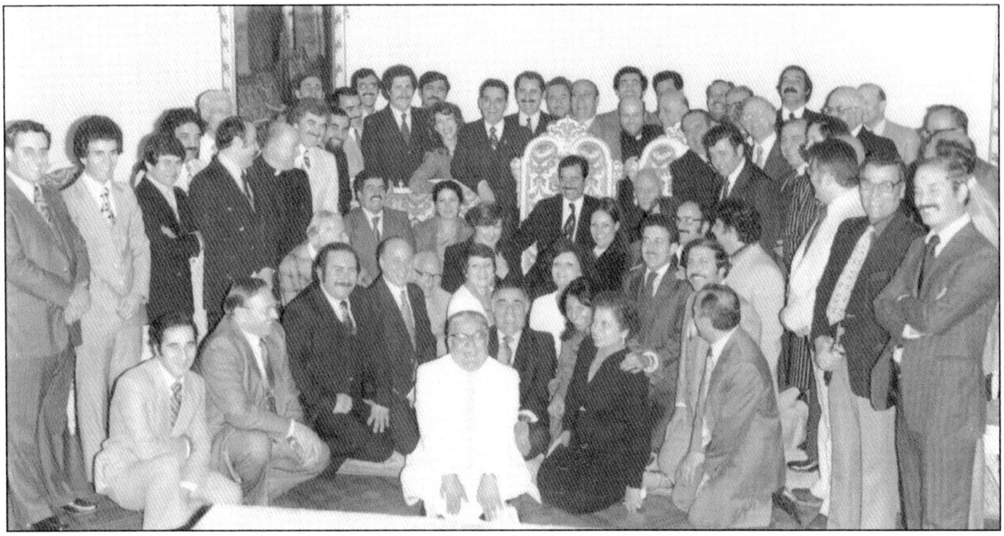

GUESTS OF PRESIDENT SADDAM. At the end of the 1970s, Iraq experienced a period of prosperity due to nationalizing its oil. The ruling Arab Baath Socialist Party aimed to promote an attractive image of Iraq and the party. The charge d'affaires of the Iraqi Embassy in Washington invited foreigners and Iraqis to visit Iraq, leading to a delegation from Michigan visiting Baghdad in 1979. (Courtesy of Raad Kathawa.)

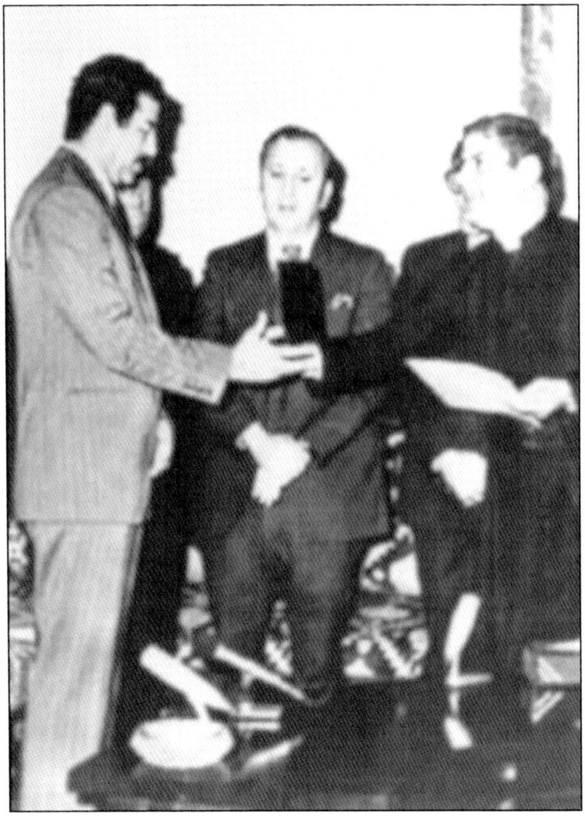

SADDAM HUSSEIN—DETROIT HONORARY CITIZEN. In 1979, Father Jacob Yasso, pastor of Sacred Heart Church, received a $250,000 donation from Iraqi president Saddam Hussein. When the news reached Detroit mayor Coleman Young, he allowed Father Yasso to present the Key to the City of Detroit to President Hussein. Additionally, Father Yasso received $200,000 to renovate his church. Other Chaldean churches also accepted Saddam's donations, including $400,000 for Saint Ephrem Parish in Chicago (Father Edward Bikoma), and $250,000 each for Saint Peter Parish in San Diego (Father Putrus Kattoula), Saint Paul Parish in North Hollywood (Father Ibrahim Ibrahim), and Saint Thomas Parish in Turlock (Father Ablahad Najjar). Shortly after, Father Najjar was shot while sleeping, likely due to accepting the money. He survived but never resumed to his normal life, retiring and later passing away in Detroit. (Courtesy of Father Jacob Yasso.)

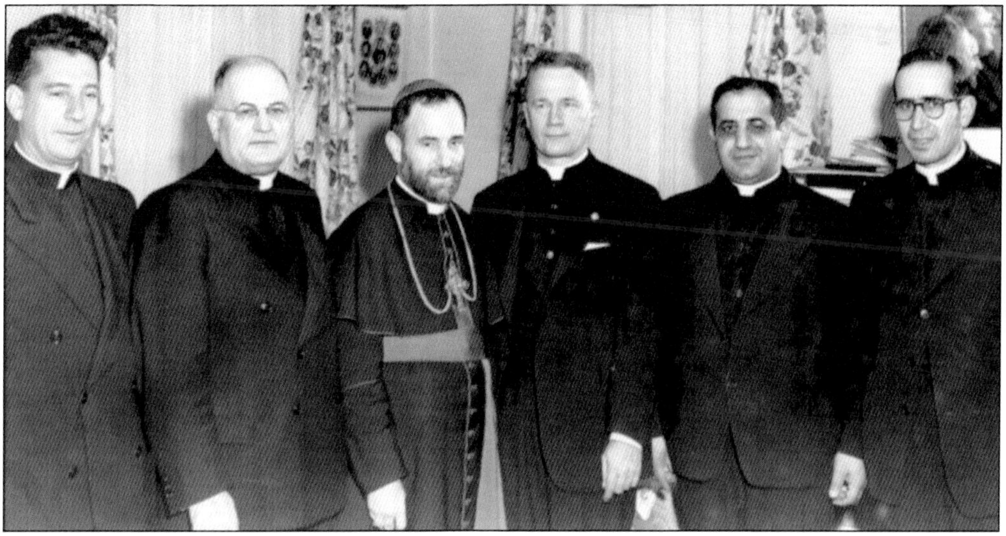

CHALDEAN VS. LATIN RITE. "The rituals of the Chaldean Rite differ considerably from the Latin Rite. Those differences were particularly strong in the country of origin and could be seen in the early churches in Detroit," said Mary C. Sengstock in her book *Chaldeans in Michigan*. The Chaldean Rite of the Eastern Catholic Church is in full communion with Rome, and each rite has some regional and local variations in the way mass is celebrated. Worshiping in the Aramaic language, which was used by Jesus, remains the most distinct difference between the Chaldean and Latin Rites. In this photograph, priests from three rites gather, Latin, Maronite, and Chaldean, representing different Catholic sects. (Courtesy of Tobia Hakim.)

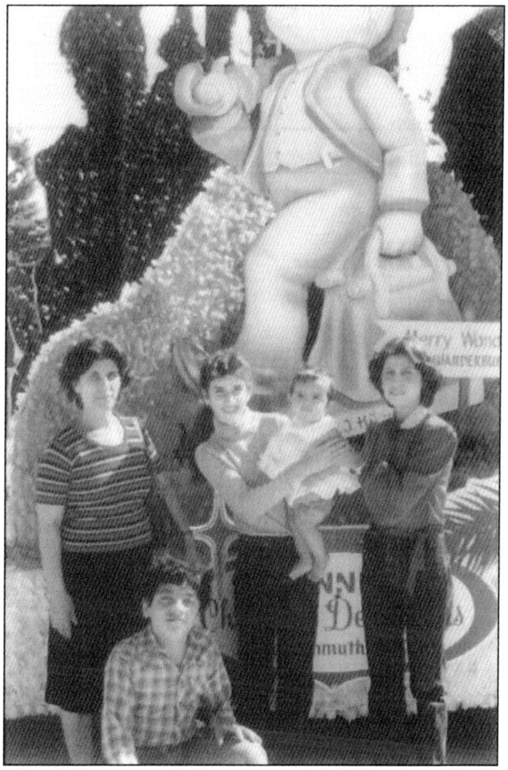

BRONNER'S CHRISTMAS WONDERLAND. Christians all over the United States take advantage of this one-of-a-kind store located in the city of Frankenmuth, about 80 miles north of Detroit. The well-stocked store has something for everyone. Today, people tend to think of Christmas as "The Most Wonderful Time of the Year," as the hit song from 1963 calls it. A word of caution: visitors the landmark store during the Christmas holiday week should prepare for long lines and two-hour waits. Pictured here is a Chaldean family visiting Bronner's Christmas Wonderland in 1981. (Courtesy of Jacob Bacall.)

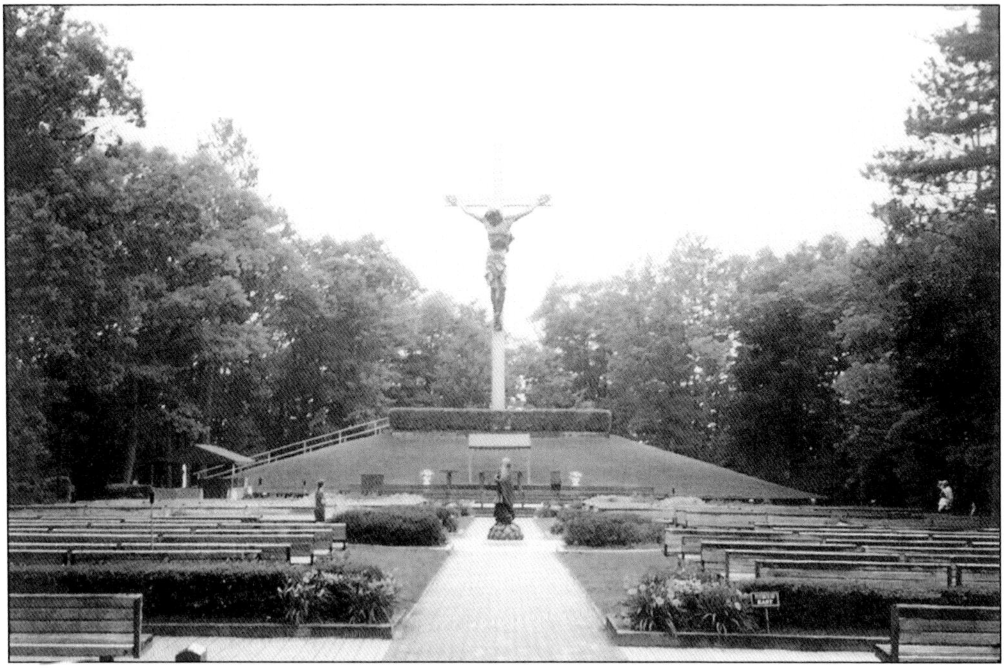

CROSS IN THE WOODS. Every year on September 14, known as "Chaldean Day," crowds gather at the National Shrine of the Cross in the Woods in Indian River, Michigan, to celebrate Holy Cross Day. For over 30 years, Chaldeans have made the pilgrimage to this shrine. They arrive in the morning in the small town with a population of around 2,000. Before the Chaldean mass at noon, they walk the quiet and peaceful grounds, visiting the Stations of the Cross laid out across the wooded area. They also observe the 55-foot-tall outdoor crucifix and climb the Holy Stairs leading up to the base of the cross. (Both, courtesy of Jacob Bacall.)

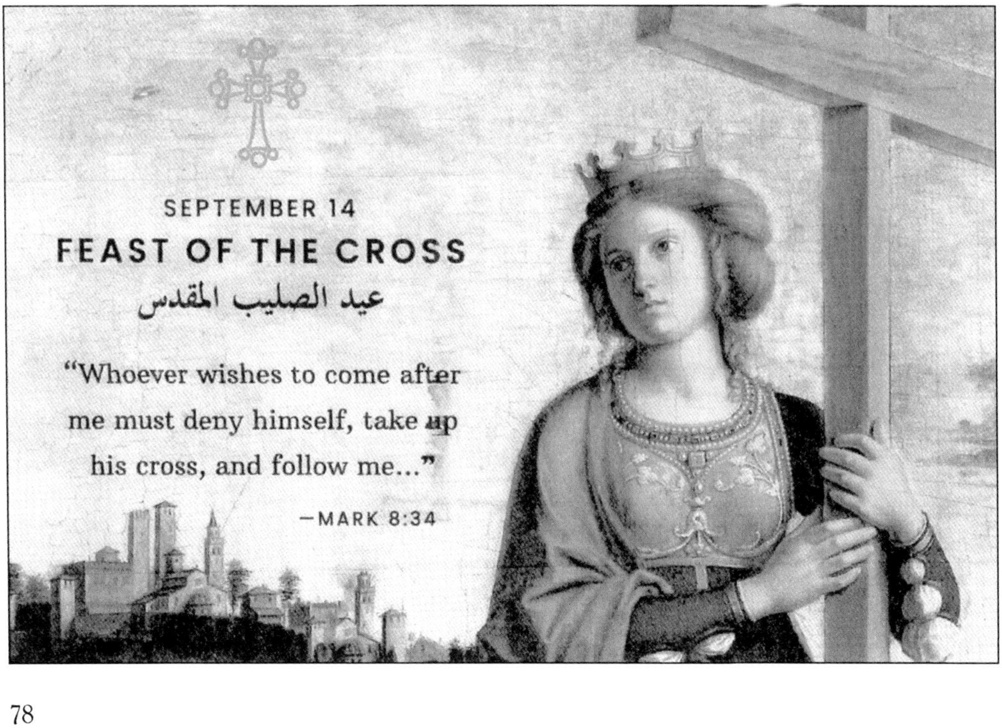

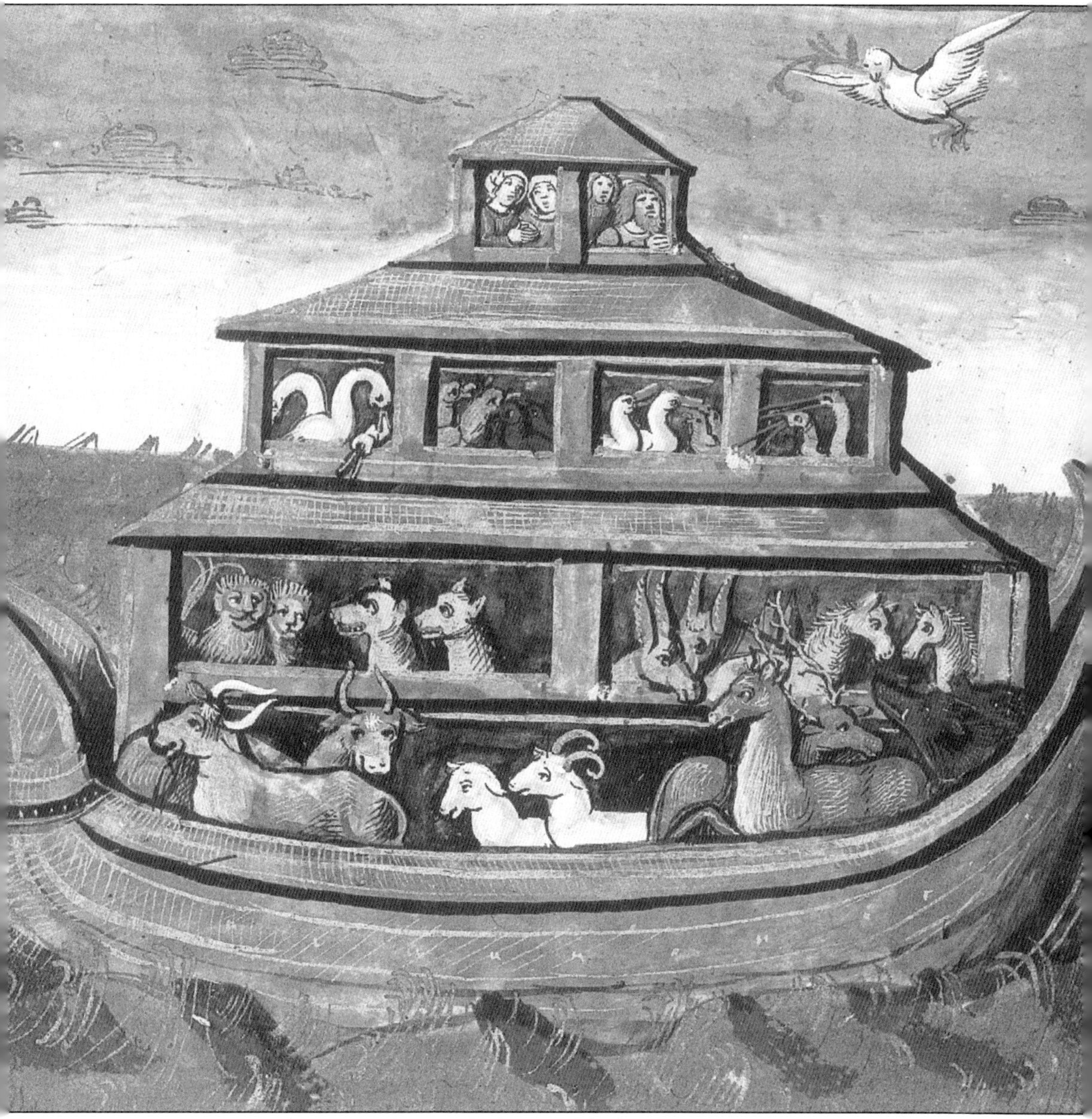

Worldwide Flood? Bible experts debate whether Noah's flood covered the entire globe or just the ancient world's known region. Civilization began in the fertile valleys of the Tigris and Euphrates, where massive floods once destroyed cities. Around 4500 BCE, a deluge near Mount Ararat turned the Black Sea from a lake to an ocean. Flood stories exist in 70 cultures, including the *Epic of Gilgamesh*, which parallels Noah's tale of survival and a dove's return. (Courtesy of Chaldean Catholic Diocese of Saint Thomas the Apostle.)

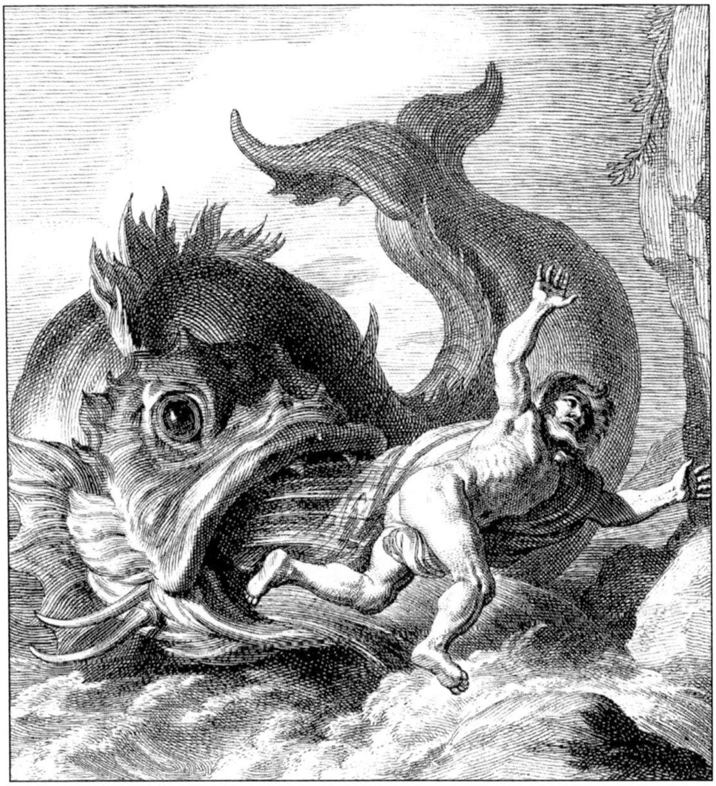

Ba'utha **(Pleading).** In the sixth century, a devastating plague struck Nineveh, prompting the bishop to recall the story of Jonah, where the Ninevites fasted, wore sackcloth, and repented to God for mercy. Inspired by Jonah's three-day repentance inside the fish, the bishop called for a similar fast and prayer. The plague eventually subsided, and the Ninevites continued the fast annually. Ba'utha, meaning "pleading" in Aramaic, and observed by Chaldean Catholic, Assyrian Church of the East, and Syriac Christian communities. (Both, courtesy of Crystal Kassab-Jabiro.)

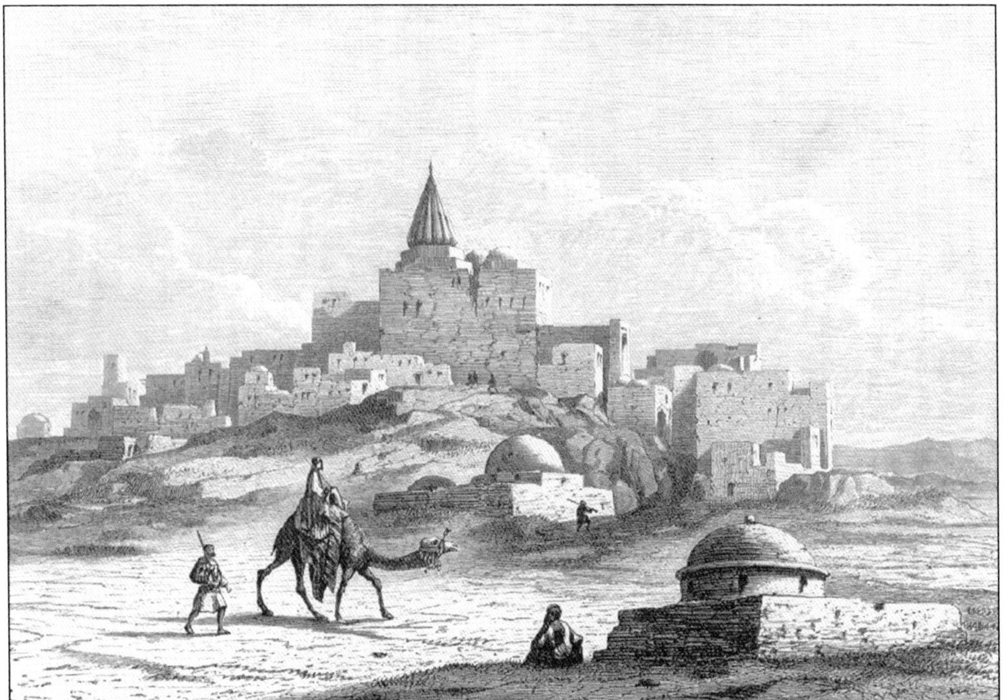

THE "TOMB OF JONAH," NEAR THE MOSQUE, ON THE ARTIFICIAL MOUND OF NEBBI YUNIS, NINEVEH.

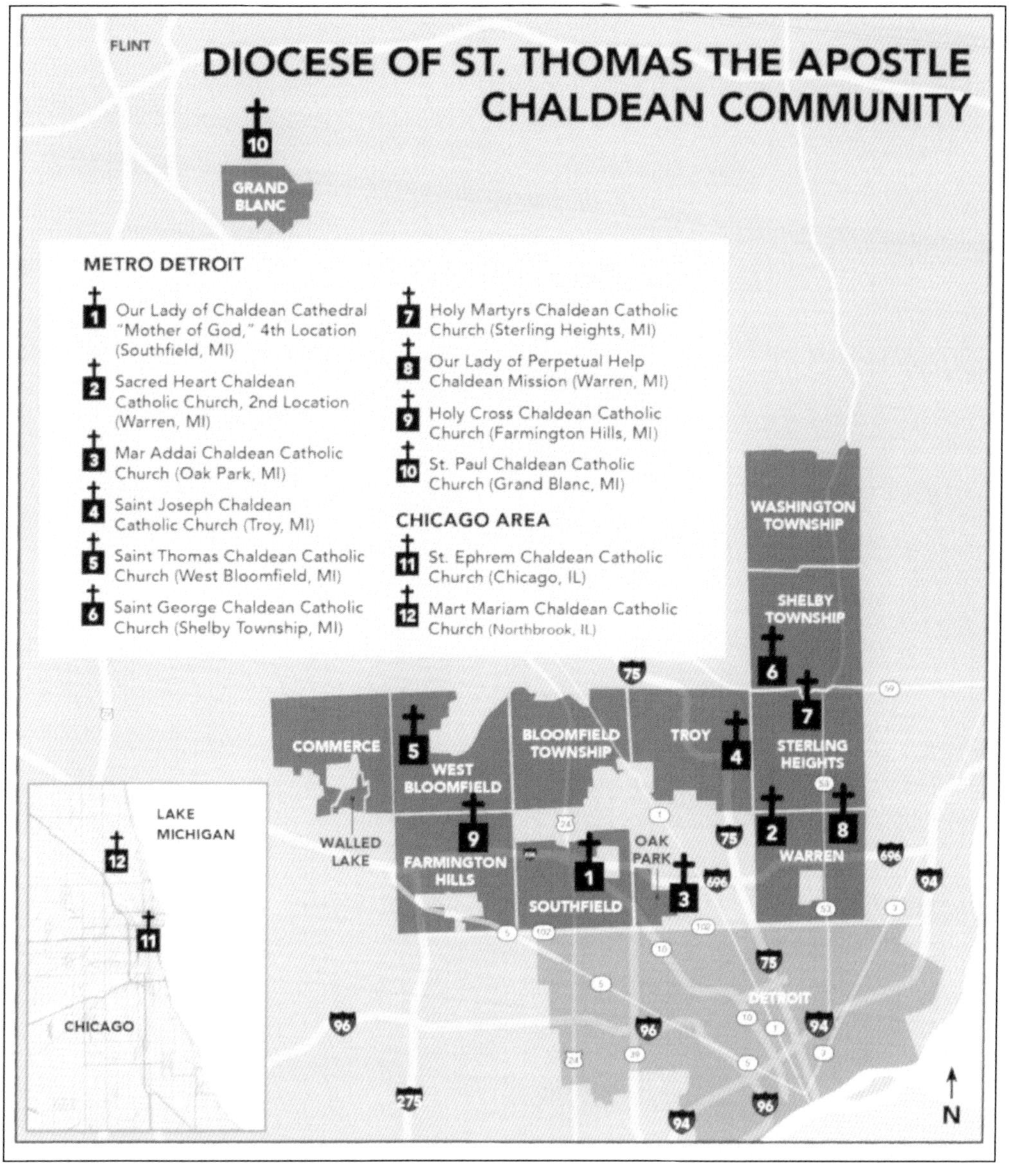

Upon This Rock I Shall Build My Church (Matthew 16:18). The early faithful Chaldeans celebrated their mass at Saint Maron Church in Detroit. In 1948, they moved to their first church, at Euclid Street and Hamilton Avenue, and in 1953 they relocated to 10213 Hamilton Avenue in Detroit. In 1972, they moved to Southfield. On May 15, 1973, the Chaldean patriarch, Bishop Paulus II Cheikho, dedicated the new Mother of God Church (the actual church hall). On September 13, 1980, he dedicated the present church. "Identification with the Chaldean religion and language remains strong, even among those who no longer speak the ancestral language," said Mary Sengstock in *Chaldeans in Michigan*. On January 26, 1982, the first apostolic exarchate in the United States was established by Pope John Paul II, and Ibrahim Ibrahim was ordained its first bishop. As religion continues to play a vital role in Chaldean life, the church serves as the center of many community activities and occasions. The 2016 annual directory listed Saint Thomas the Apostle Eparchy as the largest in the world with over 180,000 members. Today, there are 12 churches under the Diocese of Saint Thomas the Apostle. (Art by Alex Lumelsky.)

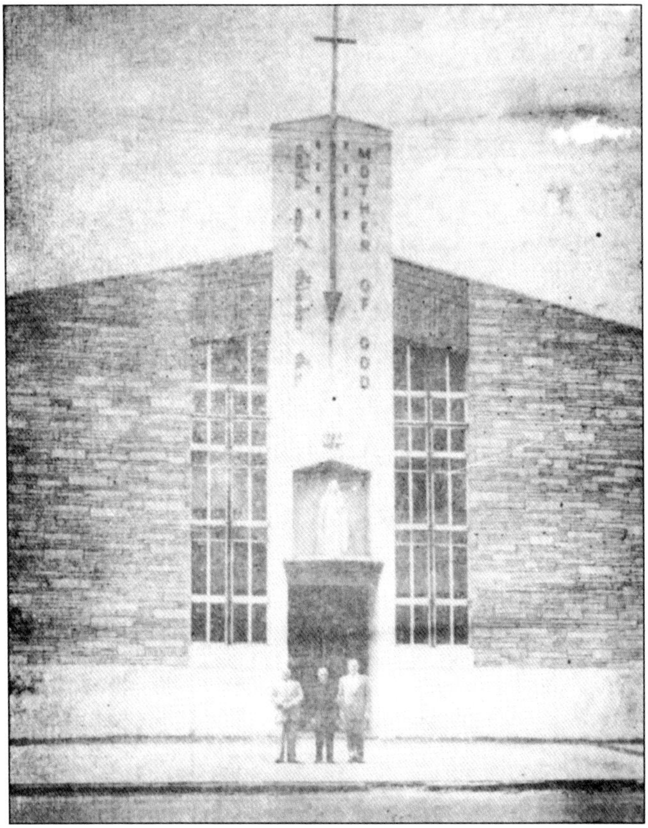

MOTHER OF GOD CHURCH (1953–1972). The second Chaldean church is often confused with the first since both were located on Hamilton Avenue in Detroit. The former funeral parlor at 10213 Hamilton Avenue at Glynn Court was purchased in 1953 and remodeled to serve as a church. A few years later, a new church was built and consecrated on April 6, 1956, by Henry Donnelly, auxiliary bishop of Detroit. Father Toma Reis became the first priest to serve at this location. (Courtesy of *Chaldean Directory*.)

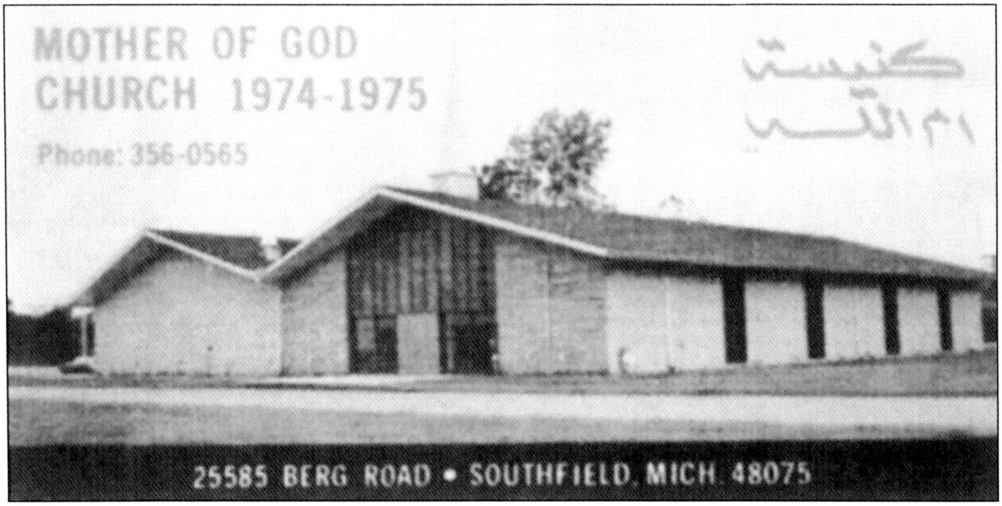

MOTHER OF GOD CHURCH (1973–1980). The third location of Mother of God Chaldean Church served the community from 1973 to 1980. The original plan was to build a much larger church to accommodate the growing congregation in Oakland County. Construction began in late 1971, with plans for a church, rectory, and a hall for community events. In 1964, Father George Garmo purchased 10.3 acres at Berg Road and Ten Mile Road in Southfield for $50,000. The church was consecrated on May 15, 1973, by Patriarch Paulus II Cheikho. Today, the third location serves as a hall for church and community events. (Courtesy of *Chaldean Directory*.)

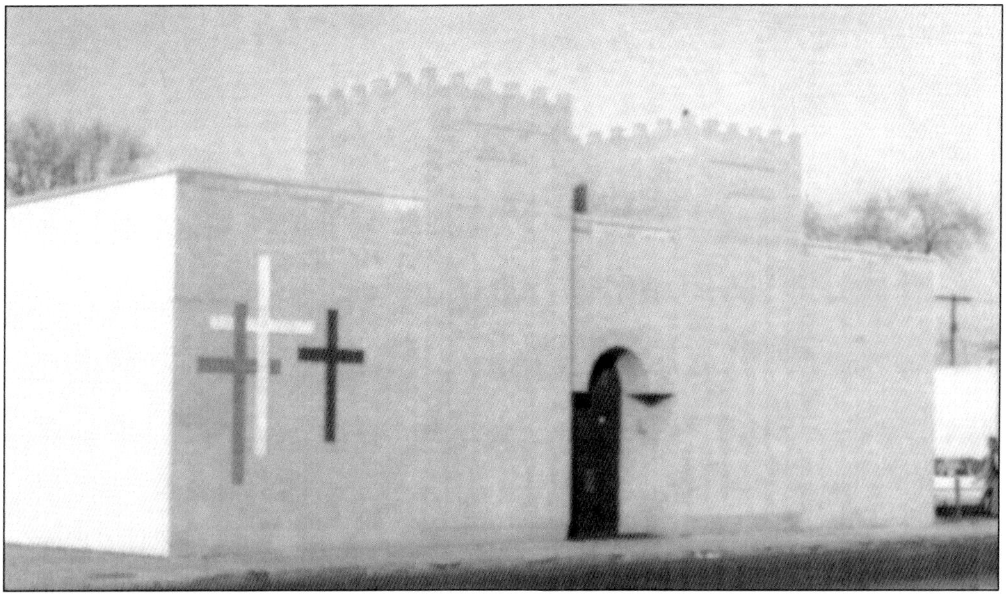

SACRED HEART CHURCH (1975–2014). In May 1973, Chaldean patriarch Bishop Paulus II Cheikho met with the Archdiocese of Detroit to establish a new Chaldean church. Father Jacob Yasso was assigned to serve the growing Chaldean immigrant community, leading to the founding of Sacred Heart Parish at 310 West Seven Mile Road. Father Yasso named it Sacred Heart Parish after Sacred Heart Church in Telkaif, Iraq. It was consecrated on June 5, 1975, by Bishop Emmanuel Delly, auxiliary to the patriarch. (Courtesy of Bryon Perry.)

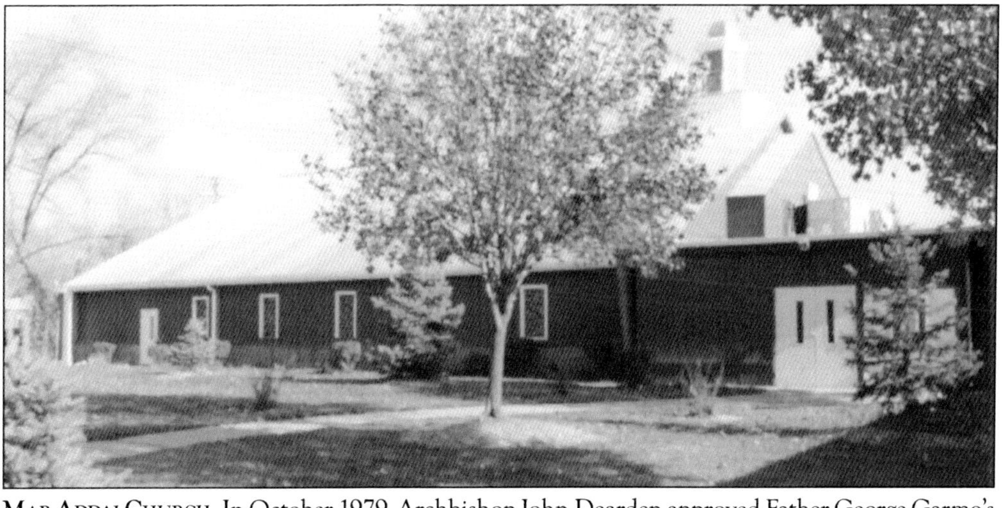

MAR ADDAI CHURCH. In October 1979, Archbishop John Dearden approved Father George Garmo's request to establish a third Chaldean parish in Oak Park, Michigan, using the former Our Lady of Fatima Church. The first mass was celebrated by Father Michael Bazzi in July 1979, and the parish was named Mar Addai. In 1981, the parish purchased the east wing of the former school, and the church was consecrated on September 24, 1983, by Patriarch Paulus II Cheikho. It was consecrated on September 24, 1983, by Patriarch Paulus II Cheikho in the presence of Bishop Ibrahim Ibrahim. (Courtesy of Bryon Perry.)

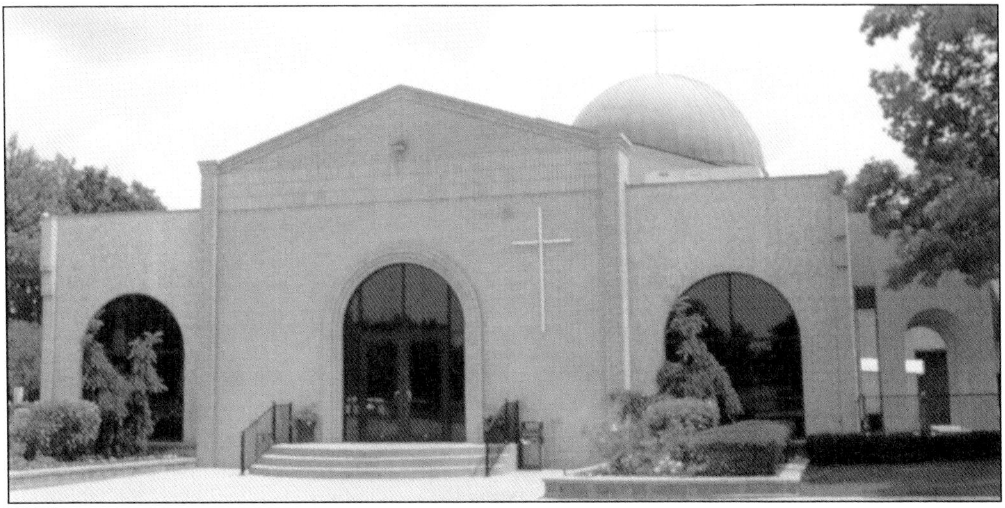

OUR LADY OF THE CHALDEANS CATHEDRAL (1980–PRESENT). The fourth location of Mother of God is adjacent to the third location and is identified by its dome. The ground-breaking was on Easter day 1979. It was consecrated on September 13, 1980, by Patriarch Paulus II Cheikho of Babylon. The first pastor was Msgr. George Garmo, and he was assisted by Father Sarhad Jammo. This is the longest-serving Chaldean Catholic church at the same location. It has been elevated to the status of cathedral, indicating its function as a bishop's church, while keeping the name Mother of God. It is the first Chaldean cathedral in the United States and in the western hemisphere. Also known as Our Lady of Chaldeans Cathedral, Mother of God is blessed with many faithful volunteers. They come not only to deepen their faith in various ways but also to share their time and talents throughout the church. Some of these volunteers are part of established groups such as the Parish Council, instructors of catechism and First Communion classes, Bible study participants, altar service members, and choirs singing in Arabic, English, and Sourath. Many other dedicated, goodhearted volunteers contribute as well. (Both, courtesy of Bryon Perry.)

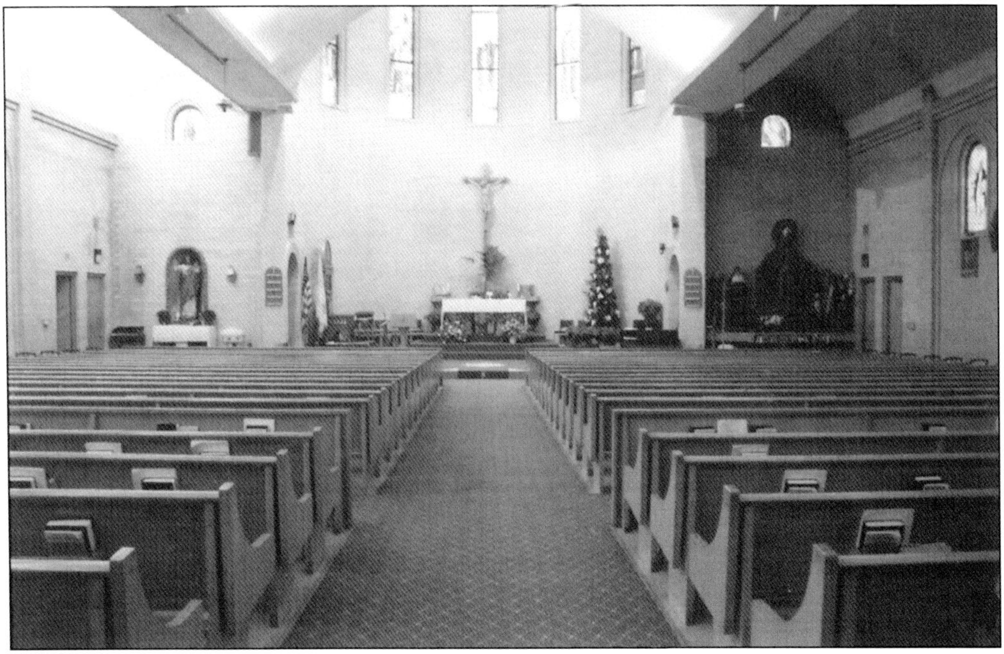

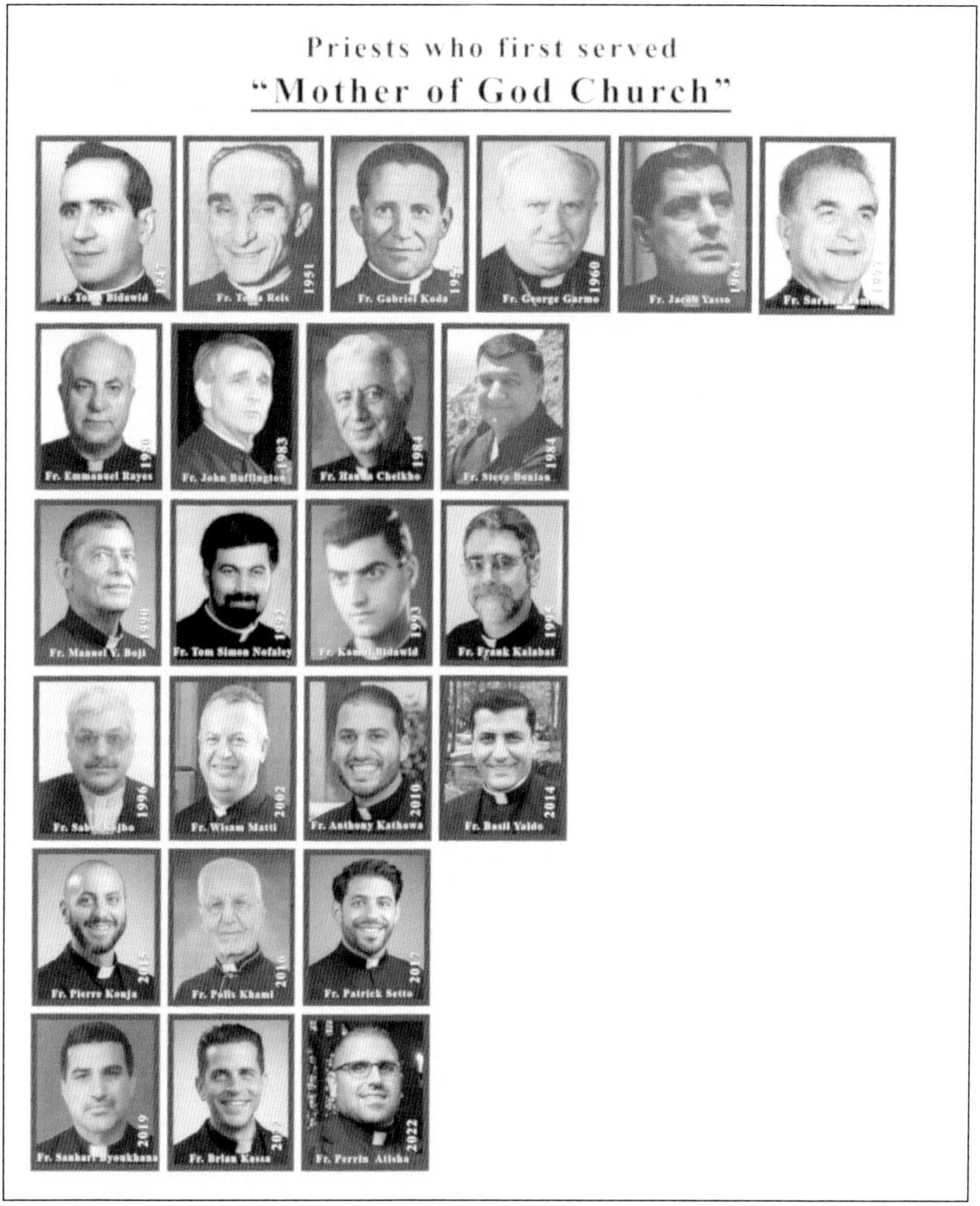

Priests Who Served Mother of God. By the 50th anniversary of Mother of God in 1993, 13 priests had served the parish. Father Toma Bidawid was the first. In 2023, the congregation celebrated the 75th anniversary of the church. The number of priests who have served has almost doubled due to the community's population growth, surpassing all expectations and projections. Mother of God currently holds the distinction of being the longest-serving Chaldean parish in America, with a seating capacity of 900 people. Its priests, deacons, and bishops continue the mission of the apostles through their work of teaching, leading the church in worship, and serving the community. As noted in Mark 10:43, "Whoever wishes to be great among you will be your servant." (Art by Lamar Sulaka.)

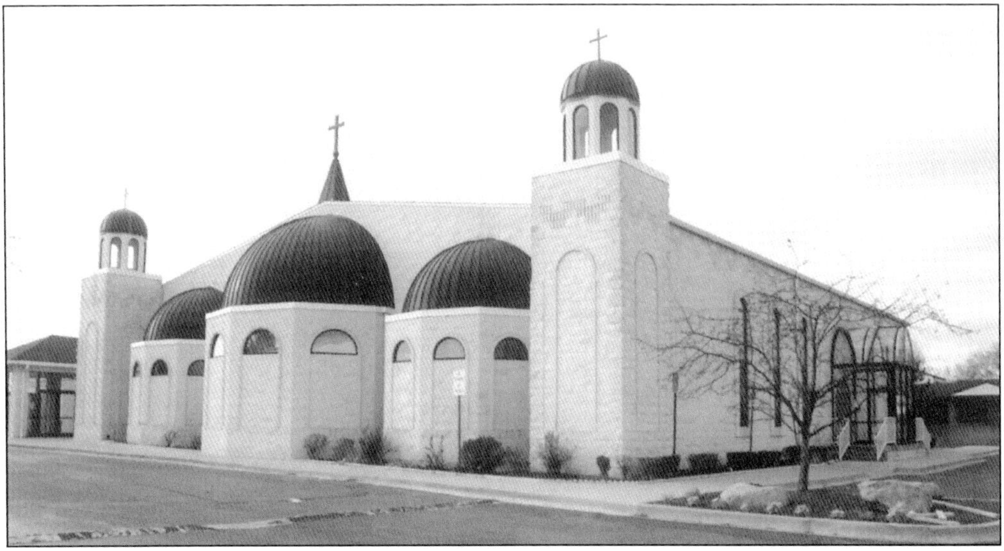

SAINT JOSEPH CHURCH. As the Chaldean community expanded, Father Michael Bazzi established Saint Joseph Church in Troy, Michigan, in 1981, purchasing Santa Anastasia Church and adding a residence for the priest. In 1982, Father Sarhad Jammo became pastor, and he oversaw the construction of a new hall, completed in 1985. Plans for a new church with Eastern architectural domes were implemented, and the church was consecrated on November 30, 1996, by Patriarch Bidawid and Patriarch Dinkha IV alongside Bishop Ibrahim Ibrahim and Bishop Bawai Soro. Saint Joseph Church is located at 2442 East Big Beaver Road in Troy. (Both, courtesy of Bryon Perry.)

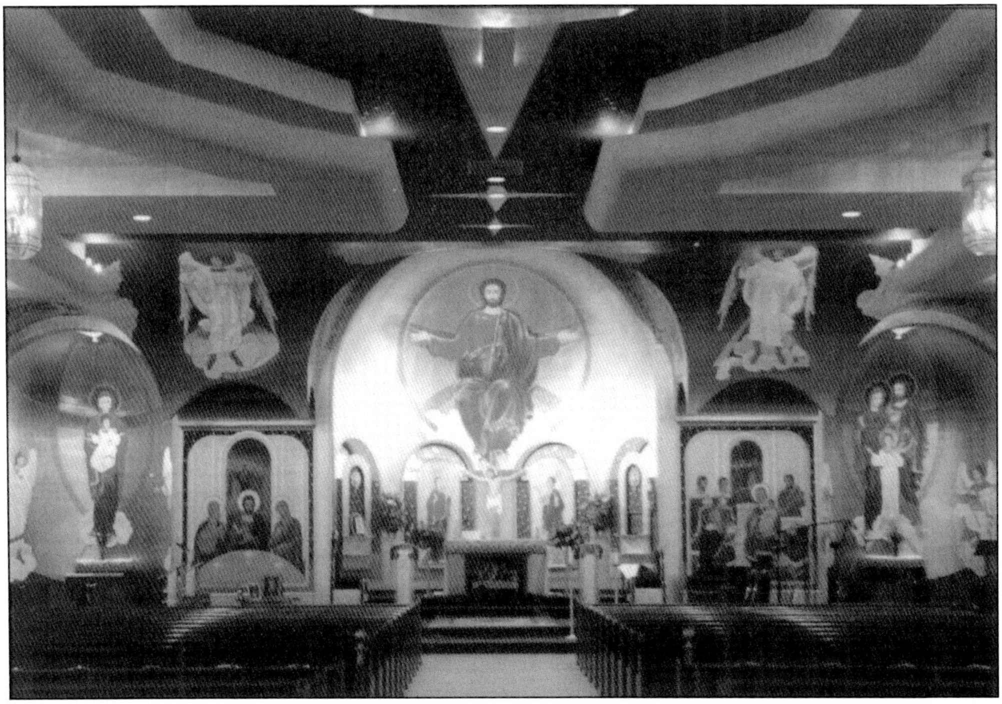

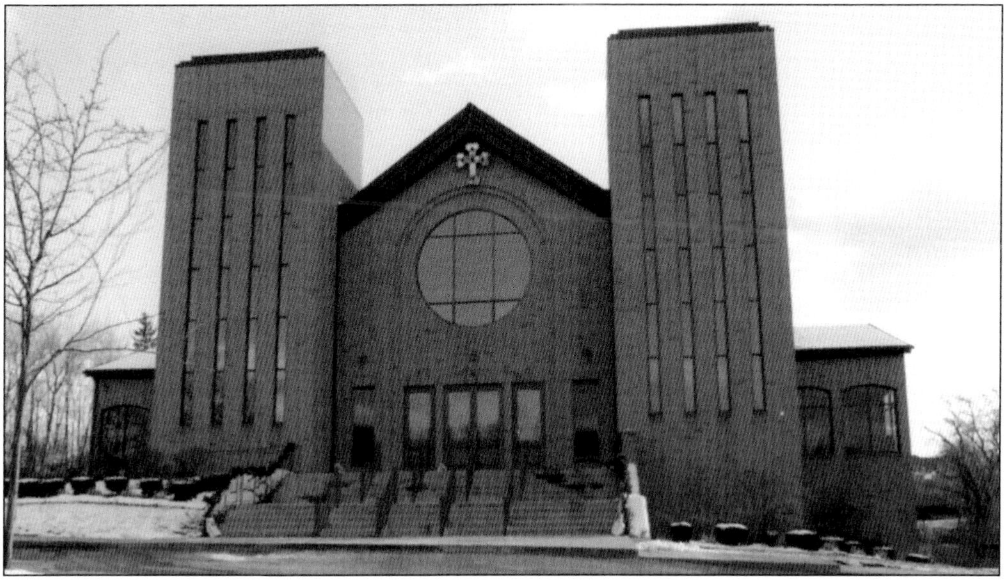

SAINT THOMAS CHURCH. In 1995, Bishop Ibrahim Ibrahim tasked Father Hanna Cheikho with establishing a new church in West Bloomfield. Land was purchased in 1996 on West Maple Road, and renowned Chaldean architect Victor Saroki designed the church with an Eastern facade inspired by the ancient city of Ishtar. Construction began in 1997, and Saint Thomas Church was completed and consecrated on April 4, 1999, by Bishop Ibrahim Ibrahim, Archbishop Cardinal Adam Maida, and Father Cheikho, the first pastor. (Courtesy of Bryon Perry.)

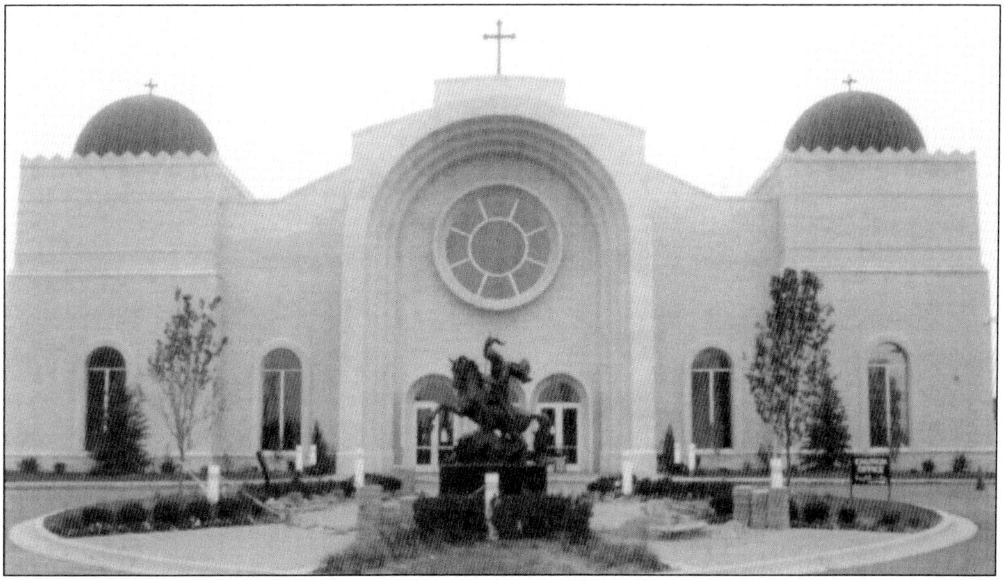

SAINT GEORGE CHURCH. Father Sarhad Jammo began the efforts to establish a new church in Michigan's Shelby Township. Bishop Ibrahim Ibrahim approved the recommendation to purchase the former Chaldean Club land east of Woodward Avenue, which had been vacant for approximately 10 years. The construction of Saint George Chaldean Church, located at 45700 Dequindre Road, began in 2003. The church was consecrated on April 24, 2005. Saint George is the largest Chaldean church in North America, with a huge rectory and classrooms. Father Emmanuel Shaleta became its first pastor. (Courtesy of Bryon Perry.)

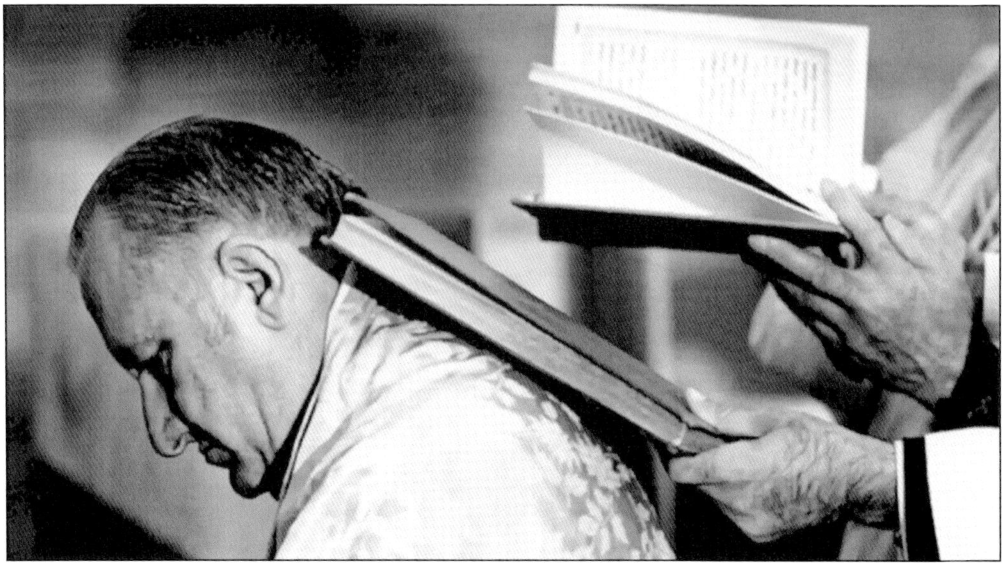

On a Mission to Serve. Bishop George F. Garmo was born in Telkaif, Iraq, in 1921 and ordained in Rome in 1945. In 1960, Patriarch Paulus II Cheikho sent him to the United States to serve at Mother of God Church. In 1964, he purchased 10.3 acres of vacant land at Berg and 10 Mile Roads in Southfield, Michigan. He served at three Mother of God locations before being consecrated as archbishop-designate of Mosul, Iraq, on September 14, 1980. During the ceremony, the Book of Gospels was placed on his shoulders, symbolizing his new responsibilities. After retiring, he returned to the United States, and he passed away in Detroit on September 9, 1999. (Courtesy of Paul Manni.)

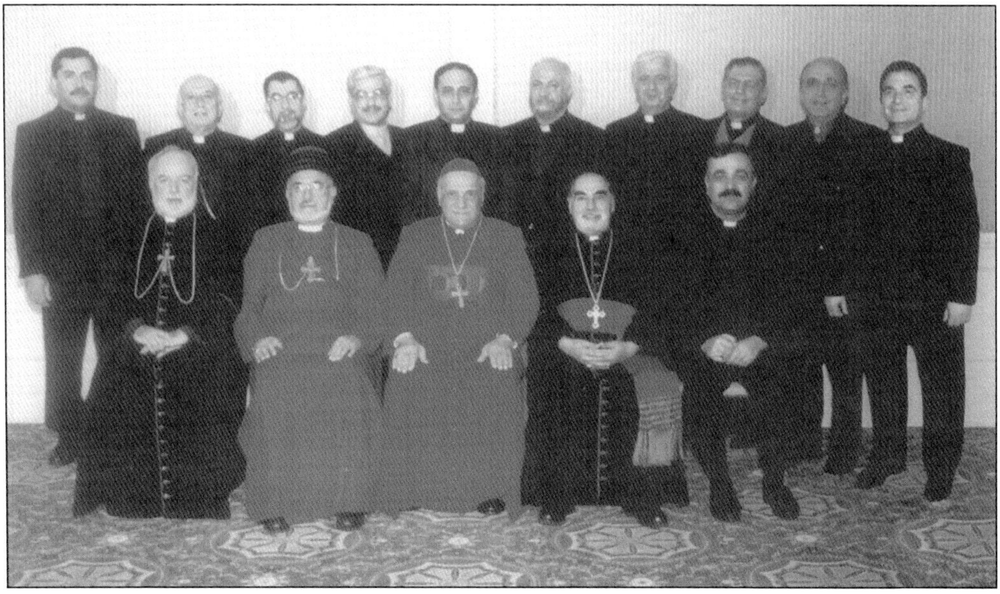

Ecumenical Dialogue. Following the Common Christological Declaration between Mar Dinkha IV and Pope John Paul II, the Church of the East began dialogue with the Chaldean Church. In 1996, Patriarch Mar Dinkha IV and Chaldean patriarch Raphael I Bidawid met to initiate cooperation on pastoral and practical matters. However, little progress was made, and much remained unchanged. (Courtesy of Raad Kathawa.)

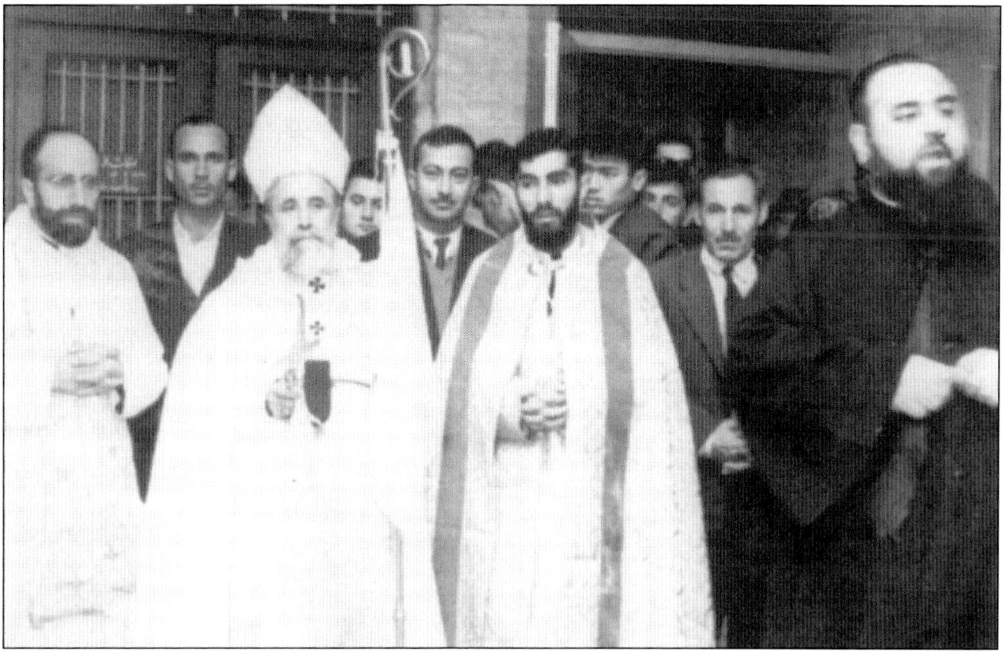

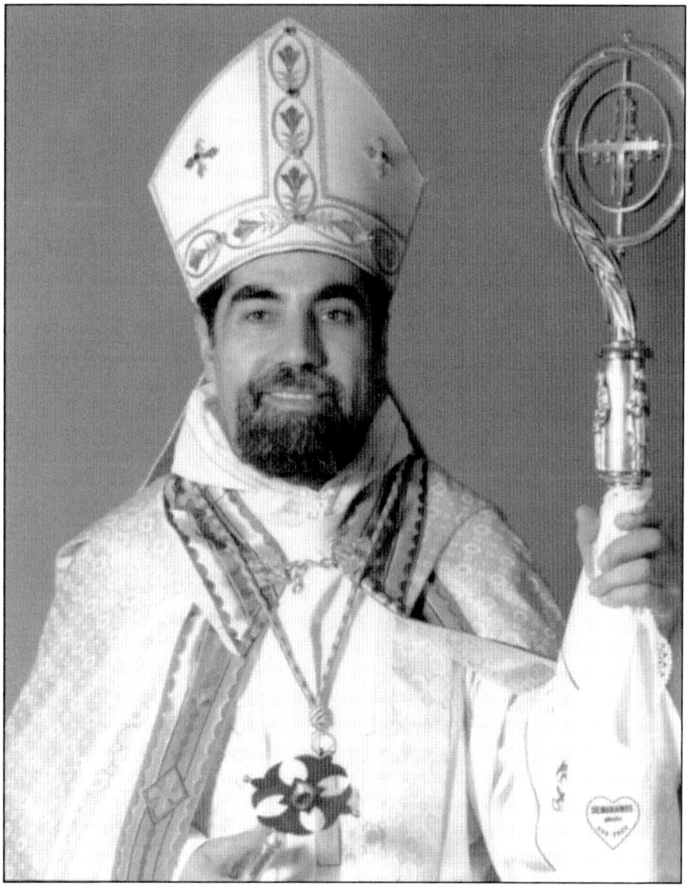

First Chaldean Bishop to America. On January 26, 1982, Pope John Paul II confirmed the election of Rev. Ibrahim N. Ibrahim as the first Chaldean bishop in the United States. He was consecrated on March 7, 1982, in Baghdad, Iraq, and installed in the Chaldean cathedral in Southfield on April 18, 1982, with Bishop Paulus II Cheikho officiating. Born on October 1, 1937, in Telkaif, Bishop Ibrahim was ordained in 1962. In 1978, he moved to the United States to assist Father Putrus Kattoula in San Diego. Serving as bishop of the Saint Thomas Chaldean Eparchy from 1982 to 2014, he laid a strong spiritual and financial foundation for the church. (Both, courtesy of Chaldean Catholic Diocese of Saint Thomas the Apostle.)

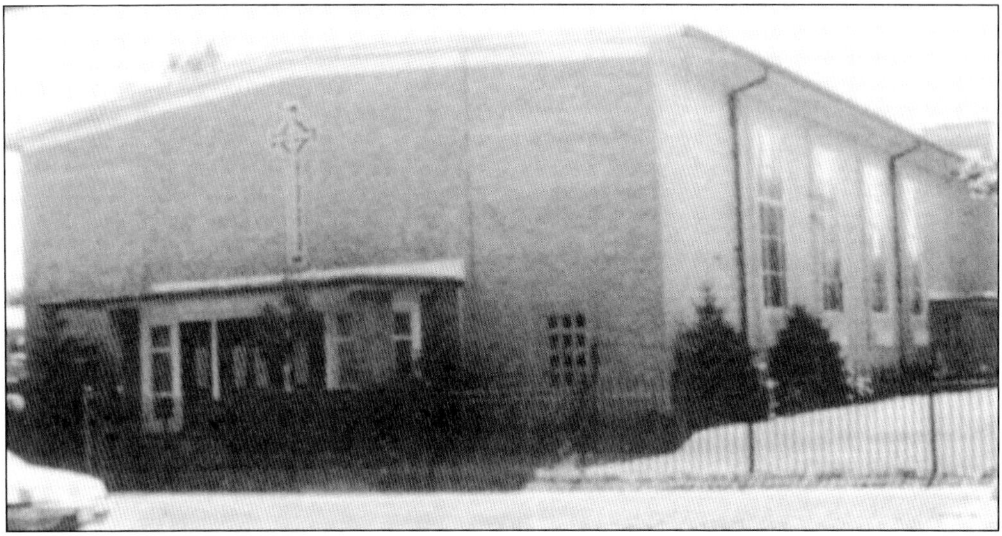

Mart Mariam Church (1986–2011). In 1986, Rev. Edward Bikoma purchased Mart Mariam Chaldean Catholic Church, located at 2849 West Chase Avenue in Chicago. At the time, he was the pastor of Mar Ephrem Chaldean Church in Chicago. He served both churches until his retirement in 2006. Mart Mariam Church was consecrated on December 14, 1986, and was blessed by Bishop Ibrahim Ibrahim in the presence of Bishop Dinkha IV, patriarch of the Assyrian Church of the East. (Courtesy of Father Hermiz Haddad.)

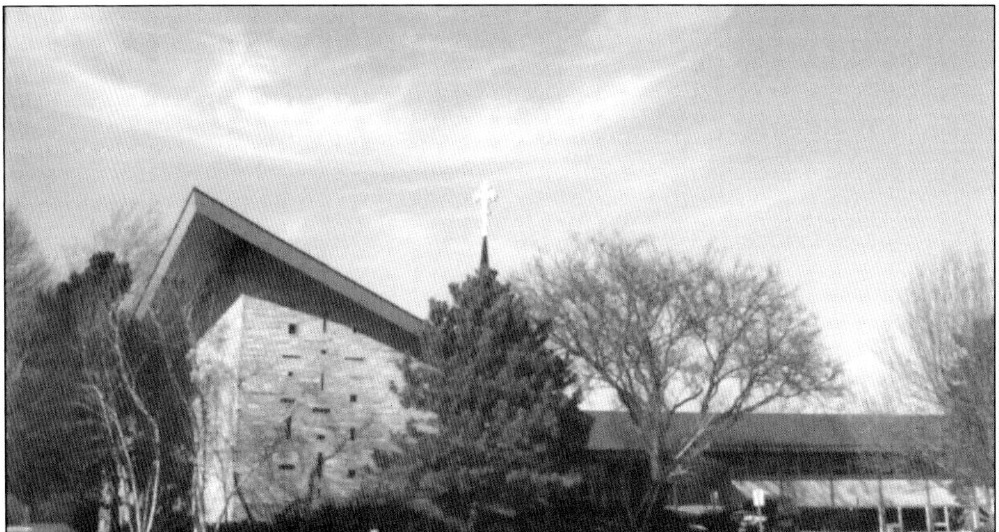

Mart Mariam Church (2011–Present). In 2011, Mart Mariam Chaldean Catholic Church in Chicago was sold for $2.1 million. A new church was purchased for $3 million at 2700 Willow Road in Northbrook, just north of Chicago. Situated on seven acres, it features a rectory, several classrooms, and a beautiful hall. Father Edward Bikoma was appointed as its first pastor. The church was blessed by Bishop Ibrahim Ibrahim and inaugurated on December 14, 1986, in the presence of Bishop Dinkha IV, patriarch of the Assyrian Church of the East. (Courtesy of Father Hermiz Haddad.)

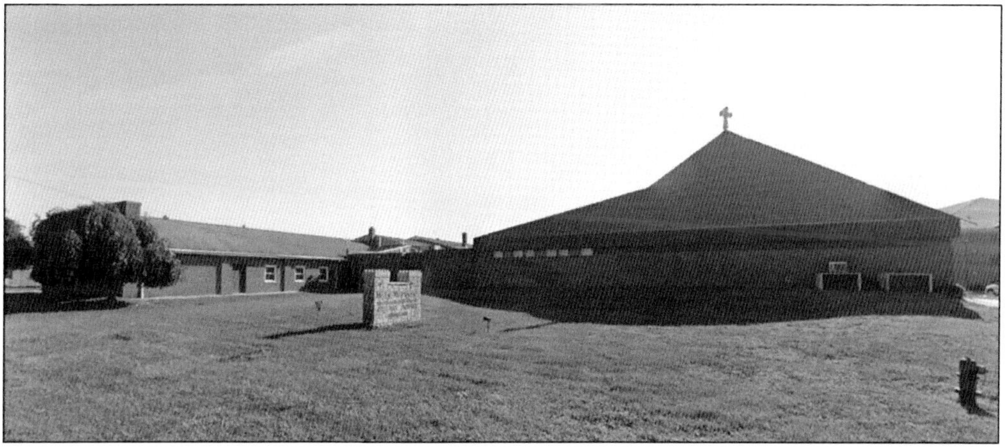

HOLY MARTYRS CHURCH. An old church situated on 12 acres of land at 43700 Merrill Road in Sterling Heights, Michigan, was listed for sale. While the location was not ideal for everyone, the attractive sale price garnered attention. After a brief period of negotiation, the property was purchased for $1.1 million. It underwent remodeling, painting, and minor construction work to enhance its functionality and appearance. The church was consecrated on the Feast of the Transfiguration of the Lord, August 6, 2010, by Bishop Ibrahim Ibrahim. Father Manuel Boji served as the first pastor. (Courtesy of Bryon Perry.)

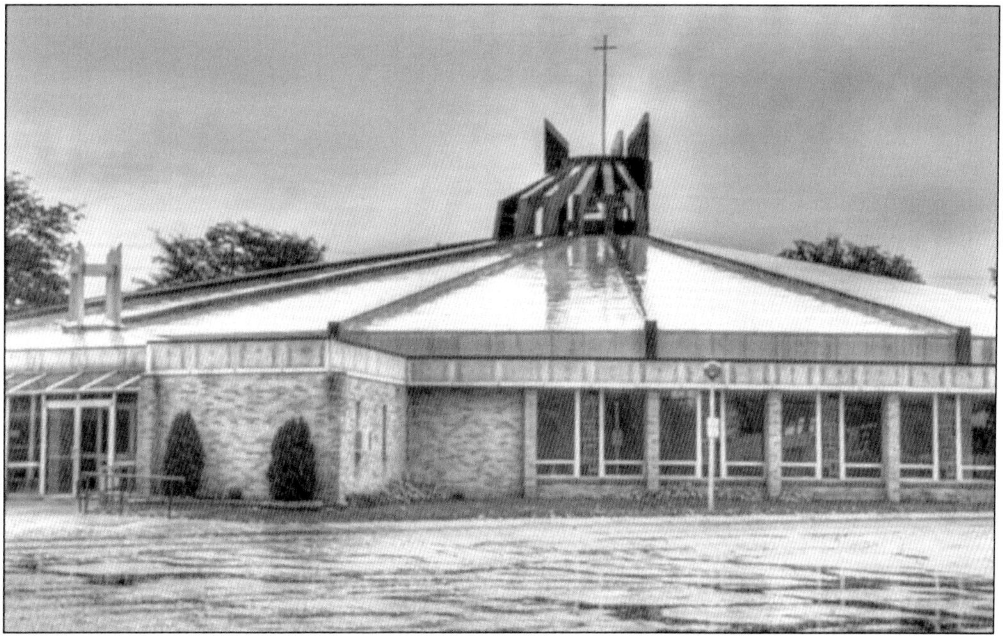

OUR LADY OF PERPETUAL HELP. In May 2010, Bishop Ibrahim Ibrahim entrusted Father Fadi Habib with establishing a new mission in Warren, Michigan, under the name Our Lady of Perpetual Help, formerly known as Saint Sylvester Church. On July 12, 2012, the mission was elevated to the status of a parish, becoming the eighth parish in the metro Detroit area. Father Habib was appointed its first pastor. The parish is located at 11200 12 Mile Road. (Courtesy of Chaldean Catholic Diocese of Saint Thomas the Apostle.)

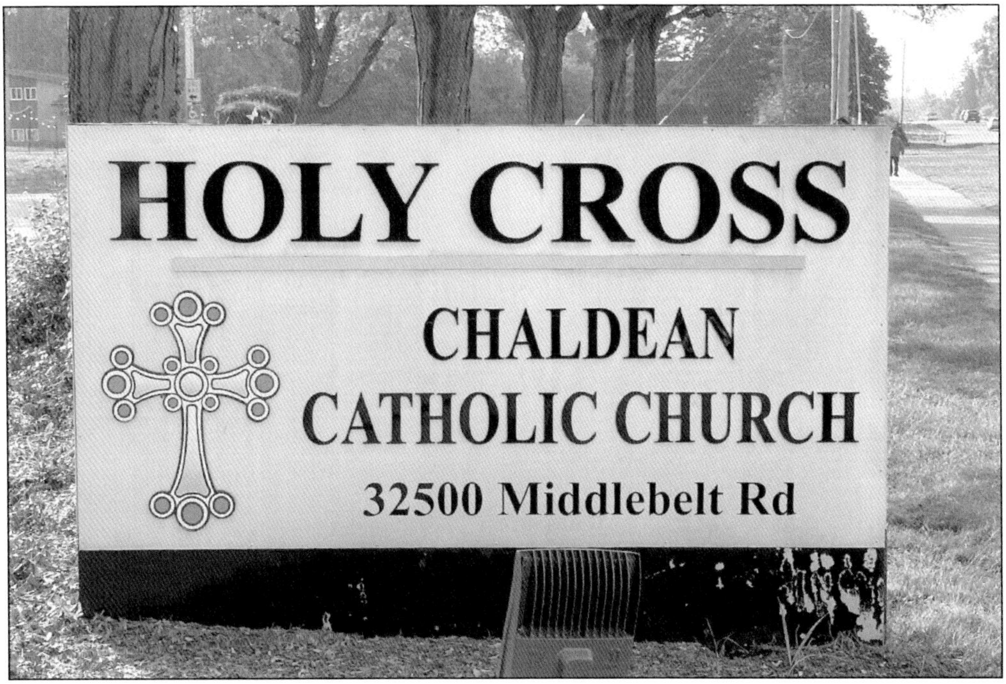

HOLY CROSS CHURCH. The former Saint Coleman Catholic Church, located at 32500 Middlebelt Road in Farmington Hills, Michigan, was purchased from the Archdiocese of Detroit on April 3, 2013. Msgr. Zouhair Toma Kejbou became the first priest to serve at the newly renamed Holy Cross Chaldean Catholic Church. A new consecration was unnecessary, as the ground had already been consecrated through Saint Coleman. (Both, courtesy of Jacob Bacall.)

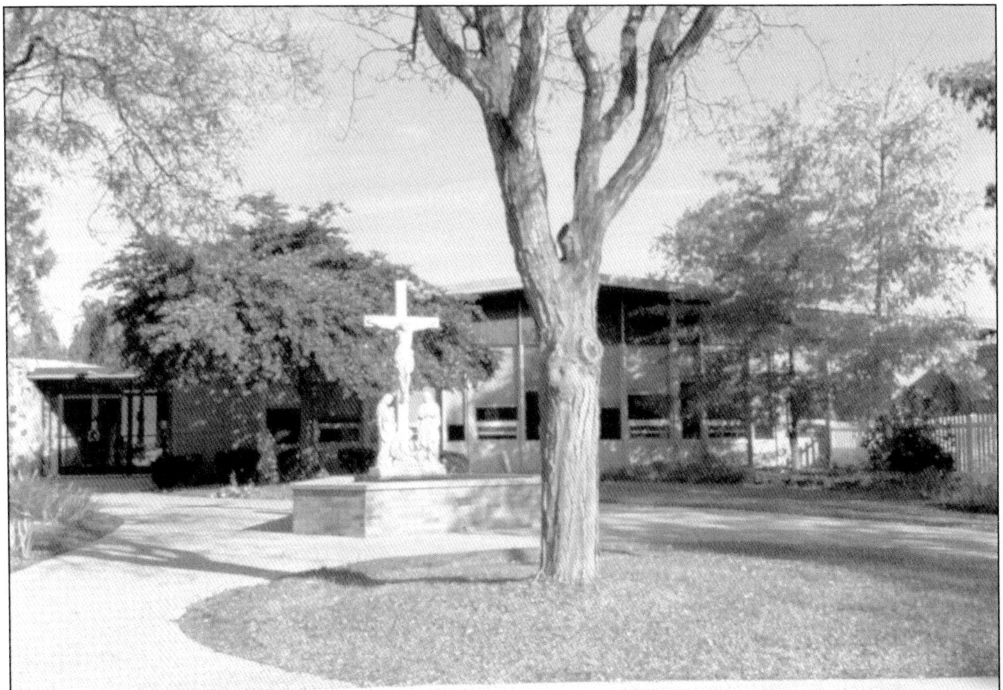

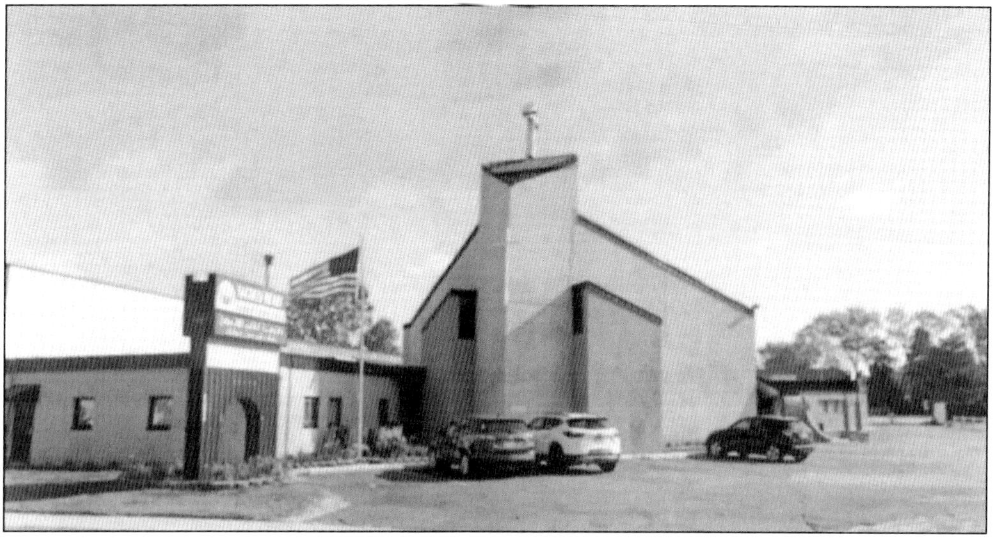

SACRED HEART CHURCH (2014–PRESENT). After Father Jacob Yasso's retirement in 2011, Father Sameem Balius became the new pastor. As the Chaldean community moved eastward, the original church was sold for $60,000. In 2014, Saint Thomas Chaldean Diocese purchased a larger church at 30590 Dequindre Road in Warren, which included a school and gym, for $950,000. It was consecrated by the newly appointed Bishop Francis Kalabat on July 1, 2014. (Courtesy of Chaldean Catholic Diocese of Saint Thomas the Apostle.)

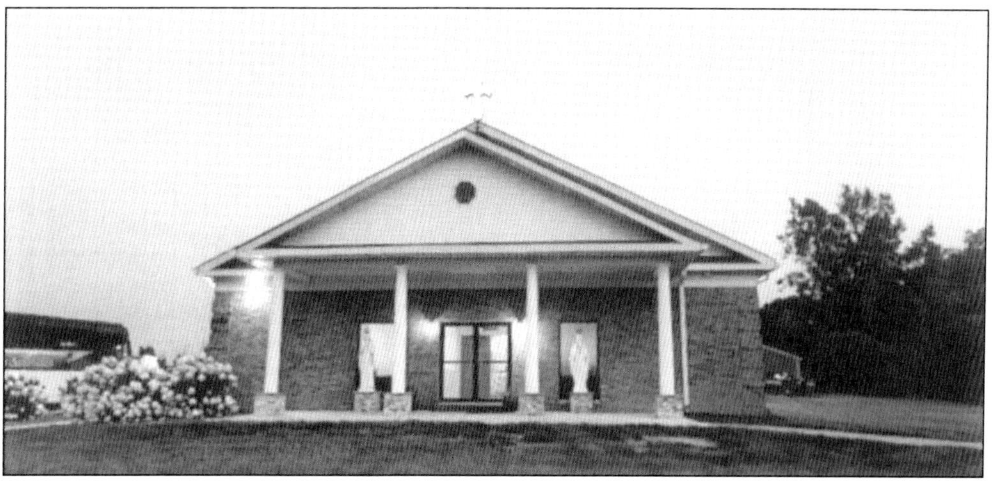

SAINT PAUL CHURCH. In 2013, the Chaldean Diocese of Saint Thomas established a new parish named Saint Paul. Located in Grand Blanc, about 40 miles north of Detroit near Flint, the property was purchased on November 5, 2013, for $380,000. The church was consecrated on the feast of Saint Paul, June 29, 2014, by Bishop Francis Kalabat. Father Ayad Hanna Khanjaro was appointed as the first pastor to serve the church, which supports a small community of approximately 60 families. It is located at 5150 East Maple Avenue. (Courtesy of Chaldean Catholic Diocese of Saint Thomas the Apostle.)

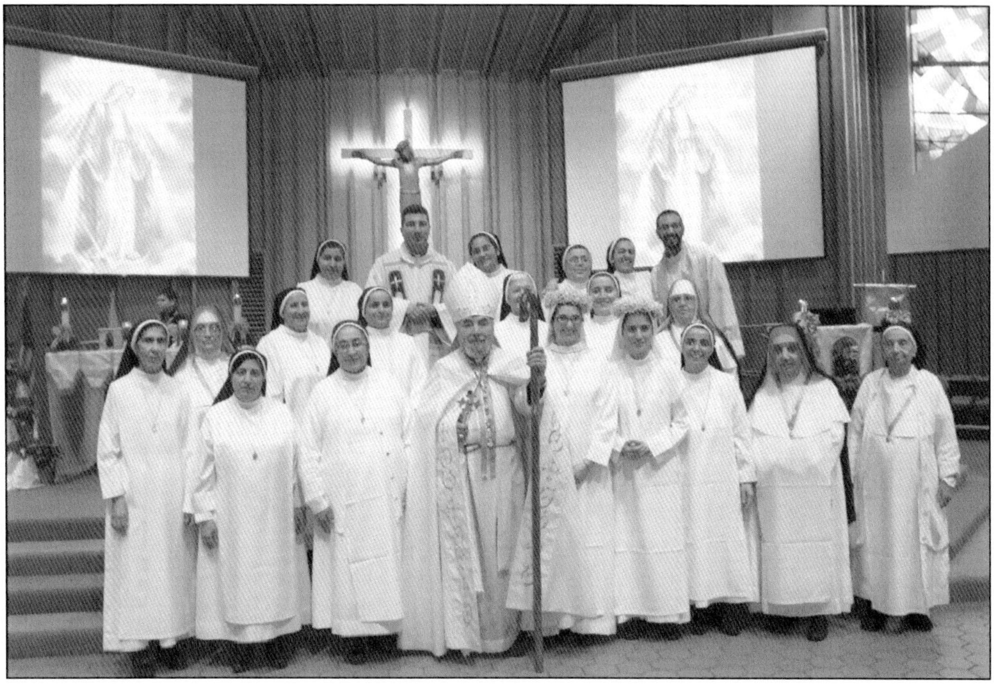

DAUGHTERS OF MARY IMMACULATE. The Daughters of Mary Immaculate, founded in Iraq on August 7, 1922, by Chaldean patriarch Joseph Emmanuel II, started with six sisters serving the poor and orphaned. Today, nearly 100 sisters serve globally, including in Iraq, Lebanon, Rome, Australia, the United Arab Emirates, and the United States. The Detroit-area convent is at 24900 Middlebelt Road. In 2022, they celebrated their 100th anniversary, raising funds for communities affected by ISIS. (Courtesy of Saher Yaldo.)

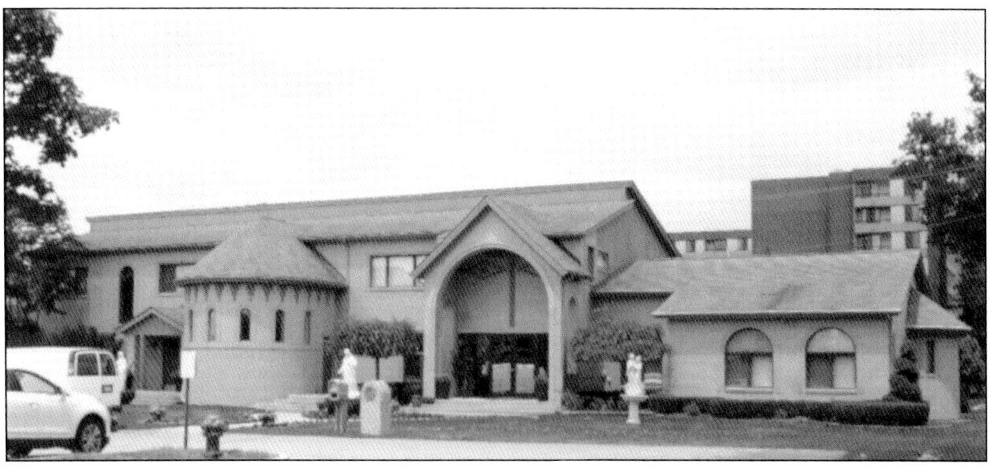

BISHOP'S HOME OFFICE. March 7, 1993, marked the dedication of the diocesan building (the chancery) at 25605 Berg Road in Southfield, next to the cathedral. It also provided accommodations for the clergy assigned to Mother of God Church. All the Chaldean parishes contributed to the construction cost. (Courtesy of Chaldean Catholic Diocese of Saint Thomas the Apostle.)

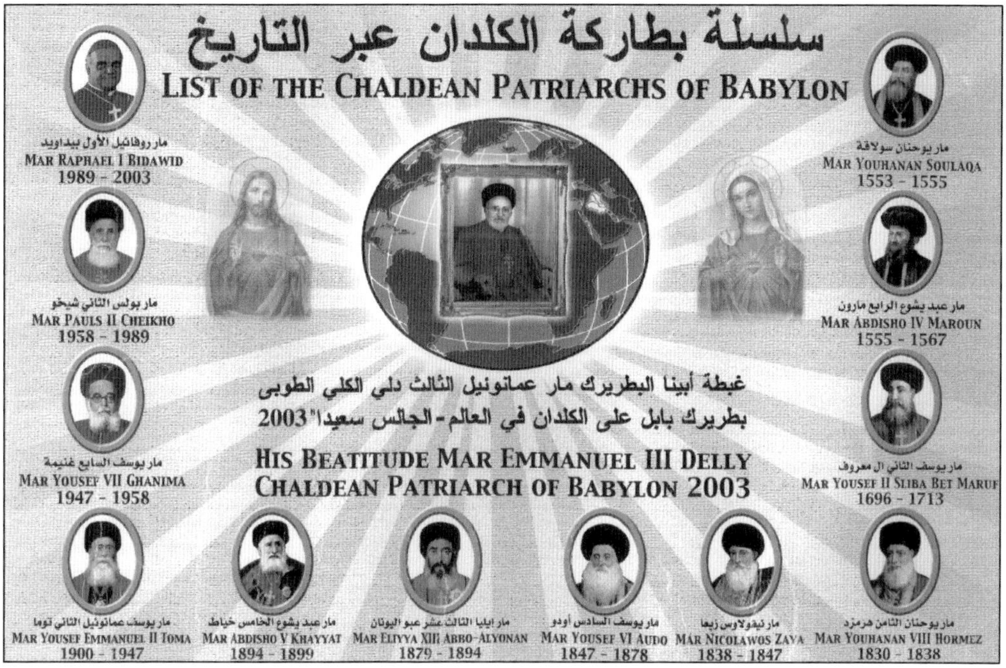

HISTORY OF THE CHALDEAN PATRIARCHS. For centuries, the Chaldean Patriarch has been the head of the largest Christian community in Iraq, playing an active and constructive role regardless of who ruled the country. The Patriarch remained a devoted patriot during both the monarchy and republican periods. His seat is in the capital, Baghdad, with Saint Joseph the Chaldean Cathedral located in Kharbanda, Baghdad. (Courtesy of Chaldean Catholic Diocese of Saint Thomas the Apostle.)

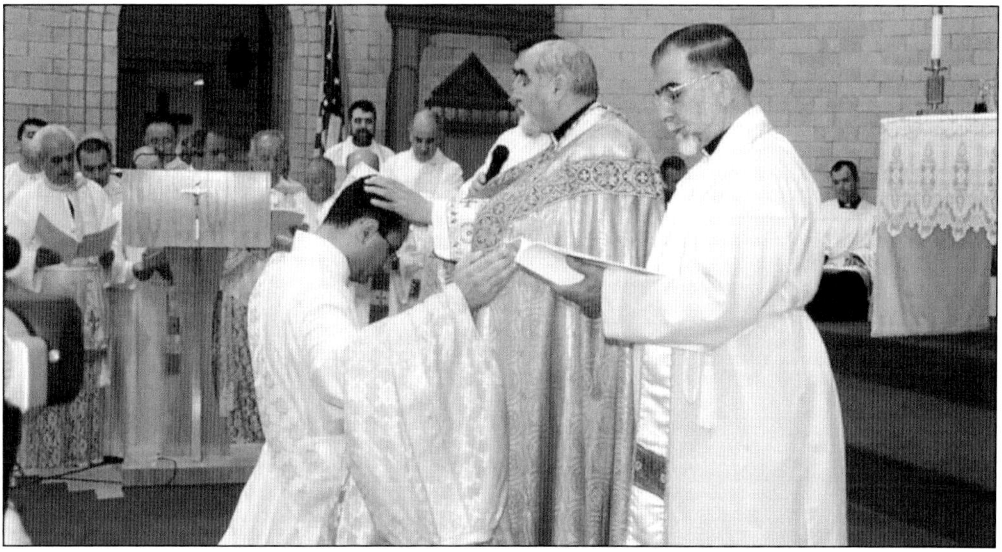
FIRST CHALDEAN PRIEST BORN IN AMERICA. In 2004, Rev. Andrew Younan became the first American-born Chaldean priest. This milestone coincided with the 100th anniversary of Saint Ephrem Church in Chicago and the 50th anniversary of Mother of God Church in Detroit. Father Younan was ordained by Bishop Ibrahim Ibrahim at Mother of God Cathedral, marking a historic moment for the Chaldean community. The bishop laid his hands upon Father Andrew's head and prayed silently; this gesture is the most important sign of the sacrament of holy orders. (Courtesy of Paul Manni.)

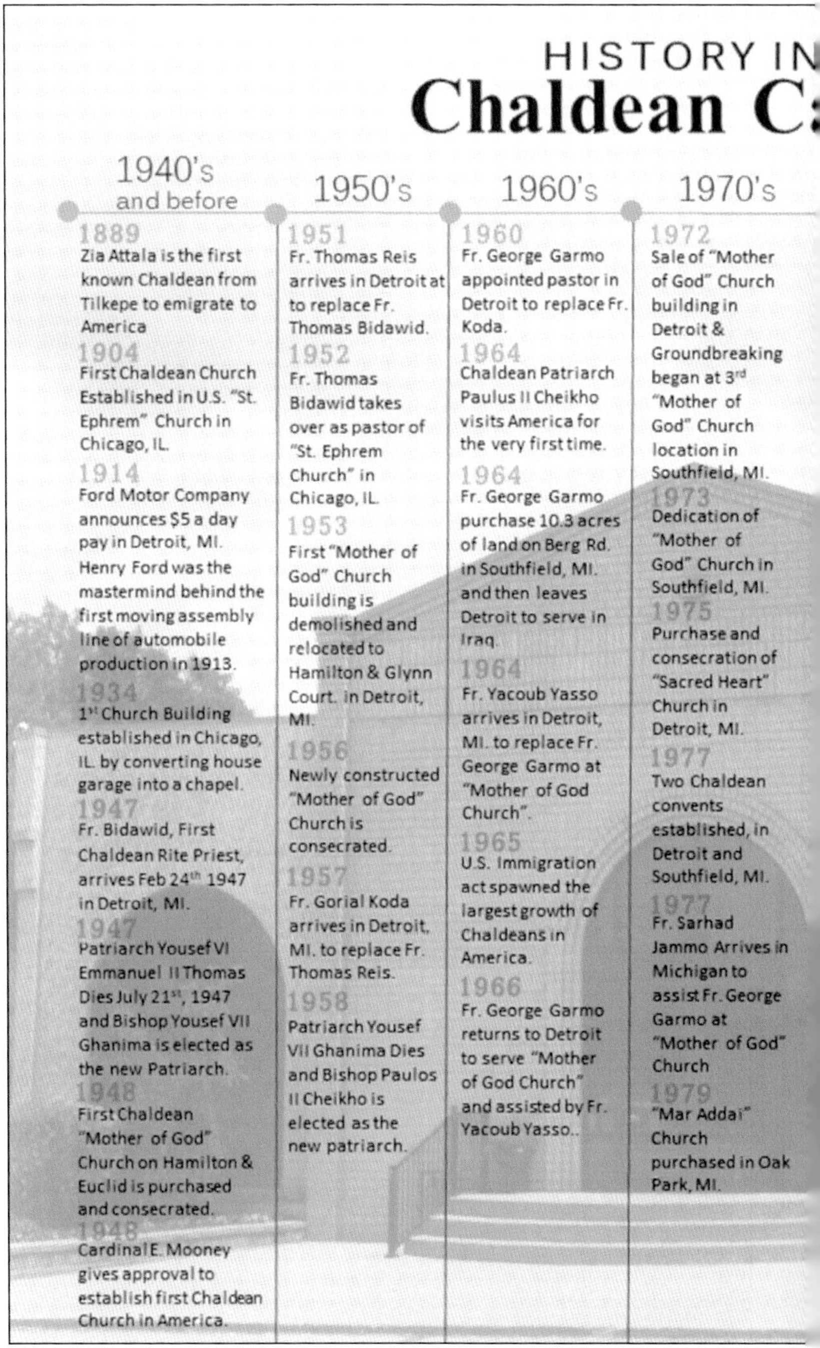

For the Records. When Father Ibrahim Ibrahim was appointed bishop of Saint Thomas the Apostle, his mission was far from easy, marked by challenges and discord within the diocese. Despite his efforts, some clergy members refused to cooperate, boycotting meetings and church activities for several years. This rift eventually led to a pilgrimage to Rome, where they sought reconciliation at the Vatican. All concerned priests, including Father Sarhad Jammo, Father Emmanuel Rayes, and Father Hanna Cheikho, traveled to Rome. After numerous meetings, Bishop Ibrahim and the clergy reached an agreement just before Easter 1992. However, tensions persisted, and history repeated

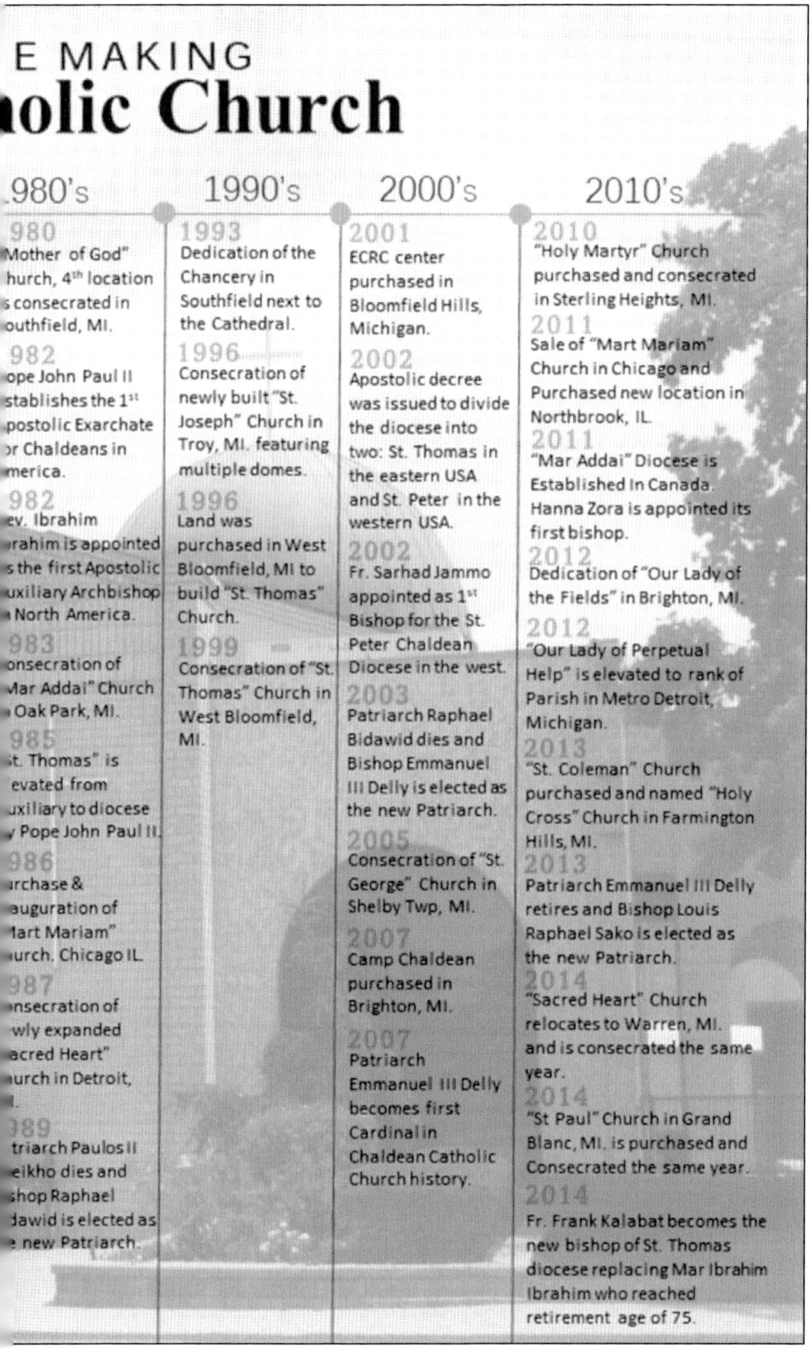

itself. Father Toma Bidawid, the first priest, faced challenges from parishioners who accused him of favoritism, with some even demanding his return to Iraq due to dissatisfaction. In his book *The History of the Iraqi Community in America*, Sam Dabish recounts these struggles: "Nevertheless, with time and a sense of collective responsibility, the community embraced flexibility and unity for their common good." On August 3, 1985, the exarchate was elevated to the rank of eparchy. (Courtesy of Chaldean Catholic Diocese of Saint Thomas the Apostle.)

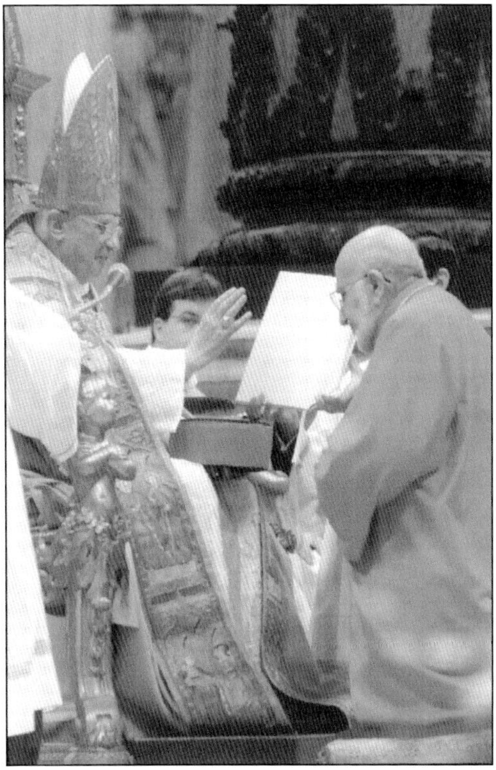

Finally! November 24, 2007, was a momentous day in the Vatican and a historic day for Chaldeans. Pope Benedict XVI elevated the patriarch of Babylon, Bishop Emmanuel III Delly, to the status of cardinal. "This honor is not for me alone, but for all of the Iraqi people," Cardinal Delly said. Bishop Delly passed away in April 2014 at the age of 86. He is the first and only Chaldean patriarch to be buried in the United States, in Holy Sepulchre Cemetery in Southfield, Michigan. (Courtesy of Jacob Bacall.)

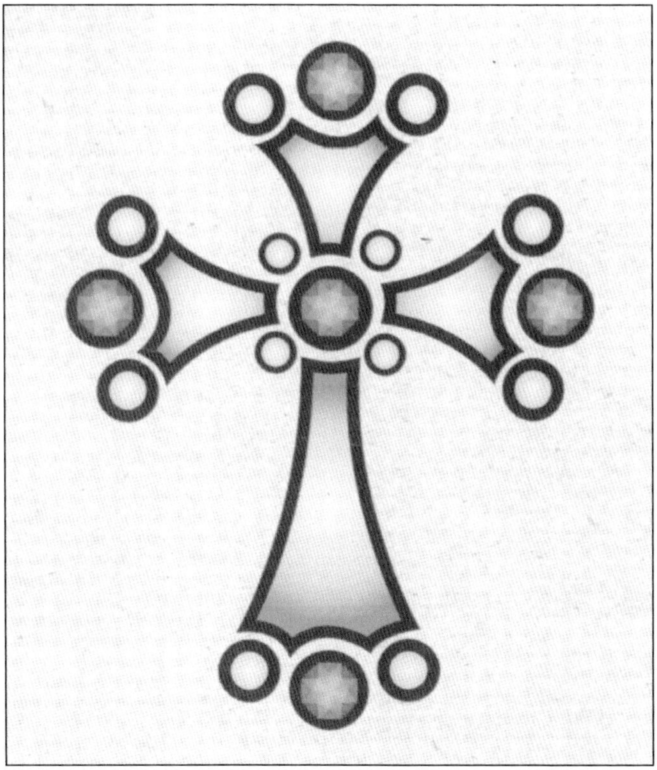

Chaldean Cross. The symbols of the Chaldean Cross place great emphasis on the Resurrection of Christ rather than his death. The fact that the cross is empty, without the corpse of Christ, signifies that Christ overcame the cross. The flowery shape of the cross symbolizes that Christ's Resurrection offers us a new life. The dot at the center of the cross represents Christ, while the four dots surrounding it symbolize the four evangelists, and the 12 larger outer dots represent the 12 disciples. An interesting distinction is that in the Latin Church, parishioners make the sign of the cross from left to right, while in the Eastern Church, the motion is from right to left. (Courtesy of Father John Jwad.)

Golden Jubilee (1948–1998). On January 10, 1998, the Chaldean community celebrated the 50th anniversary of Mother of God Church, the first Chaldean cathedral in the United States and the Western Hemisphere. From no deacons in 1948 to 20 today, the church has grown significantly. Supported by various groups and volunteers, the celebration highlighted the community's growth, cultural resilience, and unwavering faith. (Courtesy of Jacob Bacall.)

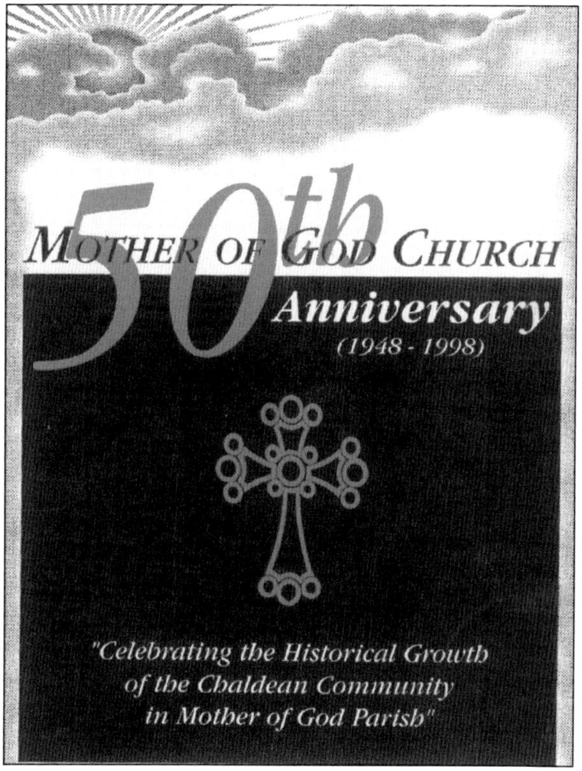

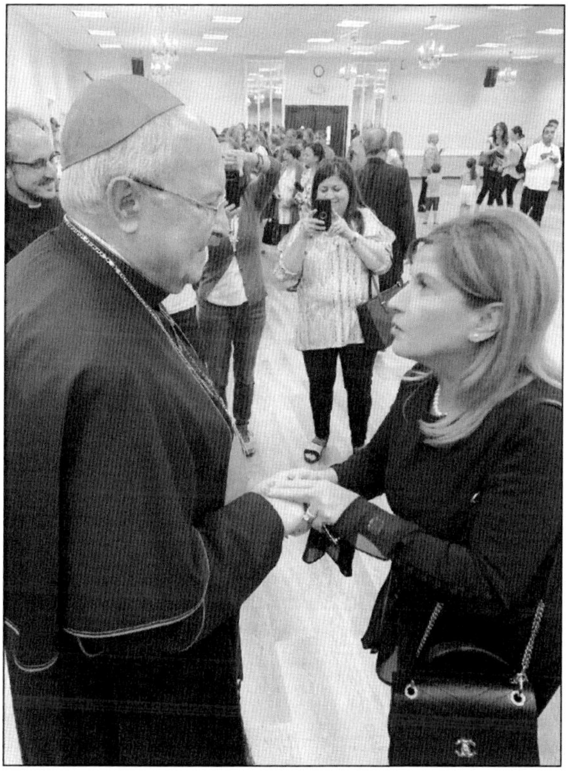

One and Only. Cardinal Leonardo Sandri, prefect emeritus of the Dicastery for the Oriental Churches and one of four copresidents of the Special Synod of Bishops for the Middle East, is shown meeting with parishioners at Mother of God Church Hall. The cardinal was on a special trip to the United States, where he also visited his personal Chaldean friend, businessman and philanthropist Akram Faraj Kareem, whom the cardinal affectionately calls "Abu Yousif." This photograph was taken at the third location of Mother of God, which now serves as a church hall. Cardinal Sandri is meeting with Anne Bacall, a member of the Chaldean parish, in 2020. (Courtesy of the *Chaldean News*.)

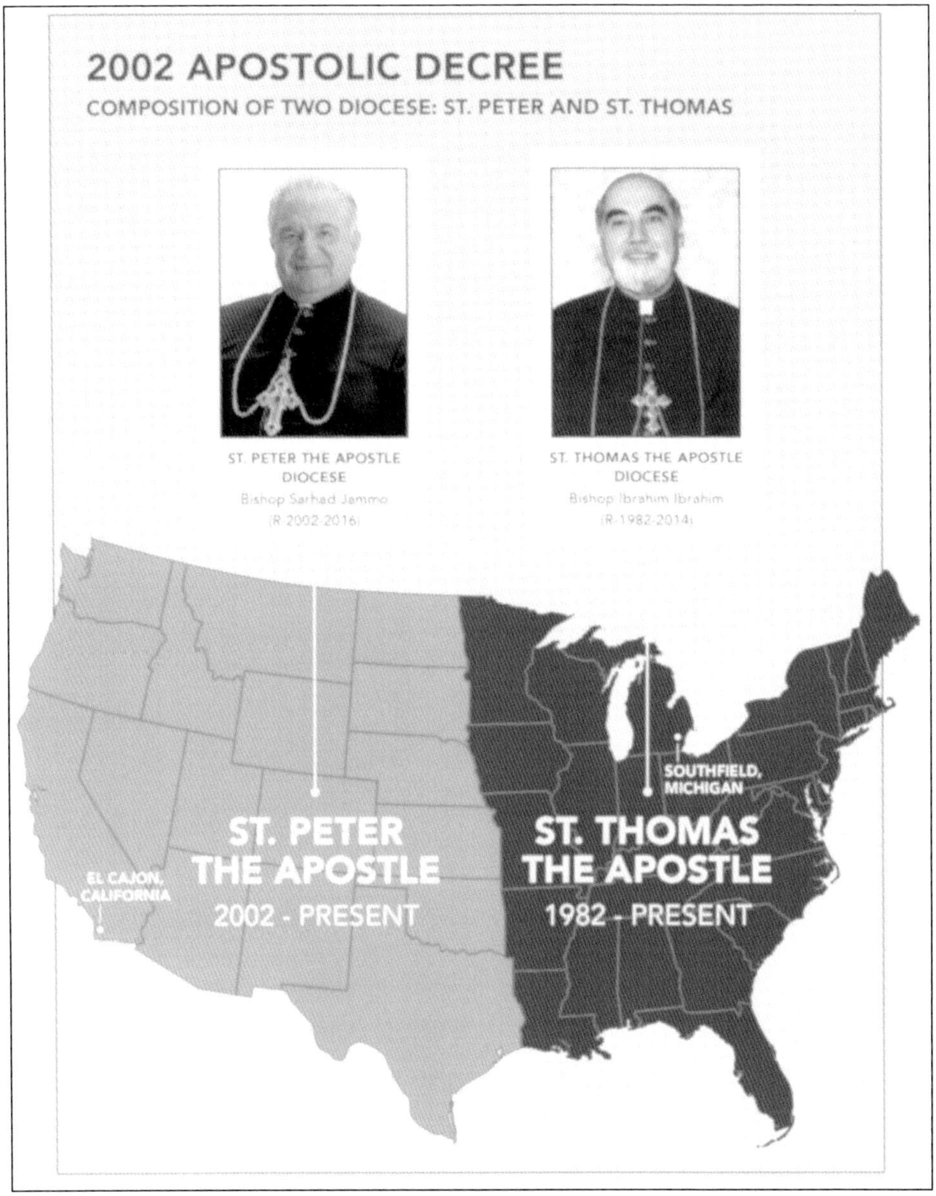

THE TWO CHALDEAN DIOCESES IN AMERICA. On May 4, 2002, an apostolic decree was issued to divide the diocese into two. Father Sarhad Jammo was appointed bishop of the new diocese in the west and was ordained at Saint Joseph Church in Troy by Patriarch Raphael Bidawid. Bishop Ibrahim Ibrahim, Bishop Emmanuel III Delly, Patriarch Dinkha IV of the Assyrian Church of the East, and Bishop Bawai Soro concelebrated the ordination on July 18, 2002. Father Jammo was then installed at Saint Peter Cathedral in San Diego on July 25, 2002. Clergy ministering in the eastern states were incardinated in the Diocese of Saint Thomas the Apostle, while those assigned to the western United States became part of the Diocese of Saint Peter. These dioceses are also known as eparchies, a term used to refer to dioceses in the Eastern Rite Chaldean Church. The Diocese of Saint Thomas the Apostle was named in honor of one of Christ's original 12 disciples who is credited with the conversion of Chaldeans to Christianity. The Diocese of Saint Peter was chosen to honor Saint Peter, whom the Church considers the first pope. (Art by Alex Lumelsky.)

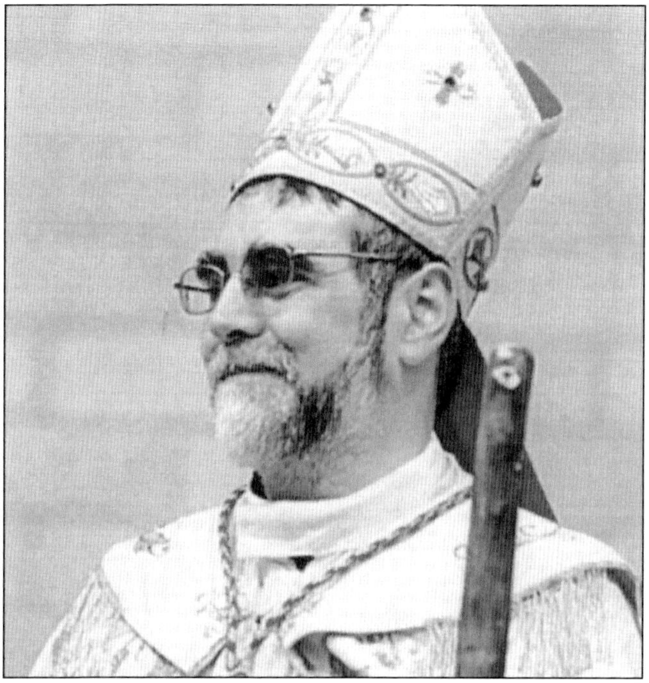

Our Priest, Our Bishop. "Now, I carry you in my heart whenever I celebrate Mass." Bishop Francis Kalabat recited these meaningful words during his homily at his ordination on June 14, 2014, at Mother of God. Born in Kuwait on May 13, 1970, he was ordained a priest on July 5, 1995. "We're confident that God will do many great things through him and will strengthen him as a good shepherd," said Archbishop Allen H. Vigneron of Detroit in his speech. Well-wishers began lining up in the church parking lot as early as 5:00 a.m. to attend his installation as the bishop of the Saint Thomas Chaldean Diocese. (Courtesy of Jacob Bacall.)

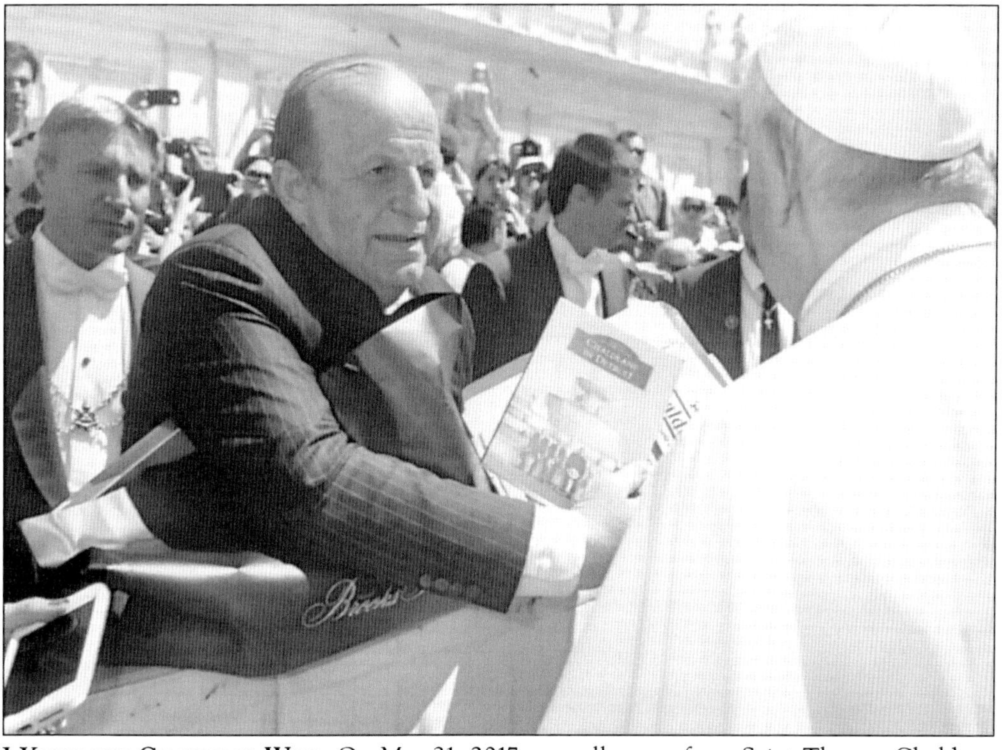

I Know the Chaldeans Well. On May 31, 2017, a small group from Saint Thomas Chaldean Catholic Church met Pope Francis at Saint Peter's Square. Among them were seminarian Junior Jwad and radio host John Zia Oram. They presented the pope with the book *Chaldeans in Detroit*. Pope Francis smiled and said, "Of course, I know Chaldeans well!" (Courtesy of John Zia Oram.)

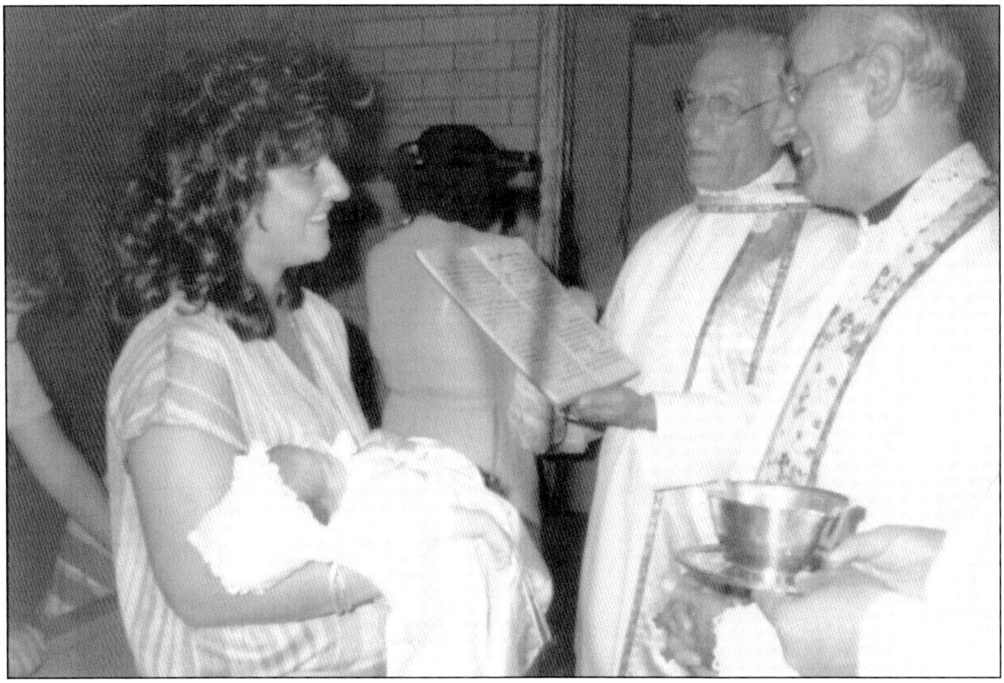

A LEGACY OF BAPTIZING THREE GENERATIONS. Father Paul Hermiz Bachi was ordained to the priesthood in Rome in 1954. He served in various churches in Iraq, Syria, and Lebanon and later ministered at a Latin church in Marseille, France, for over 40 years. He baptized Klara Jadan, the daughter of Hermiz Jadan and Naima Zoma, on March 25, 1960, at Sacred Heart Parish in Telkaif. Twenty-three years later, on July 17, 1983, he baptized Avita Kuza, the child of Amer and Klara Jadan Kuza, at Mother of God in Southfield. Avita is held by godmother Salwa Kuza Zoma in the photograph. On June 18, 2014, he traveled from France to Michigan to baptize Klara's granddaughter, Corinne Bacall, the child of Avita and Mark Bacall, at Saint Joseph Chaldean Catholic Church in Troy (below). From left to right are Avita, Corinne, and Klara. Father Bachi passed away in France in 2020 at the age of 89. (Above, courtesy of Klara Kuza; below, courtesy of Avita Bacall.)

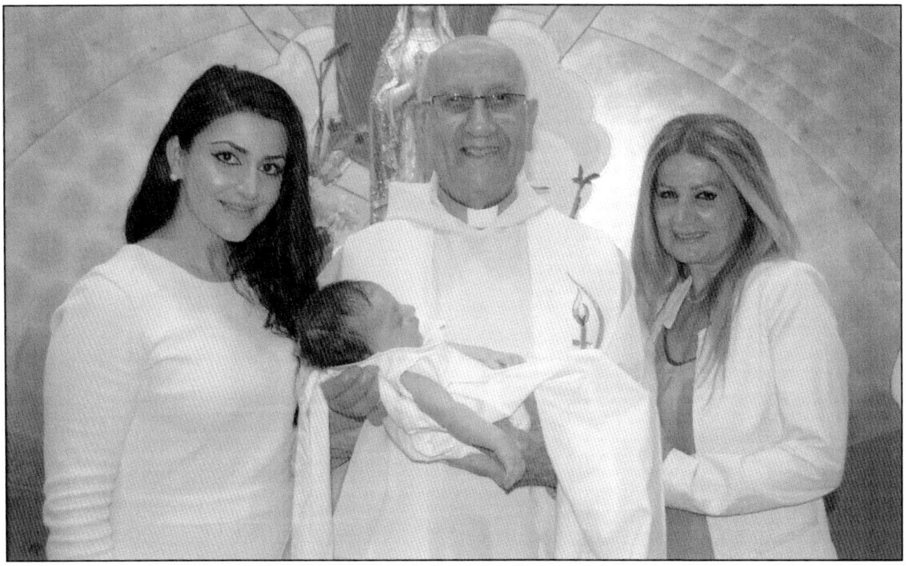

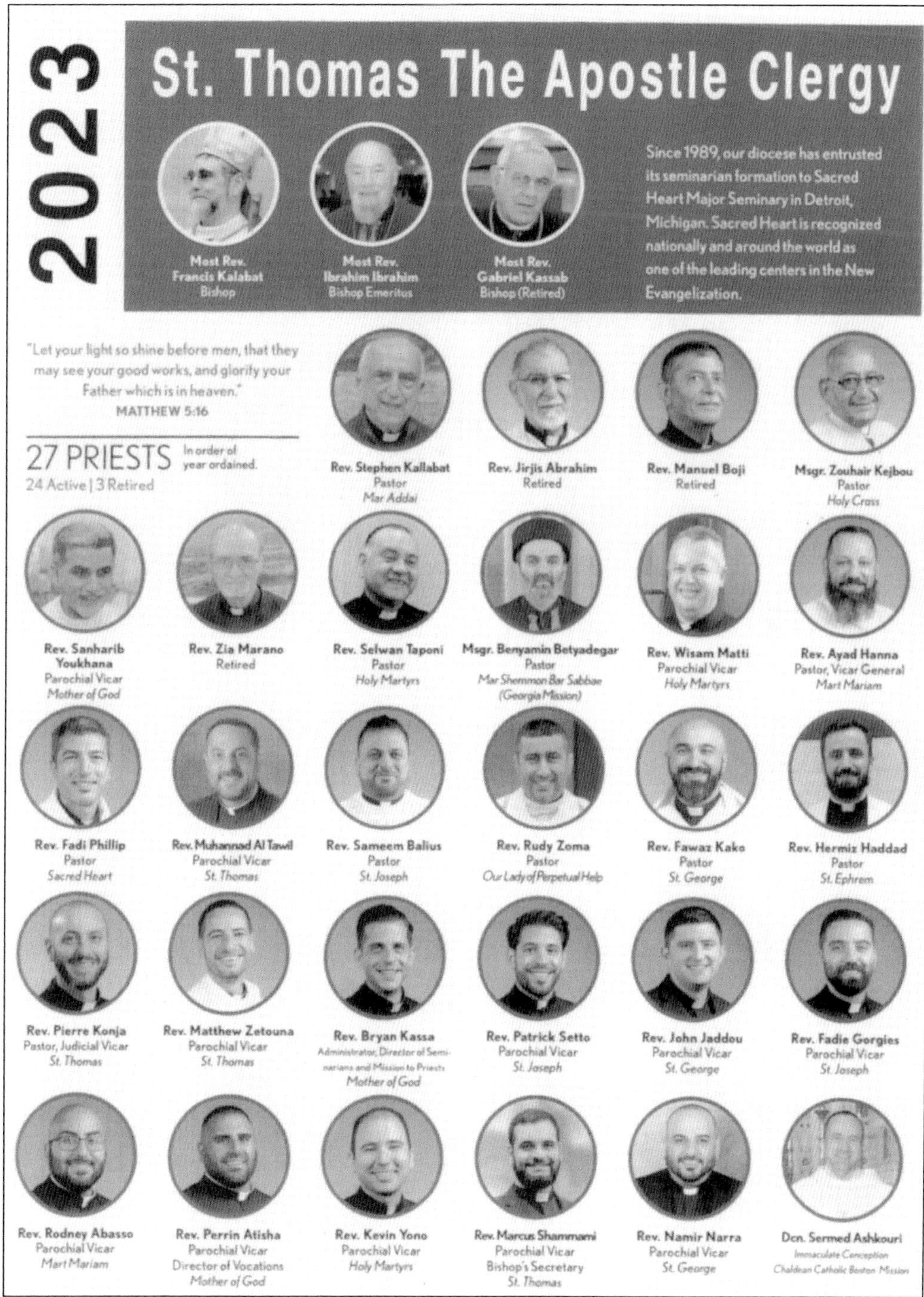

LET YOUR LIGHT SHINE. Since 1989, the diocese has entrusted its seminarian formation to Sacred Heart Major Seminary in Detroit, Michigan. Sacred Heart is recognized nationally and around the world as one of the leading centers in the New Evangelization. (Courtesy of Chaldean Catholic Diocese of Saint Thomas the Apostle.)

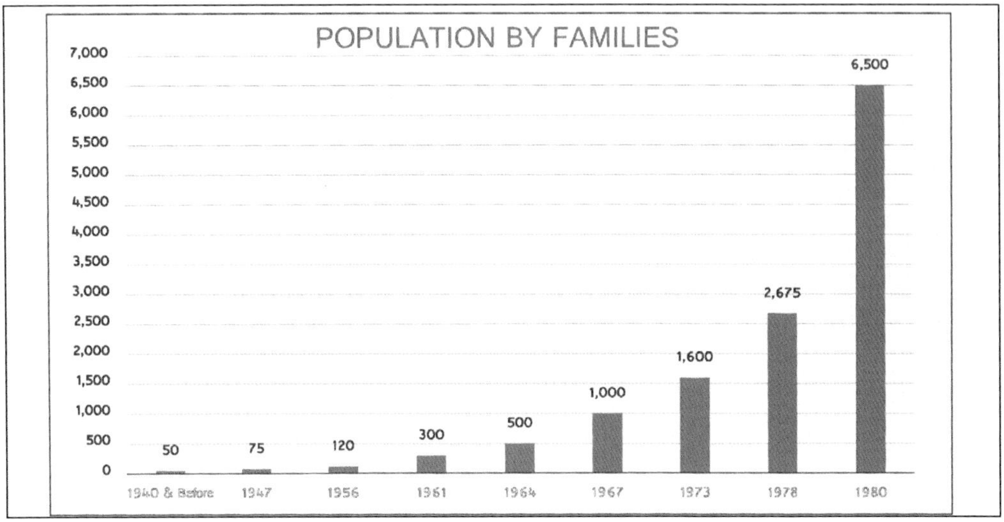

The Influx of Refugees to Michigan. The Chaldean community in Michigan grew significantly after the Immigration and Nationality Act of 1965, which allowed over 1,000 families to settle in Detroit. The first Chaldean born in the United States was Daisy Kory in 1917. Michigan became a top refugee destination, especially after the Iraq War. By 2024, Michigan had the largest Chaldean population globally, estimated at 187,000, with many believing the true number exceeds 200,000. The average Chaldean household in Michigan has 4.08 people, higher than the national average of 3.13. (Both, art by Lamar Sulaka.)

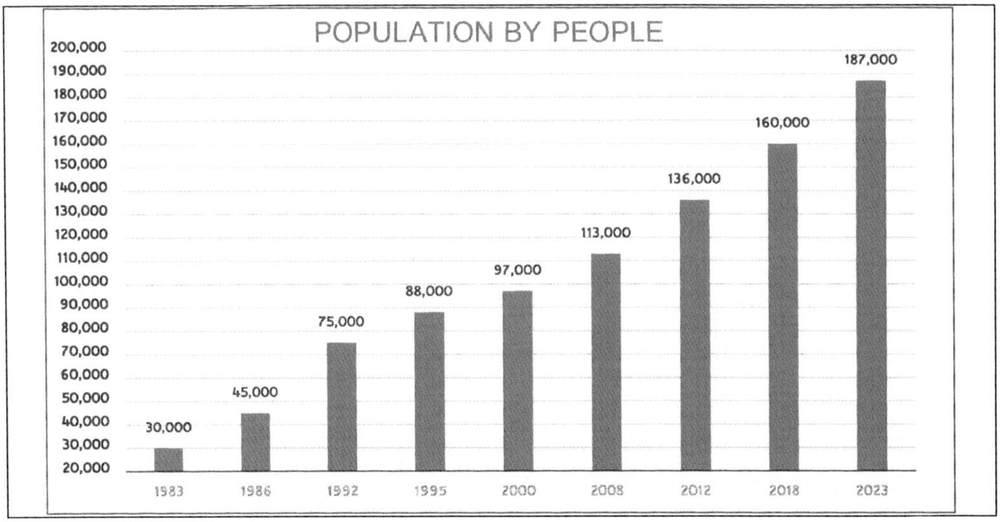

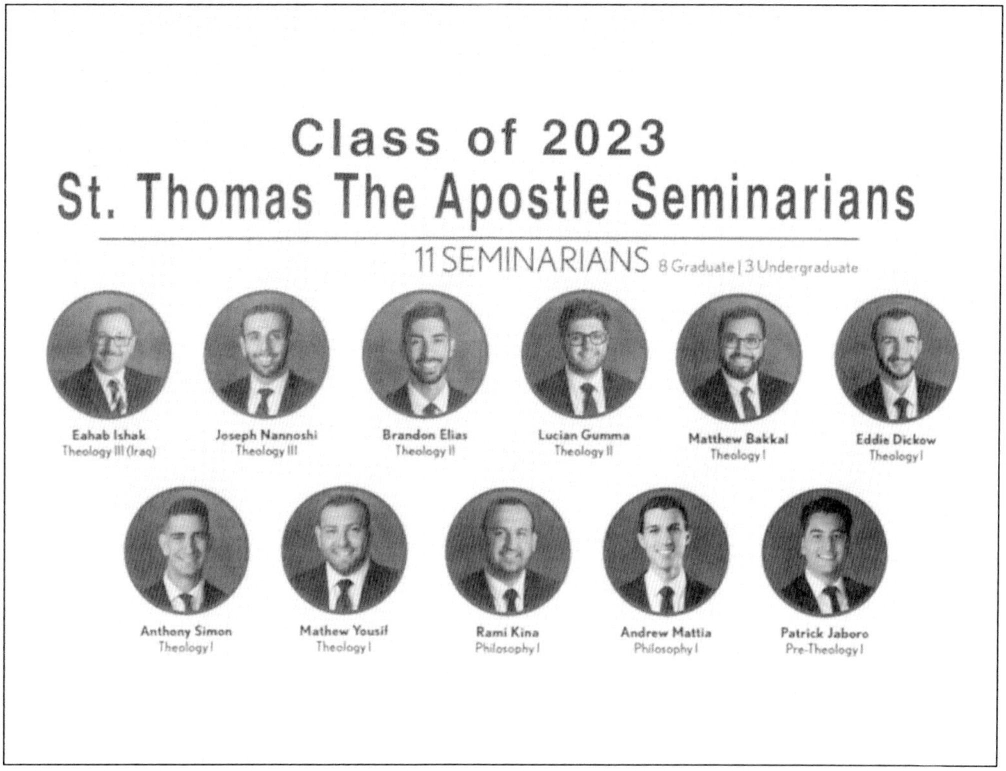

CLASS OF SPIRITUAL POWER. The 2016 annual directory of the Catholic Church's Holy See listed the Saint Thomas the Apostle Eparchy as the largest in the world, with over 180,000 members. Pictured here is the seminarian class of 2023 along with the number of sacraments performed that year. (Both, courtesy of Chaldean Catholic Diocese of Saint Thomas the Apostle.)

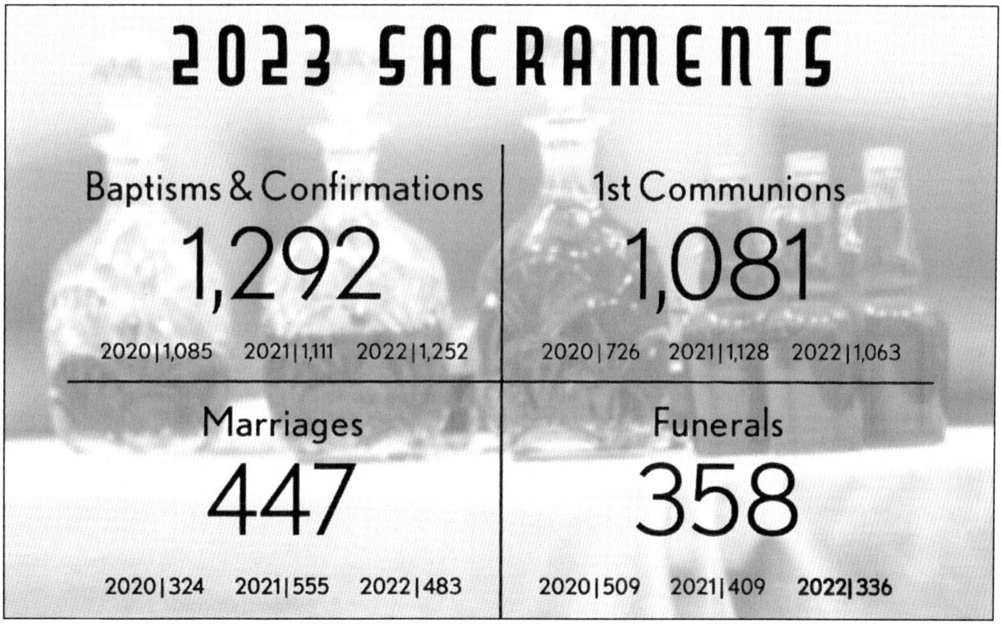

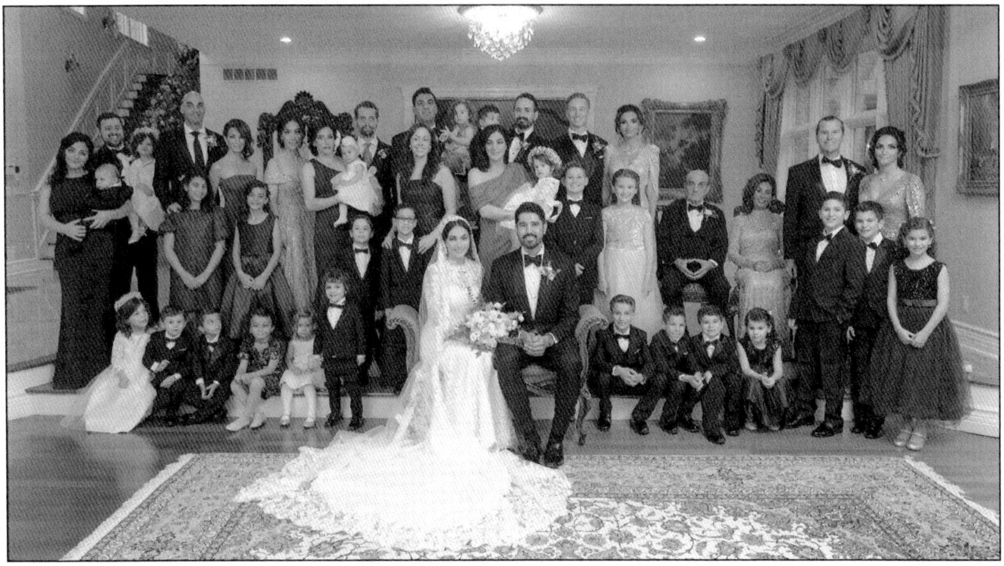

AMERICA'S MELTING POT. American-born Chaldeans with higher education often marry non-Chaldeans, reflecting the phenomenon of exogamy in the melting pot culture. Karl and Julie Kado, who emigrated from Iraq and married in Michigan in 1978, have nine children—all married to non-Chaldeans. Despite this, they uphold Chaldean traditions, celebrating weddings in Chaldean churches and maintaining cultural practices. Over time, traditions have evolved, blending old and new, such as incorporating American elements like the father-daughter dance while preserving symbolic rituals like crowning the bride and groom. (Courtesy of Karl and Julie Kado.)

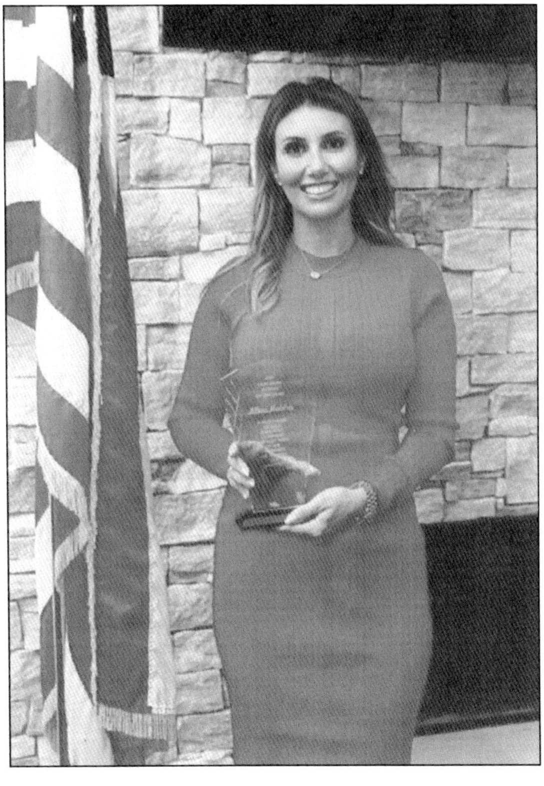

CHALDEAN APPOINTMENT BY TRUMP. President-elect Donald Trump appointed Alina Habba, his senior adviser and attorney, as counselor to the president on December 8, 2024. Trump praised her as "a tireless advocate for justice" and "a role model for women in law and politics." A first-generation American of Iraqi Chaldean descent, Habba has been a close associate of Trump since 2021. (Courtesy of Monica Yatooma.)

Six

Chaldean Catholic Eparchy of Saint Peter the Apostle in Western United States

The first known Chaldean in San Diego, Dr. Joseph Jibran, arrived in the early 1950s for academic research and later became a US citizen, practicing medicine until 1998. Other pioneers included Ramsay Alex Thomas, Sylvia Thomas, the Najors, Wadie Deddeh, Fuad Esshaki, and Farag Korkis. In 1955, Aziz Habib and his wife, Anna, opened the first Chaldean-owned grocery store, Food Fair Supermarket, in La Mesa.

By 1964, only 12 Chaldean families lived in San Diego. When Patriarch Mar Paulus II Cheikho visited again in 1973, the population had grown to 70 families. Recognizing the need for a church, Saint Peter Chaldean Catholic Church was established later that year. By 1974, the community had doubled to over 140 families, many relocating from Detroit.

In the late 1960s and early 1970s, Chaldeans migrated to California and Arizona due to safety concerns in Detroit, where many faced violent robberies. California offered better opportunities, while Arizona's dry climate, similar to Iraq's, provided a familiar environment.

Some early Chaldeans settled in Mexico before moving to the United States, while others remained, integrating into Mexican society and forming a unique Chaldean Mexican community through intermarriage and cultural blending.

Today, the Eparchy of Saint Peter, based in San Diego, serves 55,000 Chaldean/Assyrian Catholics across 26 western US states. It includes 13 parishes, 6 missions, 24 active priests, and 4 retired priests, reflecting the community's growth and resilience.

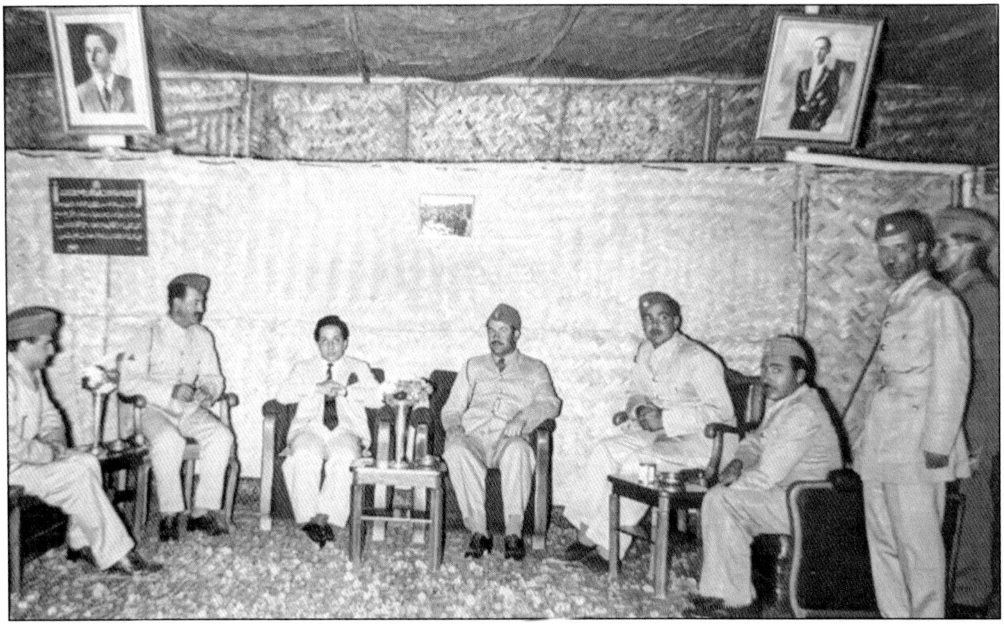

"I Smelled Something . . ." Dr. Joseph (Yousif) Jibran, MD, immigrated to San Diego from Baghdad in 1952. A physician to King Faisal II's guards, he recalled, "I smelled something wrong, so I got out of Iraq." His instincts were right. Six years later, on July 14, 1958, King Faisal II and his family were massacred in a swift coup d'état. Dr. Jibran is seated on the far left alongside Iraqi generals, with King Faisal II in a white suit. Below is Dr. Jibran at his clinic (Both, courtesy of Basil Zetouna.)

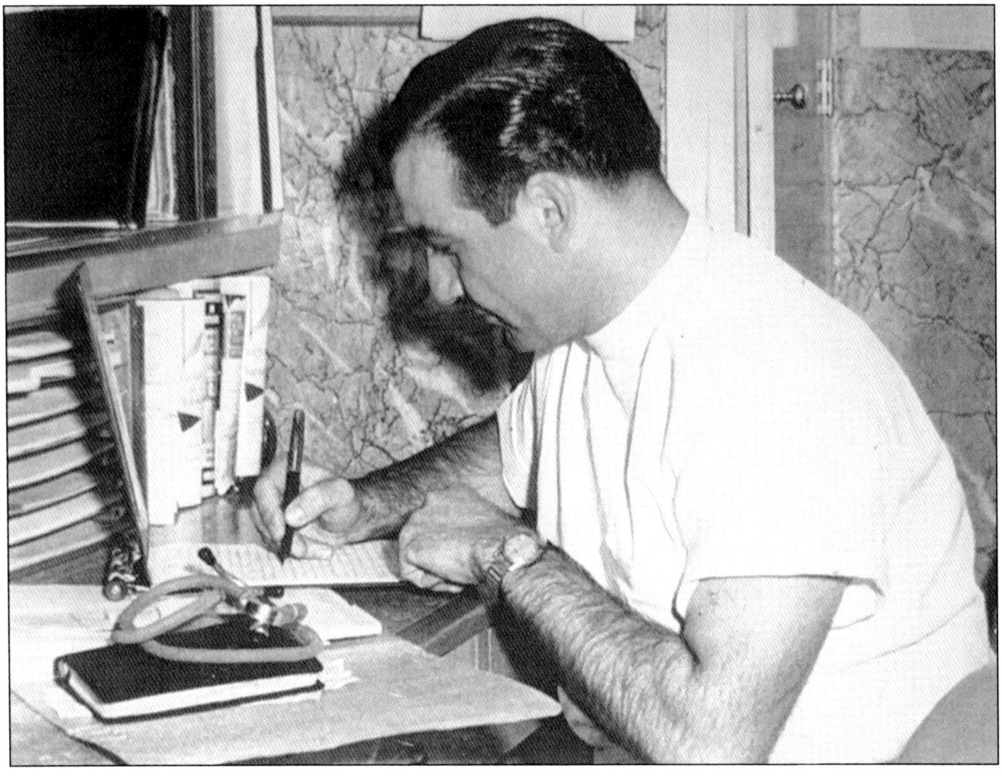

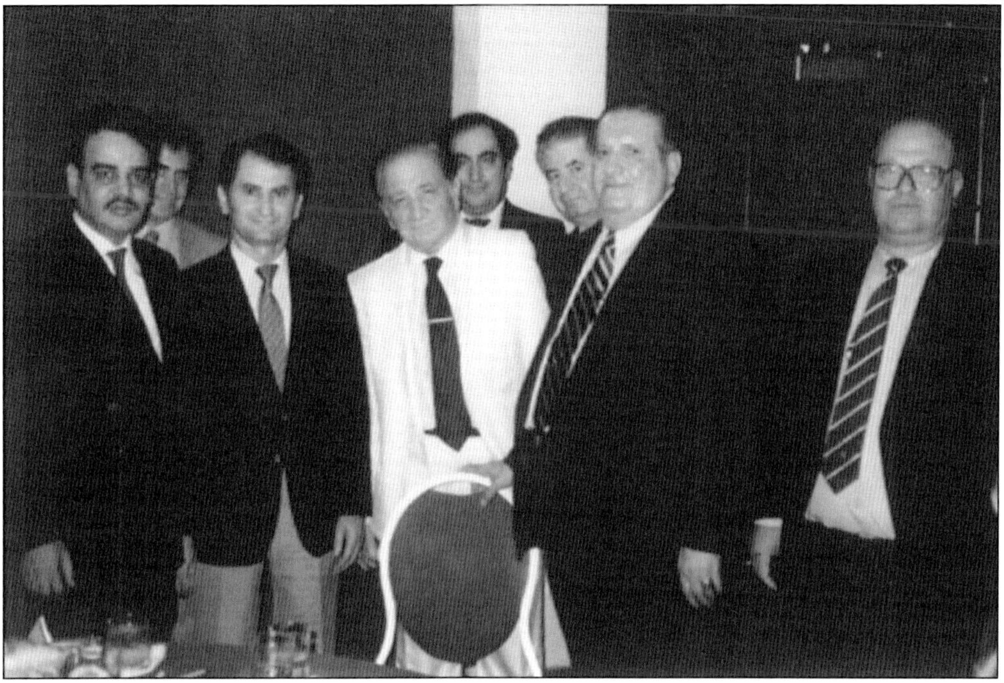

Aboard a Military Ship. Shamasha Elia Najor (1914–2010) was an early Chaldean immigrant to America. In 1946, he left Iraq aboard an American military ship, traveling from Cairo to New York before settling in Detroit. Shamasha Elia, like many other native Chaldeans from Iraq, entered the food market. Twenty-five years later, he left Detroit for San Diego to join his brothers, Frank (Francis) and Tony (Antwan). He established himself as a successful businessman, operating supermarkets and engaging in real estate development. In this photograph, Elia Najor is seen wearing a white suit. (Courtesy of Frank Najor.)

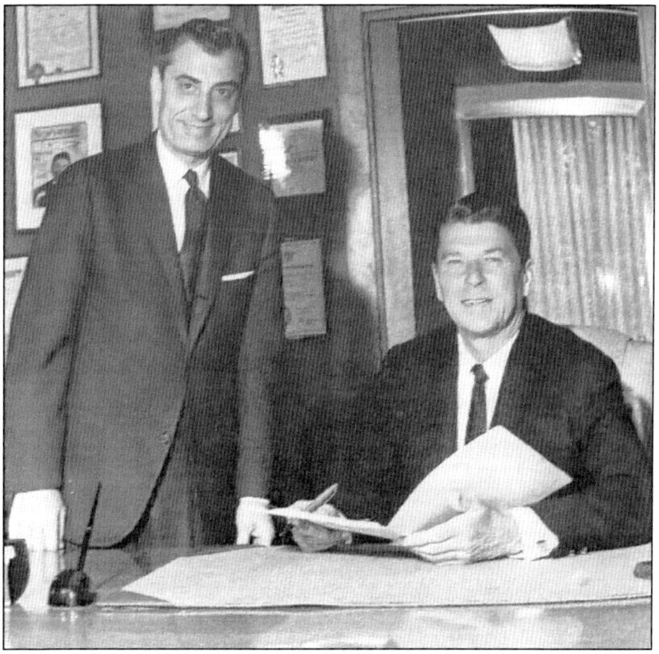

The Chaldean Senator of California. Wadie Deddeh (1920–2019) was born in Baghdad, Iraq, on September 6, 1920, and immigrated to the United States in 1947, settling in Detroit, Michigan. In the late 1950s, Deddeh moved to San Diego. His political career began in 1966. In 1982, he was elected state senator for San Diego's 40th District, becoming the only Democrat to gain a senate seat that year. He was re-elected in 1986 and 1990. After retiring, he published his memoir, *Only in America: An Immigrant Success Story* in 2018. Deddeh passed away in San Diego on August 27, 2019, at 99. (Courtesy of Wadie Deddeh.)

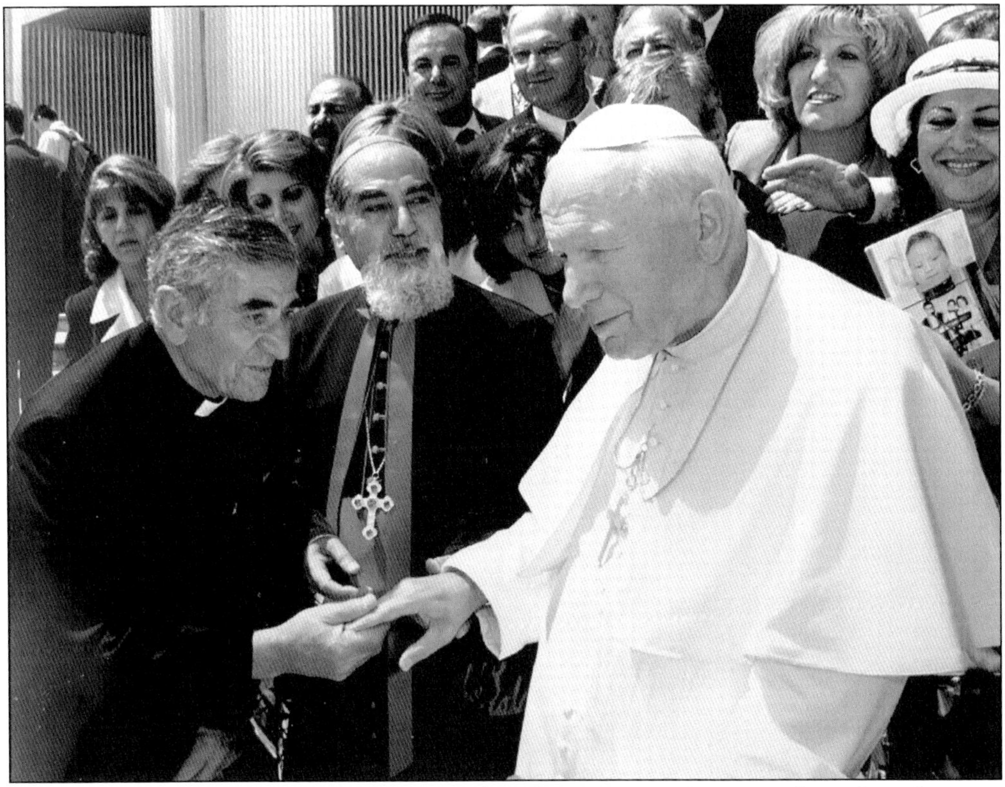

THE MARRIED PRIEST. In the Chaldean Catholic Church, married men can be ordained priests, but they cannot marry or remarry if widowed. Father Eshai Joseph, originally a married priest in the Assyrian Church of the East, joined the Chaldean Church in 1962 and founded Saint Thomas the Apostle Church in Turlock, California, in 1964. After his wife's death in 1966, he remarried and returned to the Assyrian Church. Despite efforts, he was not reinstated. Father Joseph passed away on March 17, 2012. (Courtesy of James Shamoun.)

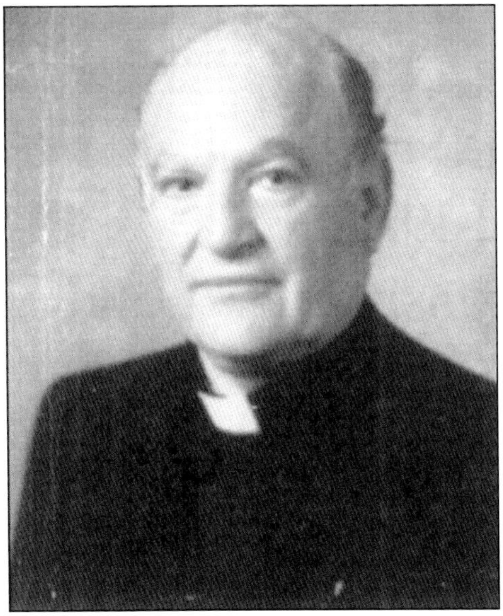

THE SPIRIT OF A BRAVE MAN. Father Ablahad Najjar was born in 1922 in Telkaif, Iraq. In 1966, he replaced Father Eshai Joseph in Turlock, California, and he frequently visited San Diego. In the early 1980s, he survived an assassination attempt, though the motive remains unclear. Many speculated it was linked to his acceptance of funding from the Iraqi government in 1980. Despite severe injuries, he continued his work. Father Najjar moved to Detroit in 1983 and served in Los Angeles before returning to Detroit, where he passed away on October 5, 2005. (Courtesy of *Chaldean Directory*.)

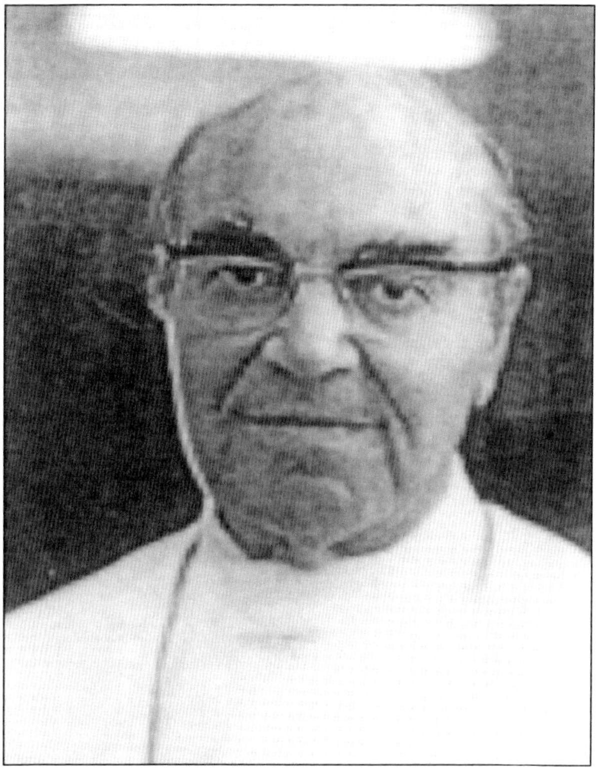

The First Priest of Saint Peter Church. Father Peter Kattoula was born in Telkaif, Iraq, in 1919. He served the Chaldean community in New Britain, Connecticut, from 1966 to 1973. In 1973, he was called to serve the growing Chaldean community in San Diego, California, where he established Saint Peter Parish and served as pastor for 14 years. Father Kattoula passed away on March 20, 1987, at the age of 69. (Courtesy of Vincent Kattoula.)

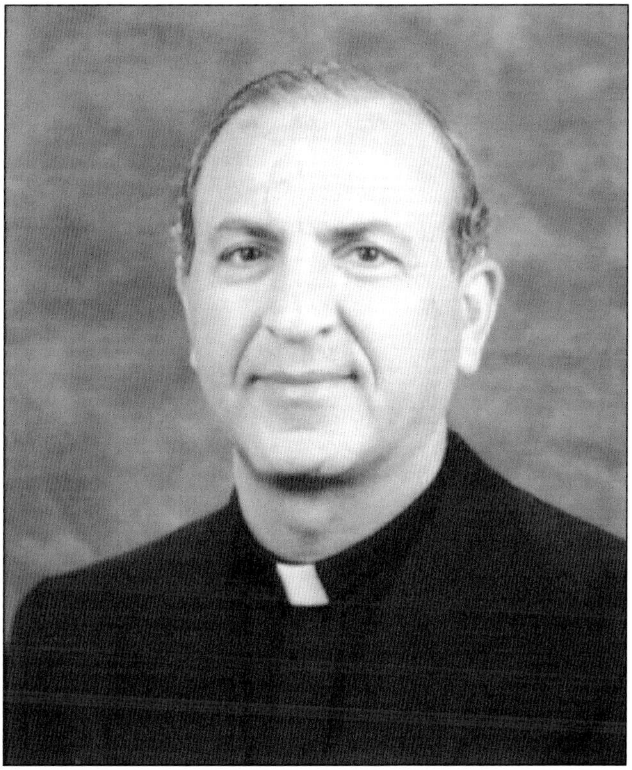

Keeping the Faith Alive. Born in Telkaif, Iraq, in 1938, Father Michael J. Bazzi was ordained a Chaldean priest on May 15, 1964. After serving in Telkaif, he moved to the United States in 1974, teaching scripture in Wisconsin. Father Bazzi established Mar Addai Church in Michigan (1979) and Saint Joseph Church (1981) before becoming pastor at Saint Peter Parish in San Diego in 1987. He later founded Saint Michael Church in El Cajon (1999). A scholar, his notable work includes *Telkepe: Past and Present* (1969). (Courtesy of Father Michael J. Bazzi.)

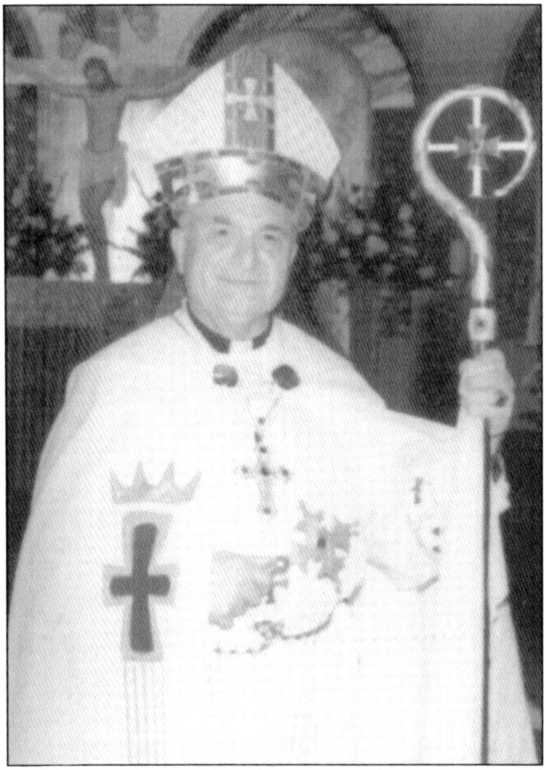

Spirited with Enthusiasm. Born in Baghdad in 1941, Sarhad Y. Jammo was ordained a priest in 1964 and immigrated to the United States in 1977. He served at Mother of God Church in Michigan and co-led efforts for unity between the Chaldean Catholic Church and the Assyrian Church of the East. In 2002, he became the first bishop of the Saint Peter Chaldean Catholic Diocese in El Cajon. Bishop Jammo retired in 2016, leaving a legacy of faith and unity. (Courtesy of Bryon Perry.)

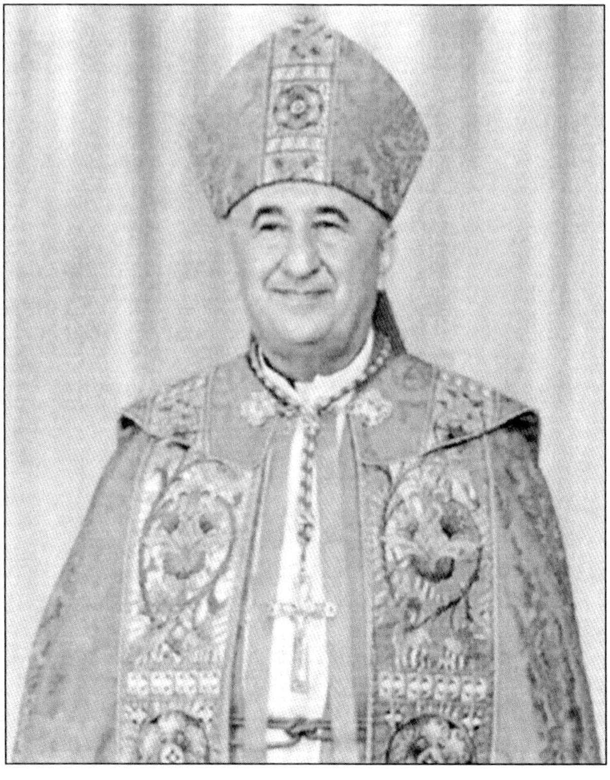

Always Ready to Serve. Emanuel Hana Shaleta, born on November 11, 1956, in Iraq, was ordained a priest by Pope John Paul II in 1984. He served in North Hollywood, California, and later in Michigan. In 2015, Pope Francis appointed him as the second bishop of the Chaldean Eparchy of Mar Addai of Toronto. In 2017, he became the second bishop of the Chaldean Catholic Eparchy of Saint Peter in San Diego, focusing on pastoral services and expanding the number of priests. (Courtesy of Chaldean Catholic Eparchy of Saint Peter the Apostle.)

The Rites of Baptism and Confirmation. In the Chaldean Catholic tradition, baptism and confirmation are conferred on infants raised in Christian faith. Only bishops and priests can administer sacraments, following Jesus's command in Matthew 28:19–20. Baby Brandon Zia Razooki is held by his uncle and godfather, Raidh Razooki, while Father Peter Kattoula performs his baptism and confirmation on June 22, 1986, at Saint Peter Chaldean Church in El Cajon, California. (Both, courtesy of Samir and Rawa Razooki.)

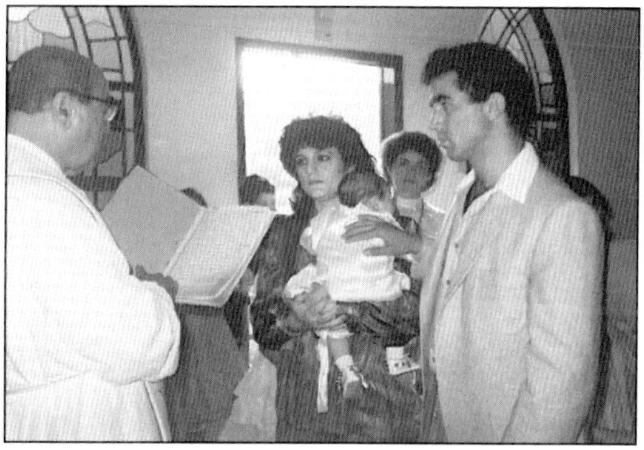

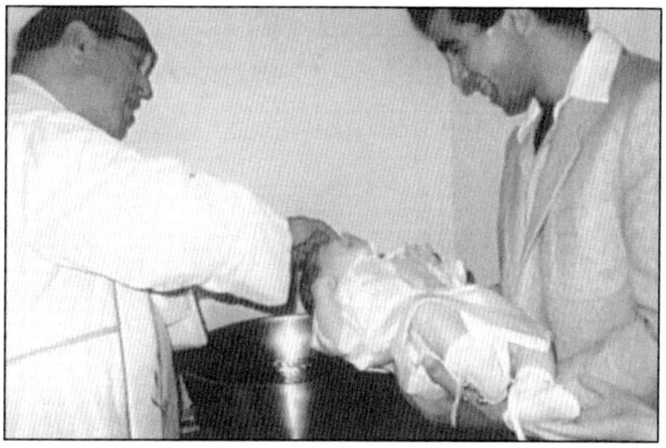

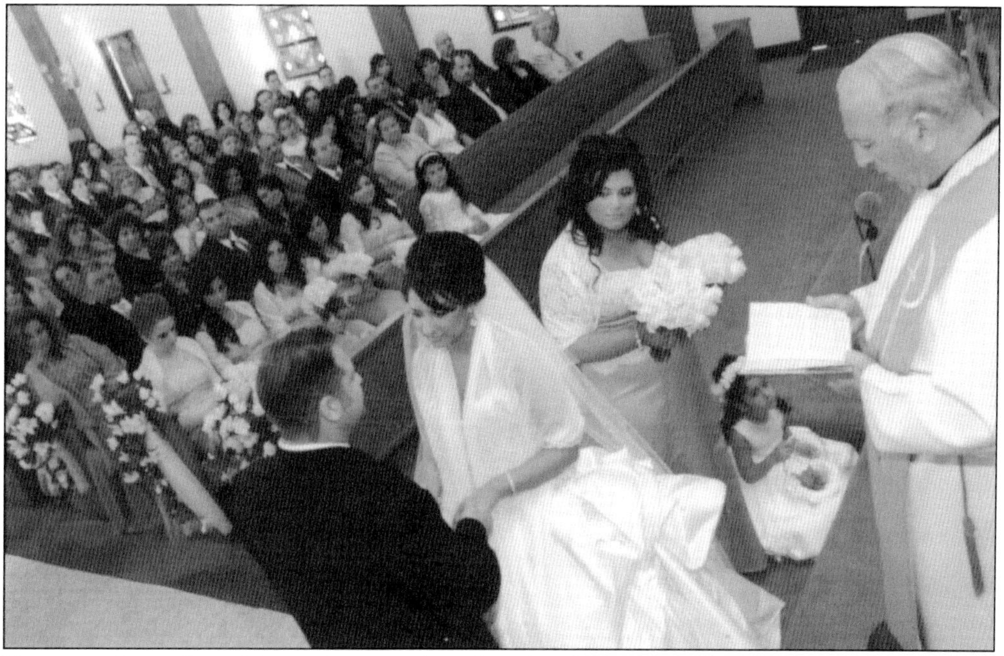

Husbands Love Your Wives. Saint Paul teaches that "the husband is the head of his wife, just as Christ is the head of the church" (Ephesians 5:23). Marriage, like holy orders, is a sacrament of service, reflecting Christ's sacrificial love for the Church. In Iraq, divorce was never an option until the 20th century, and couples had to resolve their differences. This Chaldean tradition emphasizes the enduring values of commitment and perseverance in marriage, which remain vital today. (Courtesy of Bryon Perry.)

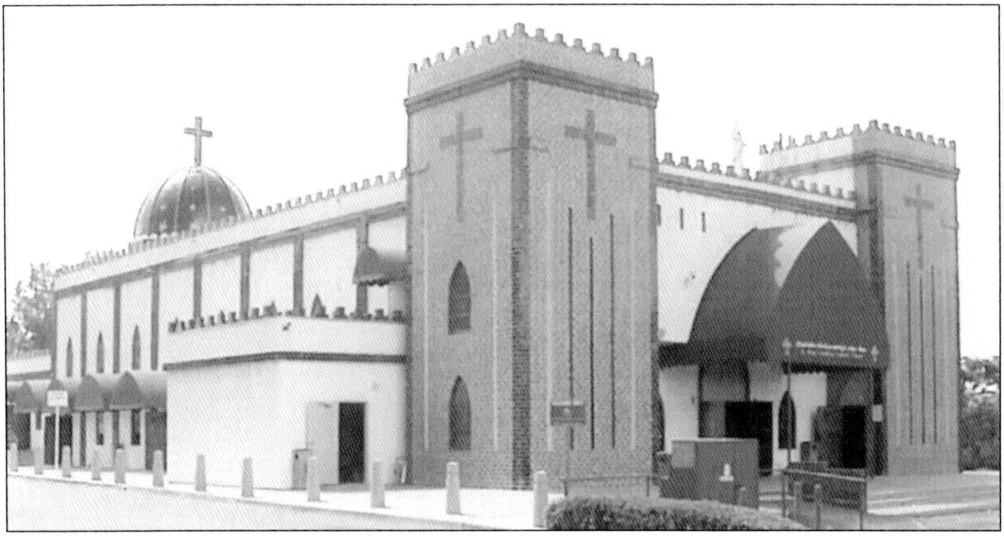

THE BELOVED SAINT PETER'S CHURCH. In the summer of 1973, Patriarch Paulus II Cheikho visited San Diego and met with over 70 Chaldean families who had mostly relocated from Detroit. On December 6, 1973, Saint Peter Chaldean Catholic Church was established, with Father Peter Kattoula as pastor. A church was built in El Cajon, California, in 1983, consecrated with the dedication of 400 families. Today, the cathedral serves over 40,000 Chaldean faithful in San Diego at 1627 Jamacha Way. (Courtesy of Chaldean Catholic Eparchy of Saint Peter the Apostle.)

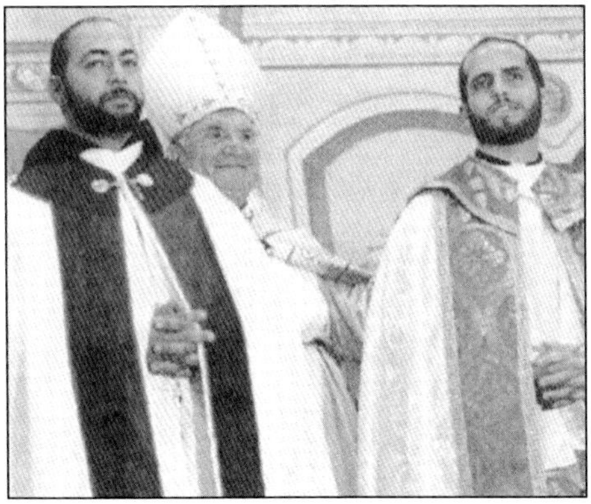

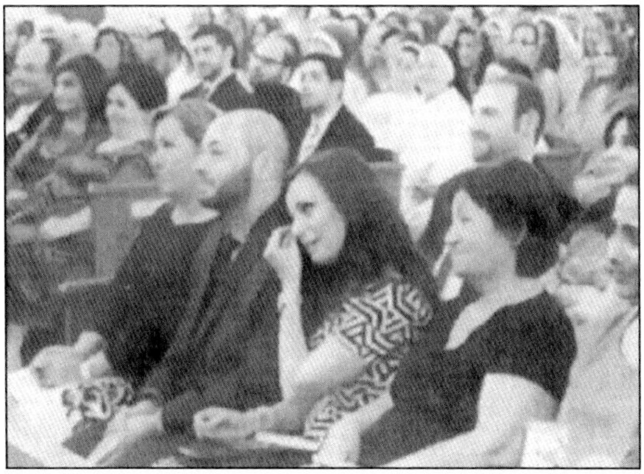

SAINT PETER DIOCESE'S FIRST-EVER ORDINATIONS. On April 10, 2015, Bishop Sarhad Jammo ordained Father Ankido Sipo and Father Simon Esshaki, the first priests from the Seminary of Mar Abba the Great in San Diego. This historic event marked the eparchy's spiritual growth and its role in nurturing a new generation of Chaldean American priests, celebrated by the community at Saint Peter's Chaldean Catholic Cathedral. (Both, courtesy of Chaldean Catholic Eparchy of Saint Peter the Apostle.)

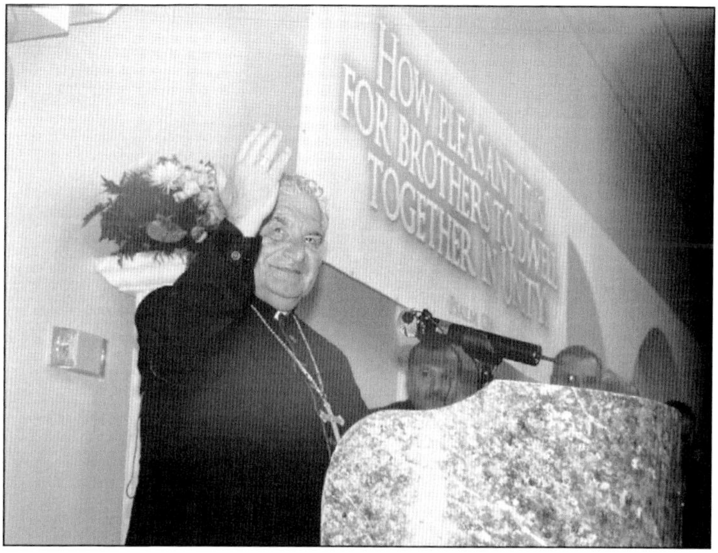

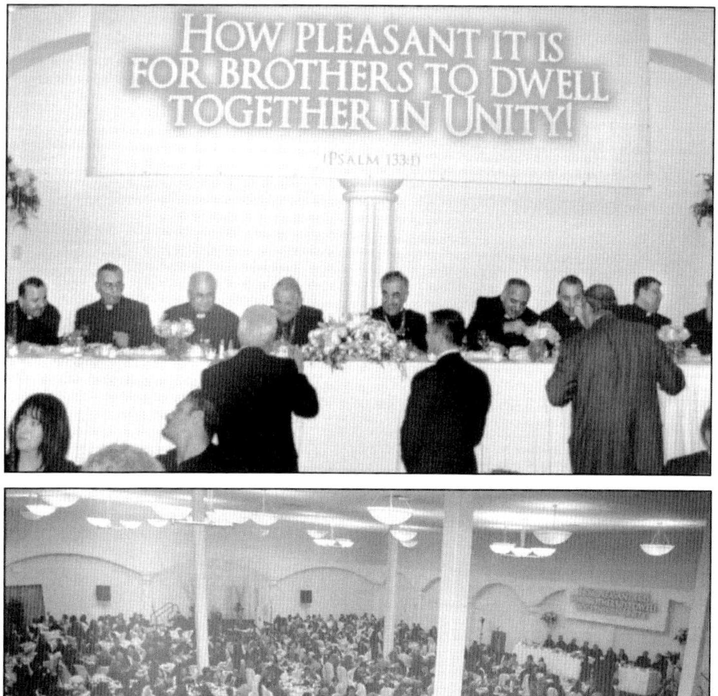

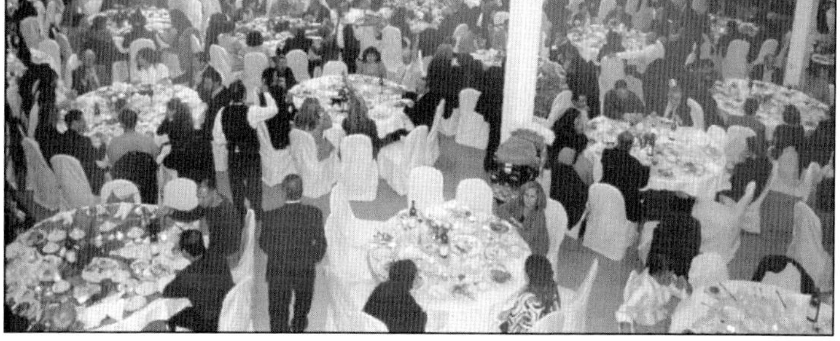

UNITY OF ASSYRIANS AND CHALDEANS. In 2008, a historic event occurred when Assyrian priests and deacons, led by Bishop Bawai Soro, joined the Chaldean Catholic Eparchy of Saint Peter the Apostle, marking a significant union after nearly 150 years. This collaboration included hundreds of Assyrian faithful from California and Chicago. In 2014, Pope Francis appointed Bishop Soro to ecclesial service, granting him the title of titular bishop of Foratiana. The first photograph shows Bishop Sarhad Jammo greeting the Chaldean and Assyrian faithful at a 2008 church unity event in San Jose, California. (All, courtesy of Bishop Bawai Soro.)

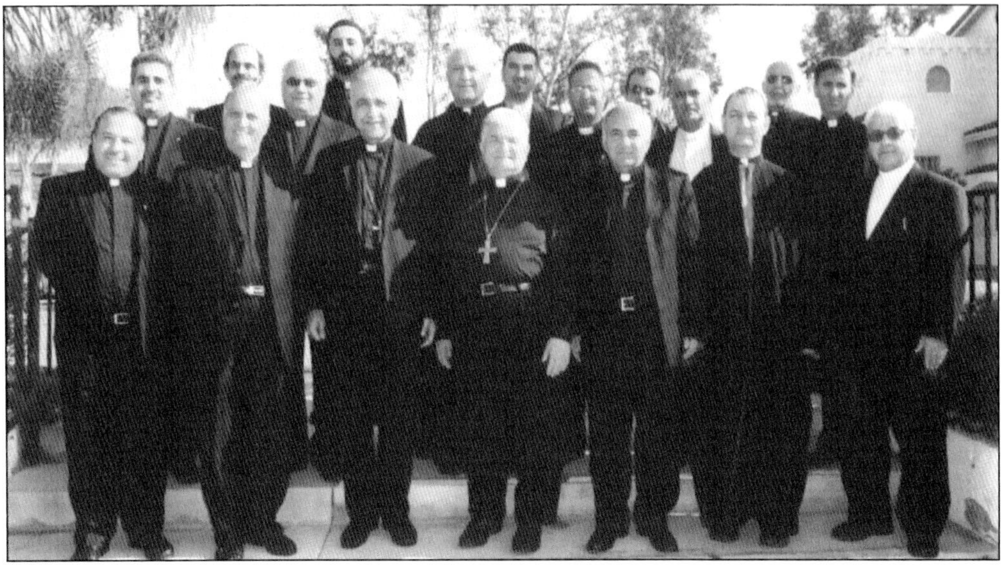

THE SPIRIT OF A PATRIOT. In May 2008, Bishop Sarhad Jammo and the Chaldean clergy welcomed Bishop Bawai Soro, Chorbishop Samuel Dinkha, and Father Michael Barota into the Chaldean Catholic Eparchy of Saint Peter. During this momentous occasion at Saint Peter Chaldean Cathedral, the clergy recited the Nicene Creed, publicly declaring the Assyrian priests, deacons, and faithful had joined the Catholic Church in full communion. (Courtesy of Bishop Bawai Soro.)

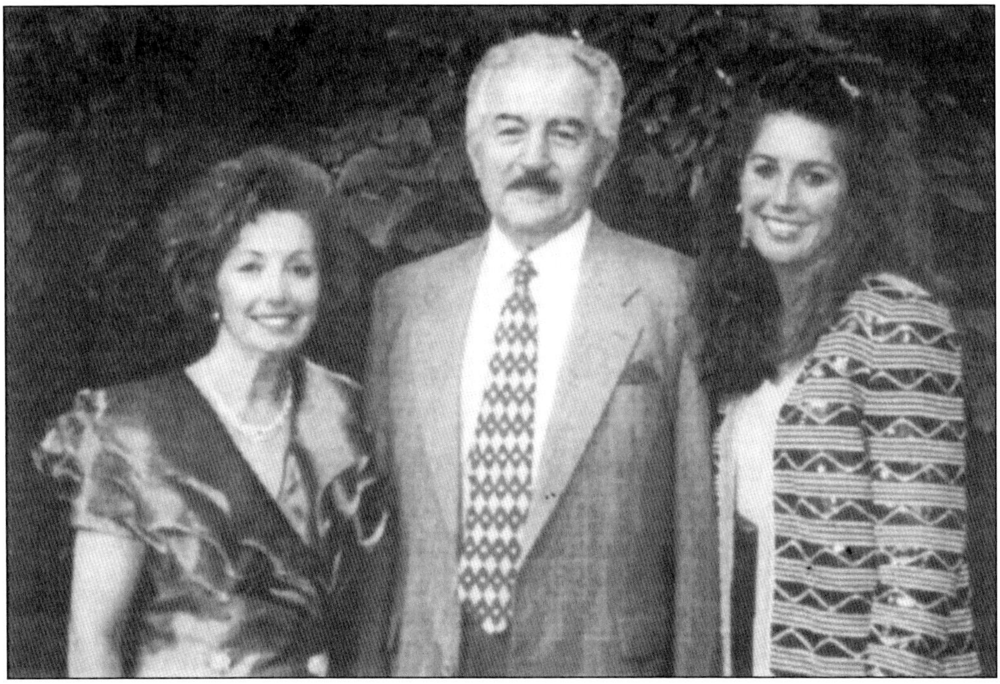

GOODBYE DETROIT: ARIZONA'S FIRST CHALDEAN FAMILY. Tom and Mary Mattia, along with their family, were the first known Chaldeans to move to Arizona, seeking relief from the harsh Michigan winters. Many Chaldeans who left Iraq after the first Gulf War also chose Arizona as their final destination. Pictured here are Tom "Toma" Mattia (center), his wife, Mary (left), and their daughter Michelle (right). (Courtesy of Paul Manni.)

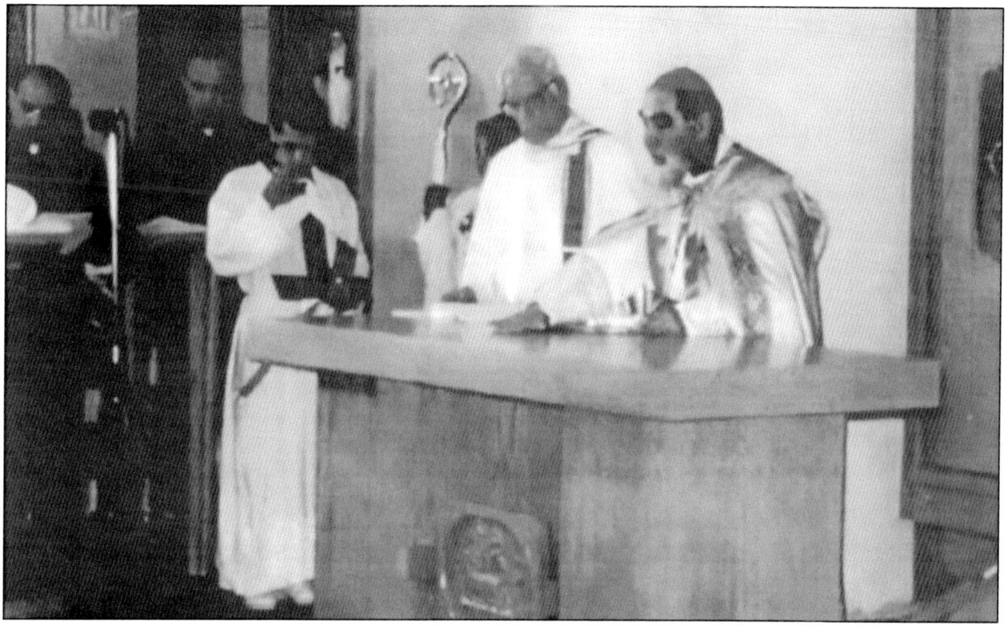

ARIZONA'S FIRST CHALDEAN CHURCH. The first Chaldean church in Scottsdale, Arizona, was originally named Mar Auraha Chaldean Catholic Church. The church was later renamed to Mar Abraham Chaldean Catholic Church, with Father Noel Gorgis as the first assigned priest. Abraham is the English equivalent of Auraha. Pictured here are His Excellency Bishop Ibrahim N. Ibrahim and Deacon Yousif Bashi anointing the altar with holy oil during the dedication of Mar Auraha on June 2, 1995. (Courtesy of Paul Manni.)

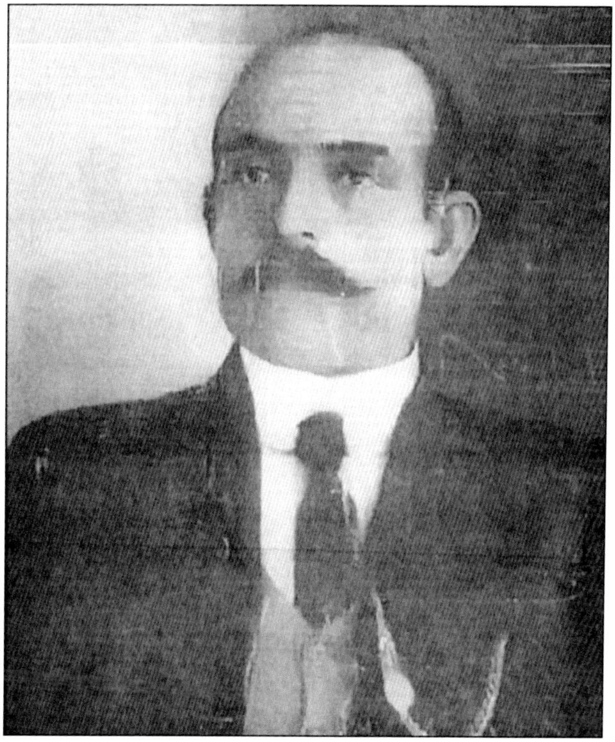

CHALDEANS OF MEXICO, PEOPLE TO REMEMBER! As a young teenager, Jajjo Hajji left his birthplace of Telkaif in search of a better life for his family. He first arrived in Adana, a city in the southern Ottoman Empire (modern-day Turkey) with a sizable Christian population. However, after witnessing brutal persecution and a large scale of massacres by the Turks against Christians, whom they called *gawer* (infidels), he was forced to flee. In 1901, Jajjo arrived at the port of San Jeronimo, Mexico. There, he quickly became a small businessman, selling clothing and saving money to support his family. Known for his kindness, he was described as a father to those in need and a mother to those who were homesick. (Courtesy of Sam Dabish.)

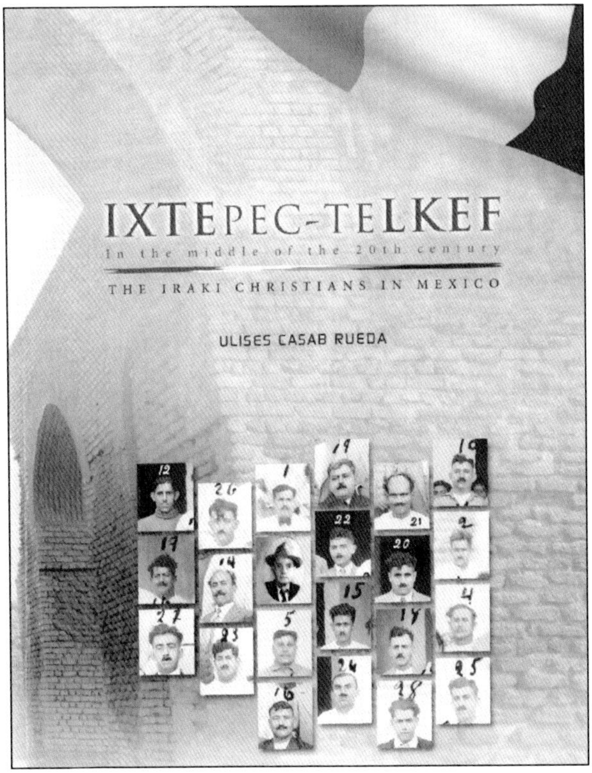

The Forgotten Chaldeans of Mexico. Physician and writer Dr. Ulises Casab Rueda authored *Tel-Kepphayas*, a Spanish-language book about northern Iraqi Christian pioneers and their migration to Mexico in the early 1900s. The book, later translated into English as *Ixtepec-Telkef* in 2021, highlights their journey. Dr. Casab Rueda, who grew up in Ixtepec, Mexico, noted that by 1929, fifty-five documented Chaldeans lived in Mexico. Some were born to Chaldean fathers and Mexican mothers, while others emigrated from Telkeppe. He hosted a book launch at Shenandoah Country Club in West Bloomfield, Michigan, on February 3, 2022. (Both, courtesy of Dr. Ulises Casab Rueda.)

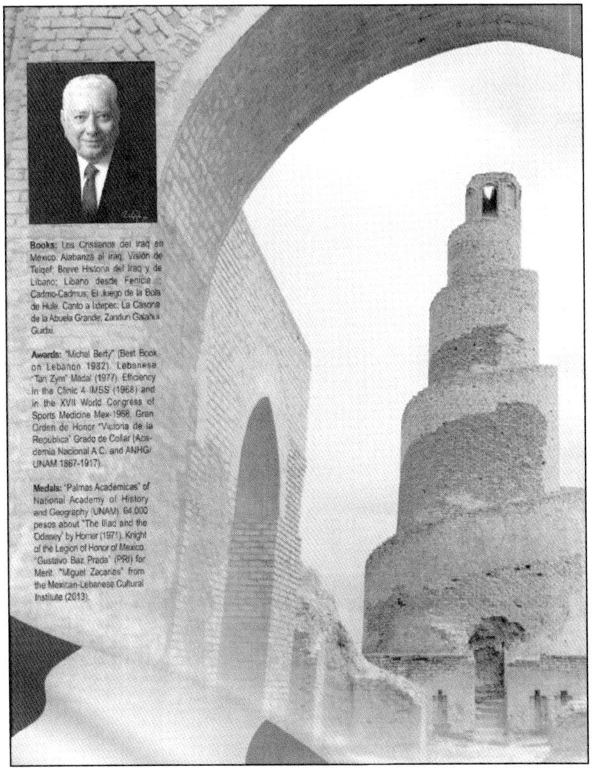

STATS ABOUT THE CHALDEAN PARISHES OF SAINT PETER EPARCHY

SAINT THOMAS ASSYRIAN-CHALDEAN CATHOLIC CHURCH	SAINT PAUL ASSYRIAN-CHALDEAN CATHOLIC CHURCH	SAINT MARY ASSYRIAN-CHALDEAN CATHOLIC CHURCH
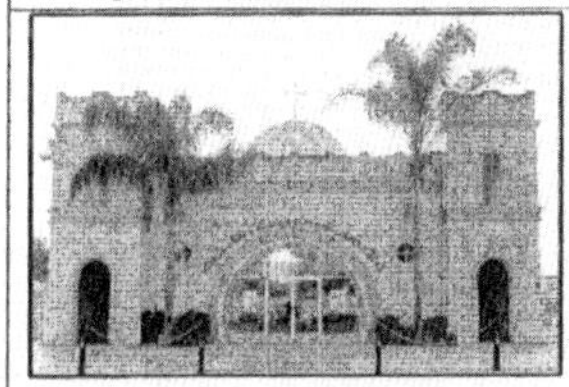 2901 N Berkeley Avenue Turlock, CA 95382 **Established:** 1964 **First Priest:** Father Eshai Seth Joseph (1961-1966) **Consecration:** 1964 **Population:** 50 Families ('64), 343 Families ('22).	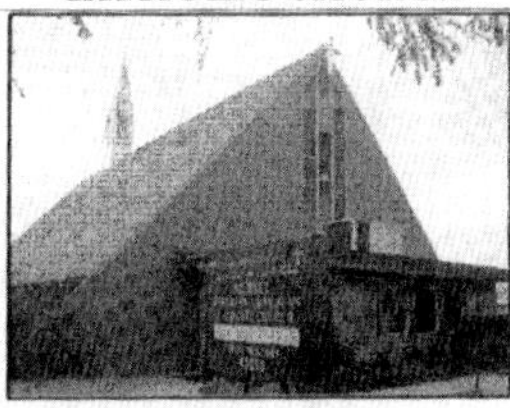 13050 Vanowen Street North Hollywood, CA 91605 **Established:** 1979 **First Priest:** Father (Bishop) Ibrahim N. Ibrahim **Consecration:** 1980 **Population:** 250 Families ('80) 545 Families ('22)	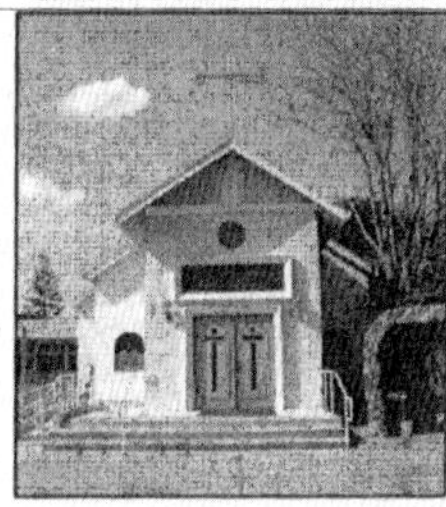 109 North First Street Campbell, CA 95008 **Established:** 1983 **First Priest:** Father Francis David **Remodeled:** 2015 **Population:** 320 Families ('22)
MAR ABRAHAM CHALDEAN CATHOLIC CHURCH	**SAINT MICHAEL CHALDEAN CATHOLIC CHURCH**	**SAINT GEORGE CHALDEAN CATHOLIC CHURCH**
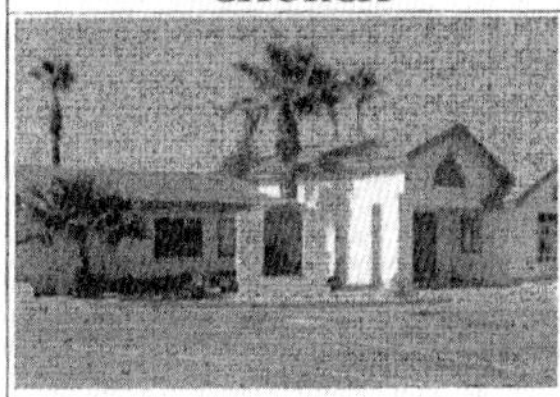 6816 E. Cactus Road Scottsdale, AZ. 85254 **Established:** 1994 **First Priest:** Father Noel Gorgis (Monk) **Consecration:** 1995 **Population:** 100 Families ('94), 350 Families ('22).	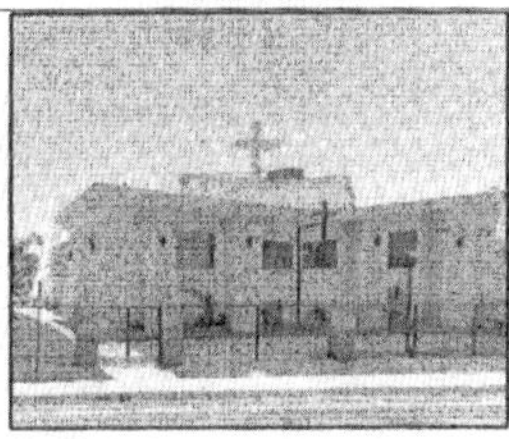 799 E. Washington Avenue El Cajon, CA 92020 **Established:** 1999 **First Priest:** Archdeacon Sabri Kejbo (1999-2021) **Consecration:** 2000 **Population:** 250 Families ('00) 2,000 Families ('22)	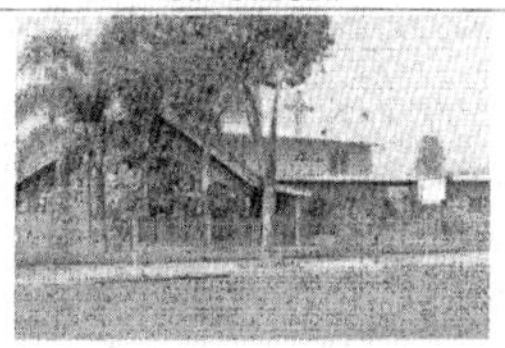 4807 W. McFadden Avenue Santa Ana, CA 92704 **Established:** 2001 **First Priest:** Father Paulos Khozairan (Monk) **Consecration:** 2001 **Population:** 120 Families ('01)

CHURCHES: PART ONE. There are 12 churches in the Chaldean Catholic Eparchy of Saint Peter the Apostle. Above are images of 6 of the 12, accompanied by notable facts highlighting the unique history and characteristics of each parish. (Courtesy of Jacob Bacall.)

STATS ABOUT THE CHALDEAN PARISHES OF SAINT PETER EPARCHY

SAINT BARBARA CHALDEAN CATHOLIC CHURCH	SAINT MATTHEW ASSYRIAN-CHALDEAN CATHOLIC CHURCH	OUR LADY OF PERPETUAL HELP CHALDEAN CATHOLIC CHURCH
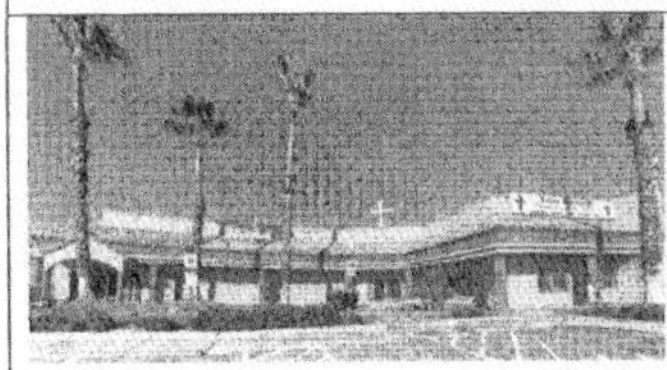	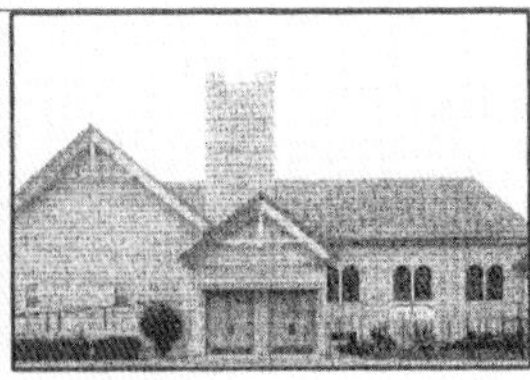	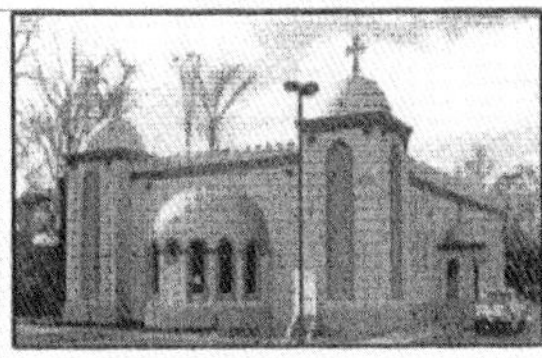
4514 Meadows Lane Las Vegas, NV 89107 **Established:** 2007 **First Priest:** Father (Bishop) Felix Shabi **Consecration:** 2007 **Population:** 170 Families ('22)	3005 6th Street Ceres, CA 95307 **Established:** 2008 **First Priest:** Father Michael Barota (2008-2012) **Consecration:** 2008 **Population:** 177 Families ('22)	7625 Hazel Avenue Orangevale, CA 95662 **Established:** 1984 **First Priest:** Father Frances Dawood (1984-1986) **Consecration:** 2011 **Population:** 120 Families ('22)
SAINT JOHN CHALDEAN CATHOLIC CHURCH	**HOLY FAMILY CHALDEAN CATHOLIC CHURCH**	**SAINT JOSEPH CHALDEAN CATHOLIC CHURCH**
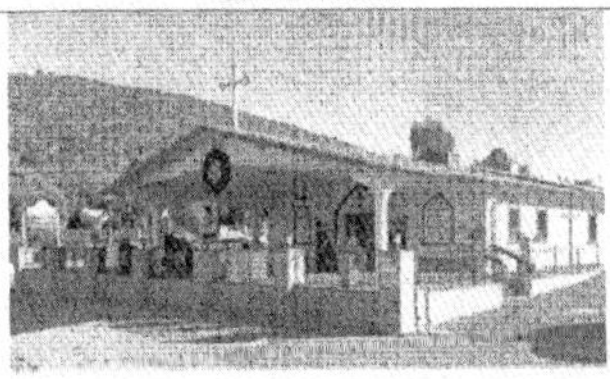	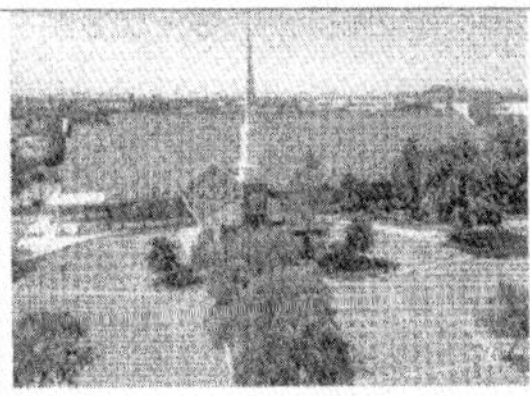	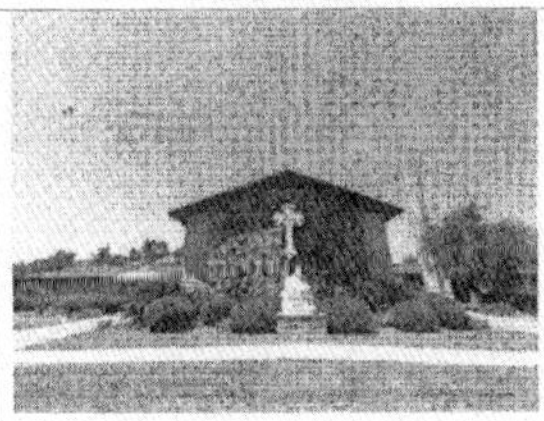
1763 N. First Street El Cajon, CA 92021 **Established:** 2017 **First Priest:** Father Abbot Ankido Sipo (2017-present) **Consecration:** 2017 **Population:** 300 Families ('22)	16612 N. 21st Avenue Phoenix, AZ 85023 Established: 2018 First Priest: Father (Bishop) Felix Shabi Consecration: 2018 Population: 950 Families ('22)	3348 Sweetwater Springs Blvd. Spring Valley, CA 91977 **Established:** 2022 **First Priest:** Chorbishop Philip Najim (2022-Present) **Consecration:** 2023 **Population:** 1500 Families ('22)

CHURCHES: PART TWO. Above are images of churches established in 2007 to date (2024) in the Chaldean Catholic Eparchy of Saint Peter the Apostle. (Courtesy of Jacob Bacall.)

Seven

Chaldean Catholic Eparchy of Mar Addai in Canada

At the turn of the 20th century, Canada housed the largest Chaldean group in North America, surpassing both the United States and Mexico. The district of Fort William, in the city of Thunder Bay, Ontario, claimed the fame of having more than 30 families who spoke Aramaic, the language that Jesus Christ himself spoke.

Sadiq Damman, from the village of Alqosh in Iraq, is mentioned as a pioneering Chaldean immigrant, having settled in Canada in 1884. However, historical records of his whereabouts are scarce, and it remains to be determined whether he returned to Iraq or lived and died in Canada.

Yousif Shammam arrived in Canada a few years after Damman and helped his family and relatives from Iraq immigrate there. His brother, Petrus, and brother-in-law, Khamo Jarjosa, joined him later. His nephew, Jameel Qashat, arrived in 1914 after being discharged from the Ottoman army just before World War I.

The automobile revolution began in Detroit, Michigan, in 1914 with the introduction of the $5-a-day wage. Within six months, most Chaldean families living in Fort William moved to Detroit. "The automobile industry was growing in Detroit, creating a magnet for immigrants," said Mary C. Sengstock in her 2005 book, *Chaldeans in Michigan*.

The Chaldean community in Canada took almost a full century to grow and become organized. It did so in the greater Toronto area in 1988, when Father Jacob Yasso became the first Chaldean priest assigned by the patriarchate to serve the Chaldeans of Canada. In 1991, the expatriated Chaldean archbishop of Ahwaz (Iran), Archbishop Hanna Zora, arrived from Rome to replace Father Yasso, who was asked to return to his diocese in Detroit.

Archbishop Zora took another decade to build in 2000 the first Chaldean church in Toronto, the Good Shepherd Chaldean Catholic Church. Over 10 years later, in 2011, Pope John Paul II established the Chaldean Catholic Eparchy of Mar Addai the Apostle and appointed Archbishop Zora as its first eparch. As of 2024, Mar Addai Eparchy has 13 parishes and missions proudly serving 40,000 Chaldeans in Canada.

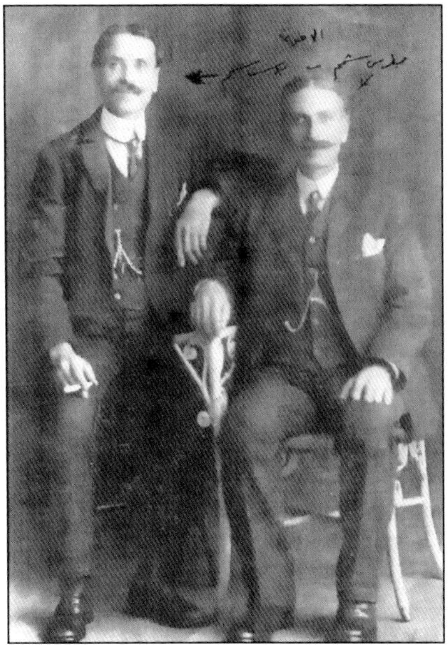

THE FIRST CHALDEAN PIONEERS. Yousif Shammam arrived in Canada in 1899. Soon after, he contacted his family and relatives in Telkaif, near Mosul, Iraq, to join him. His brother, Petrus, and his brother-in-law, Khamo Jarjosa, left for Marseille, France, via sea and then arrived in Canada. They each began working by selling household goods and food on small carts from house to house. After a short period, the first pioneers sent their friends and acquaintances in Telkaif messages to join them, and they promised to provide any assistance necessary after their arrival. This was the story until the number of Chaldeans in Canada reached more than 30 families. (Courtesy of Sam Dabish.)

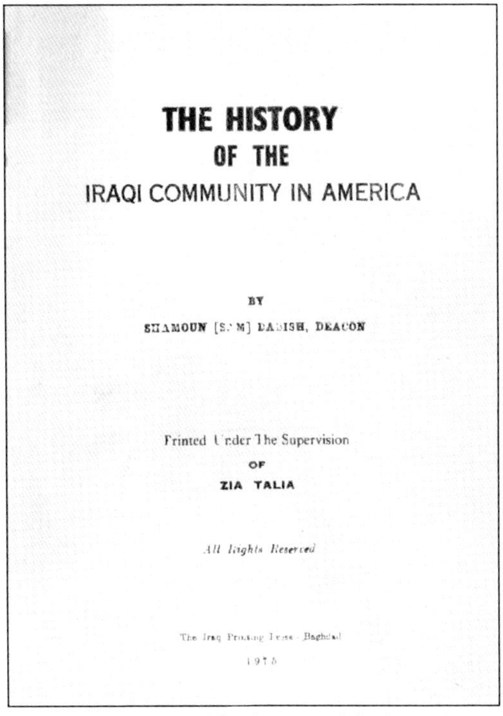

THE HISTORY
OF THE
IRAQI COMMUNITY IN AMERICA

BY

SHAMOUN [S. M] DABISH, DEACON

Printed Under The Supervision
OF
ZIA TALIA

All Rights Reserved

The Iraq Printing Press - Baghdad
1975

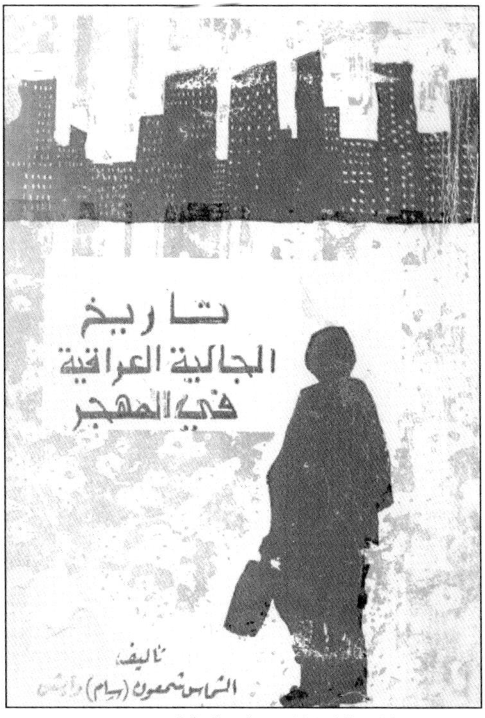

HISTORY RECORDS. *The History of the Iraqi Community in America*, published in 1975 by Shamoun (Sam) Dabish, provided a valuable account of the early Chaldean diaspora, mainly focusing on Detroit, Michigan, and Fort William District in Thunder Bay, Ontario. It highlighted the hard work and determination required to establish the first Chaldean church in Detroit and the pioneering Chaldean community organization in America, the Chaldean Iraqi Association (CIA). Dabish's dedication to his community, as evidenced by his roles as a deacon, parish council member, elected CIA member, and author, showcased his deep faith and commitment to preserving the history and culture of the Chaldean diaspora. (Both, courtesy of Jacob Bacall.)

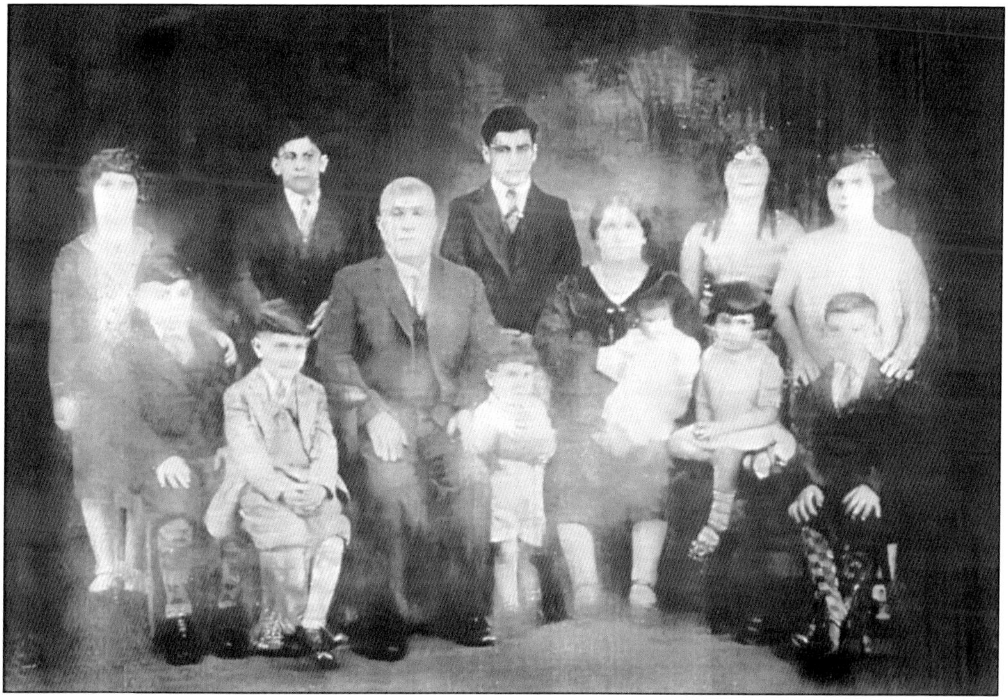

I Got My Family with Me. Homi Yalda and his wife, Amena, migrated with their 11 children from Fort William, Thunder Bay, Ontario, to Detroit, seizing the opportunities spurred by Ford's $5-a-day wage introduced in 1914. (Courtesy of Sam Dabish.)

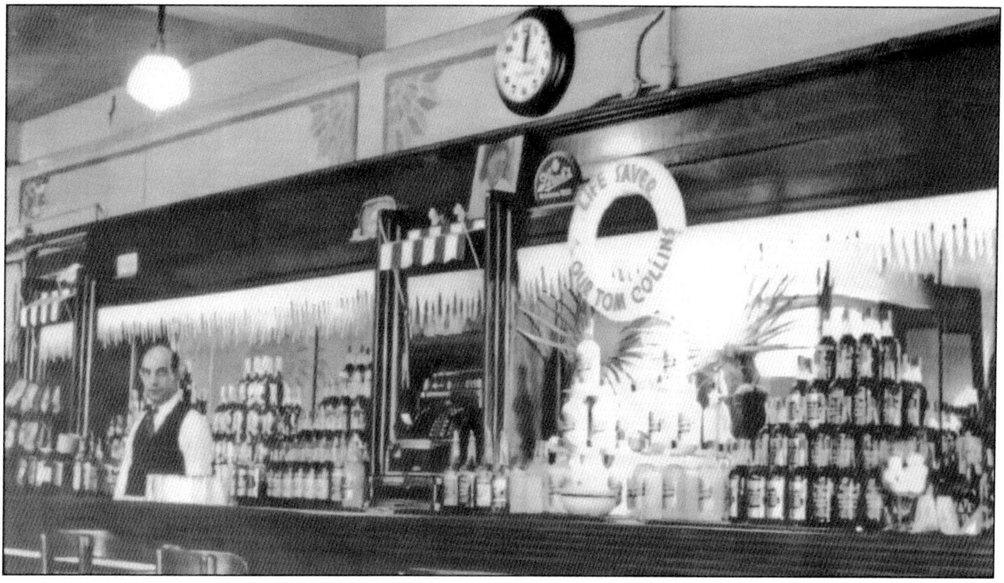

On Duty, May I Help You? David Khoury was an early immigrant to Canada around 1914 and later moved to Detroit, where he became a longtime resident. Word of the success of these early immigrants reached those who remained behind in Telkaif, and many more were induced to leave in search of economic betterment. David Khoury is Zia Attala's brother-in-law, known to be the first Chaldean emigrant from the village of Telkaif to the United States, who arrived in Philadelphia around 1889, according to Mary Sengstock's book *Michigan History*. (Courtesy of Jacob Bacall.)

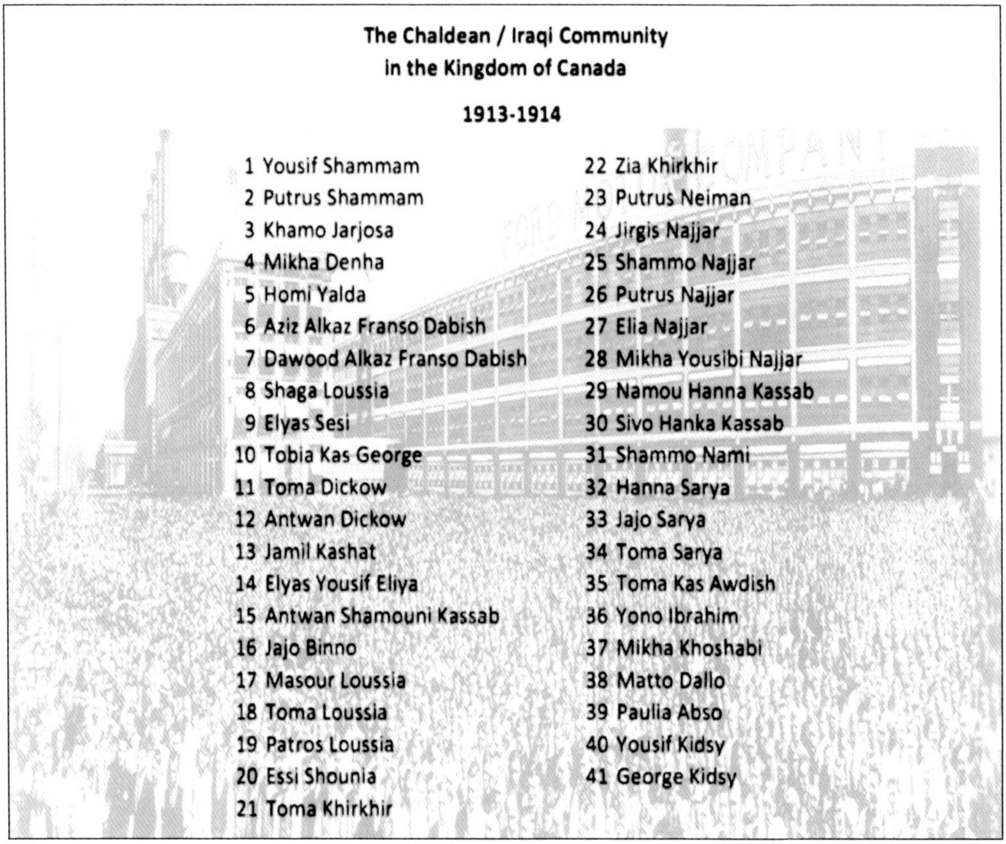

The Chaldean / Iraqi Community in the Kingdom of Canada

1913-1914

1 Yousif Shammam
2 Putrus Shammam
3 Khamo Jarjosa
4 Mikha Denha
5 Homi Yalda
6 Aziz Alkaz Franso Dabish
7 Dawood Alkaz Franso Dabish
8 Shaga Loussia
9 Elyas Sesi
10 Tobia Kas George
11 Toma Dickow
12 Antwan Dickow
13 Jamil Kashat
14 Elyas Yousif Eliya
15 Antwan Shamouni Kassab
16 Jajo Binno
17 Masour Loussia
18 Toma Loussia
19 Patros Loussia
20 Essi Shounia
21 Toma Khirkhir
22 Zia Khirkhir
23 Putrus Neiman
24 Jirgis Najjar
25 Shammo Najjar
26 Putrus Najjar
27 Elia Najjar
28 Mikha Yousibi Najjar
29 Namou Hanna Kassab
30 Sivo Hanka Kassab
31 Shammo Nami
32 Hanna Sarya
33 Jajo Sarya
34 Toma Sarya
35 Toma Kas Awdish
36 Yono Ibrahim
37 Mikha Khoshabi
38 Matto Dallo
39 Paulia Abso
40 Yousif Kidsy
41 George Kidsy

THE WAY IT WAS. From the early 1890s to 1910, many Chaldean and Arab immigrants embarked in the common trade of pack peddling, known as *qasha* or *qushshah*. This involved selling clothing, fabric, and household necessities door-to-door in rural areas. It required little training, basic English, and minimal investment. This list shows some of the 41 Chaldeans who lived in Canada from 1913 to 1914. Among them were, from left to right, Namou Kassab, Antwan Shamouni Kassab, and Sivo Hanka Kassab, pictured in 1915. At center are Toma Khirkhir (in white hat) and Abbo Essa Garmo. Also pictured at right is Elyas Yousif Eliya. (All, courtesy of Sam Dabish.)

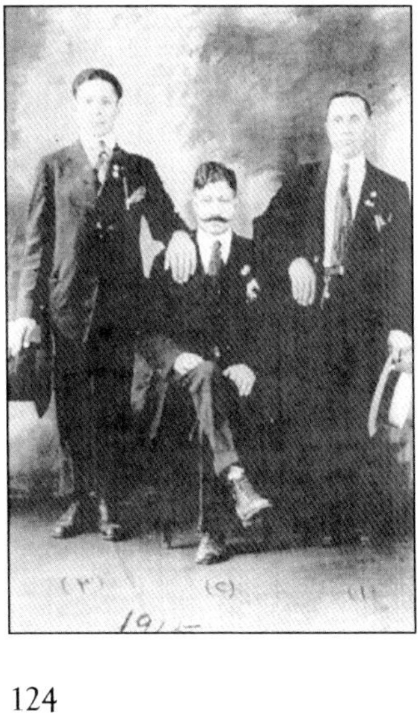

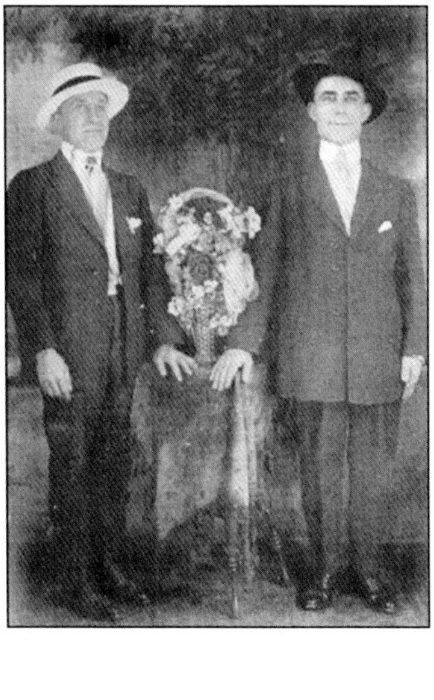

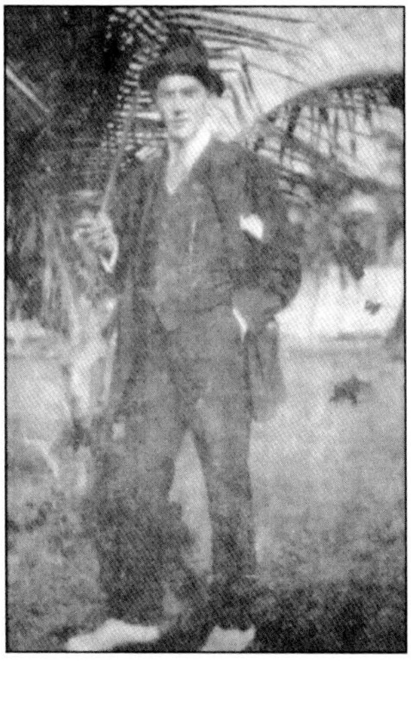

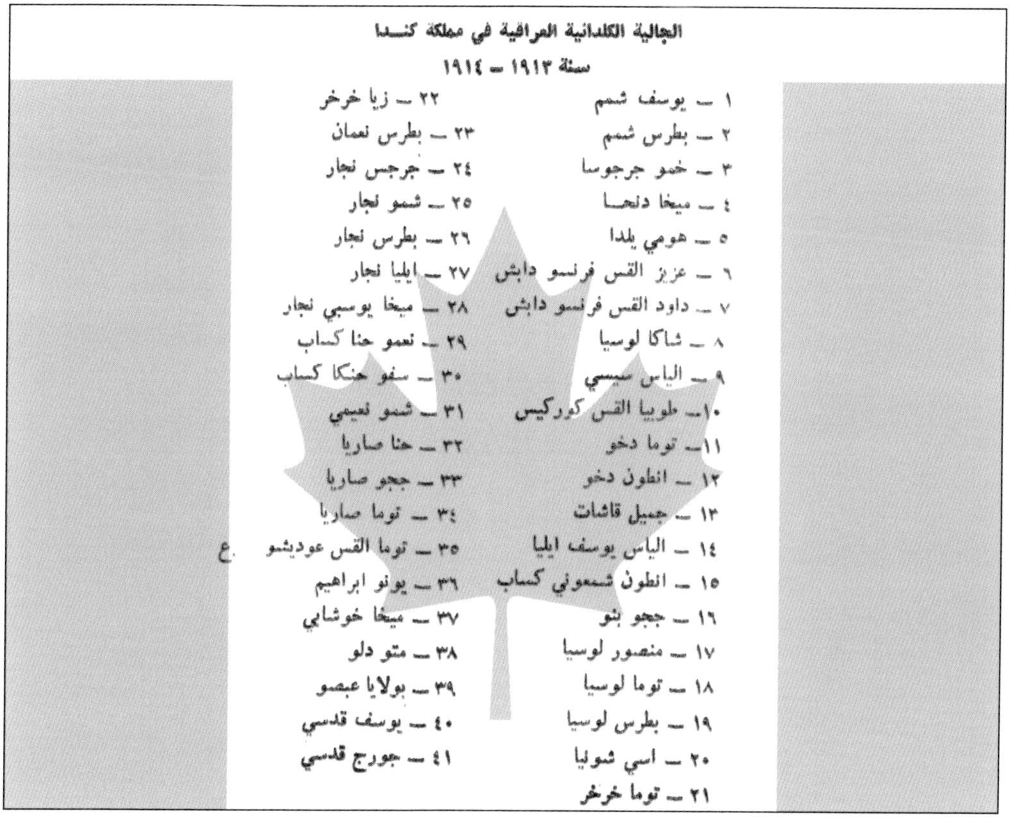

الجالية الكلدانية العراقية في مملكة كنــدا

سنة ١٩١٣ – ١٩١٤

١ – يوسف شمم
٢ – بطرس شمم
٣ – خمو جرجوسا
٤ – ميخا دنحـا
٥ – هومي يلدا
٦ – عزيز القس فرنسو دابش
٧ – داود القس فرنسو دابش
٨ – شاكا لوسيا
٩ – الياس سيسي
١٠ – طوبيا القس كوركيس
١١ – توما دخو
١٢ – انطون دخو
١٣ – جميل قاشات
١٤ – الياس يوسف ايليا
١٥ – انطون شمعوني كساب
١٦ – ججو بنو
١٧ – منصور لوسيا
١٨ – توما لوسيا
١٩ – بطرس لوسيا
٢٠ – اسي شوليا
٢١ – توما خرخر
٢٢ – زيا خرخر
٢٣ – بطرس نعمان
٢٤ – جرجس نجار
٢٥ – شمو نجار
٢٦ – بطرس نجار
٢٧ – ايليا نجار
٢٨ – ميخا يوسبي نجار
٢٩ – نعمو حنا كساب
٣٠ – سفو حنكا كساب
٣١ – شمو نعيمي
٣٢ – حنا صاريا
٣٣ – ججو صاريا
٣٤ – توما صاريا
٣٥ – توما القس عوديشو
٣٦ – يونو ابراهيم
٣٧ – ميخا خوشابي
٣٨ – متو دلو
٣٩ – بولايا عبصو
٤٠ – يوسف قدسي
٤١ – جورج قدسي

EARLY SETTLERS. Typically, peddlers obtained inventory on credit. Yousif Shammam, the first Chaldean immigrant on record to arrive on Canadian soil in 1899, started in the qasha trade for a few years. After achieving financial independence, he brought over his brother, Petrus, brother-in-law, Khamo Jarjosa, and other friends and relatives from the village of Telkaif to join him in the same trade. They established a small community in Fort William, Thunder Bay, Ontario. Above is the a of Chaldean Canadian residents in Canada. Posing for a portrait at left (from left to right) are Shaga Loussia, Masour Loussia, and Putros Loussia. Dawood Alkaz Franso Dabish is captured in a street scene at center. In the image at right (from left to right), all wearing hats, Jack Dooda, George Najjar, and Naim Shammam strike a pose. (All, courtesy of Sam Dabish.)

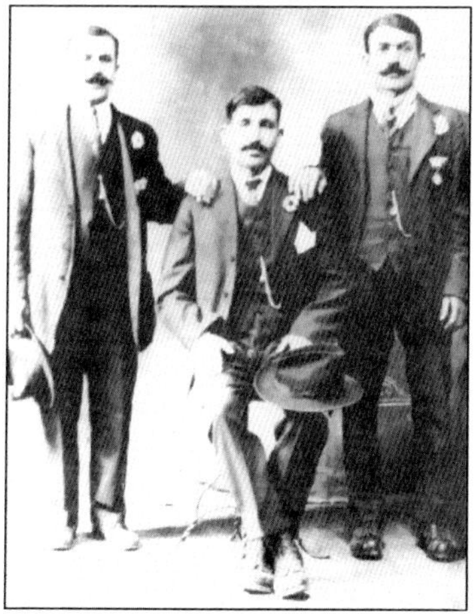
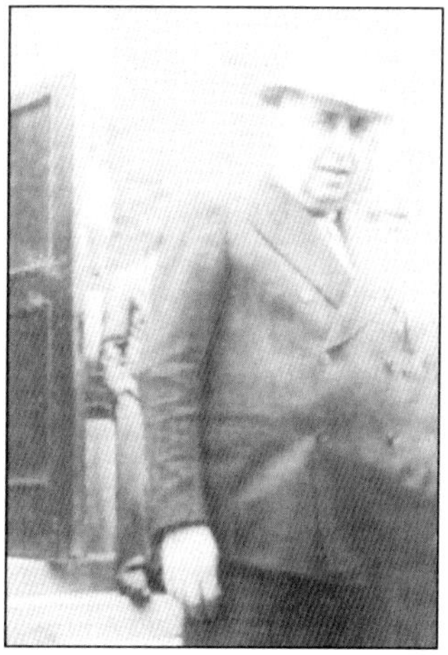
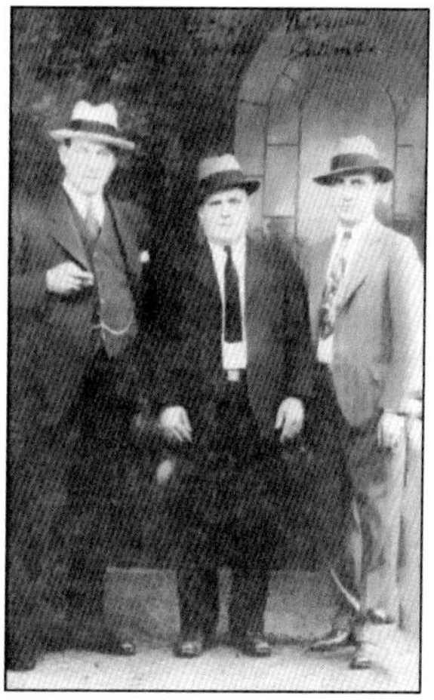

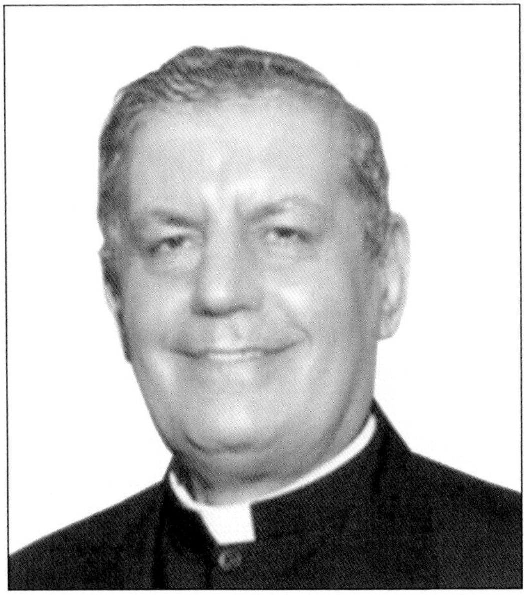

Father of Many Firsts. Father Jacob O. Yasso, born in Telkaif in 1932, was ordained in 1960. In 1964, he became pastor of Mother of God Church in Detroit. In 1988, he established the first Chaldean Catholic church in Canada. Father Yasso also served as a tribunal judge in Toronto and established Sacred Heart Church in Detroit. He passed away in 2014. (Courtesy of *Chaldean Directory*.)

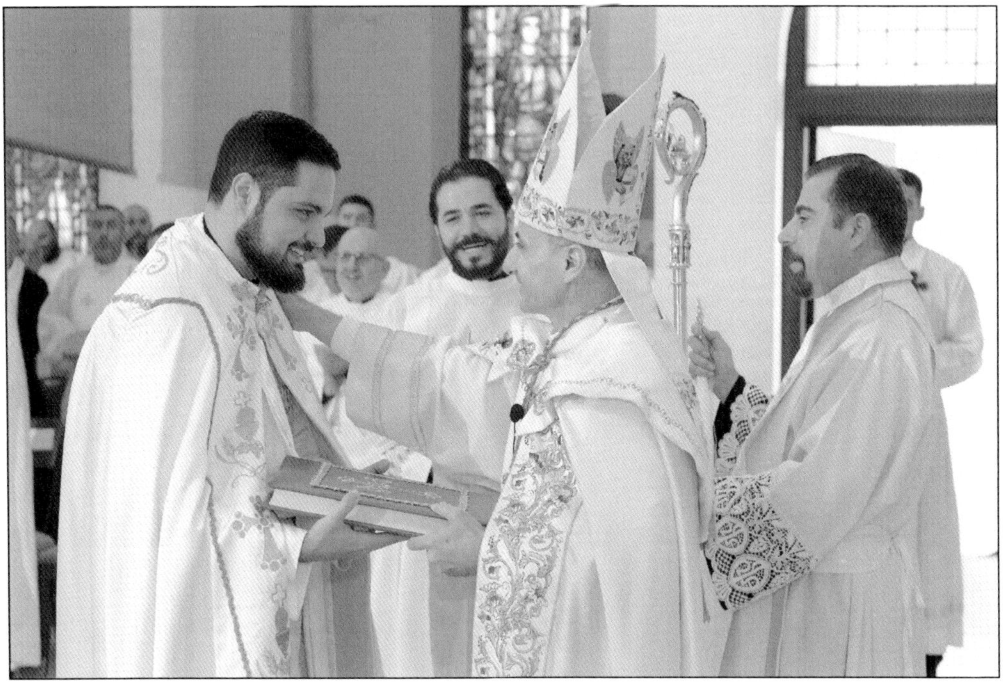

From Detroit to Calgary. Father John Jwad was born on May 7, 1996, in the suburbs of Detroit. He is the youngest of four siblings and was known as "Junior" during his youth. At 12, he learned to read and write Aramaic and began to serve the Church of Michigan in various capacities. He entered Sacred Heart Major Seminary in Detroit. After three years, he was sent on a sabbatical mission for one year in Lebanon. Afterward, he was transferred to the Chaldean Diocese of Mar Addai in Canada, where he was enrolled at Saint Philip's Seminary in Toronto. He was ordained a priest on November 1, 2023, at Holy Family Chaldean Catholic Church in Windsor, Canada. Father John is the first and only Chaldean priest born in North America and serves in the Chaldean Eparchy of Mar Addai in Canada. (Courtesy of Father John Jwad.)

FIRST CHALDEAN BISHOP TO CANADA. Bishop Hanna Zora, born in Batnaya, Iraq, on March 15, 1939, was ordained in 1962 and consecrated bishop of Ahwaz, Iran, in 1974. He moved to Toronto in 1991 and oversaw the opening of Good Shepherd Chaldean Cathedral in 2000. Appointed the first bishop of the Eparchy of Mar Addai in 2011, he retired in 2014 and passed away on October 2, 2016, in the country of Georgia. (Courtesy of Dr. Stefan Galyana.)

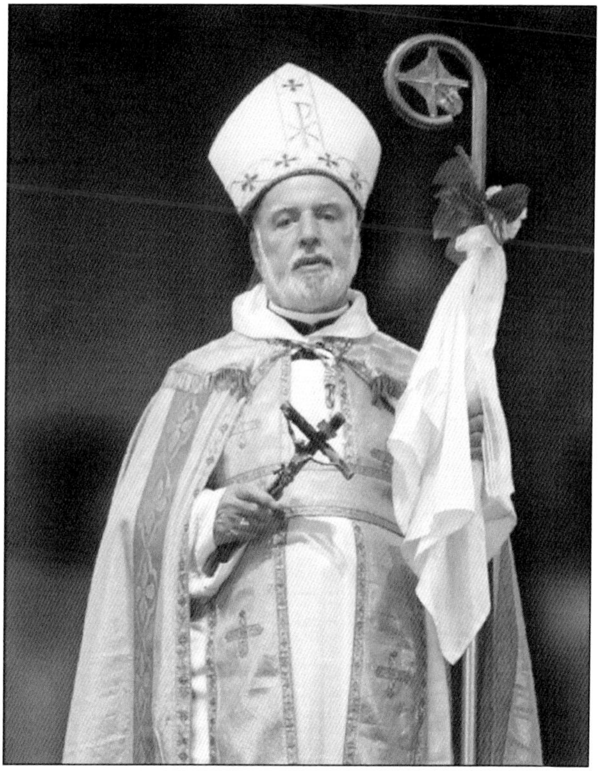

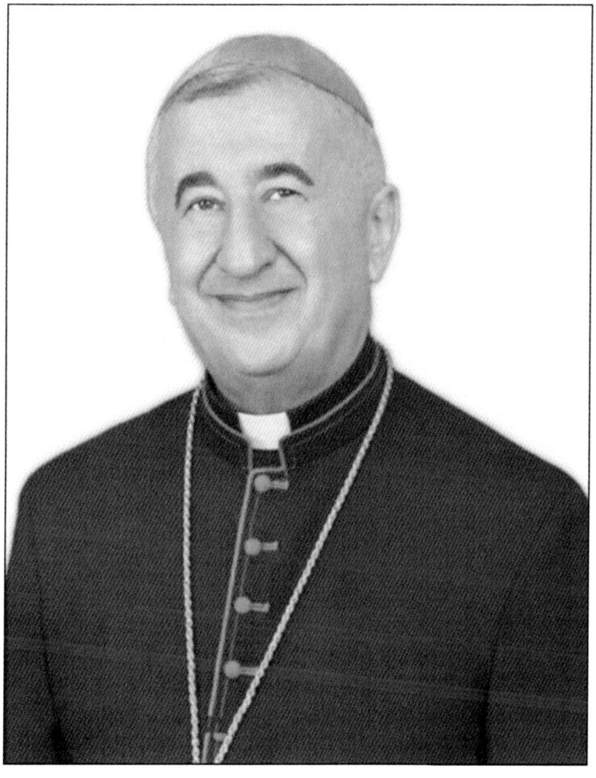

CALLED TO SERVE. Father Emanuel Hana Shaleta was born in Fishkabour, near Zakho, Iraq, on November 11, 1956. He was ordained a priest on May 31, 1984. On January 15, 2015, he was appointed by Pope Francis as bishop of the Eparchy of Mar Addai in Toronto, Canada. On August 9, 2017, Pope Francis appointed Bishop Shaleta the second eparchial bishop of the Chaldean Catholic Eparchy of Saint Peter the Apostle in San Diego, California. (Courtesy of Chaldean Catholic Eparchy of Saint Peter the Apostle.)

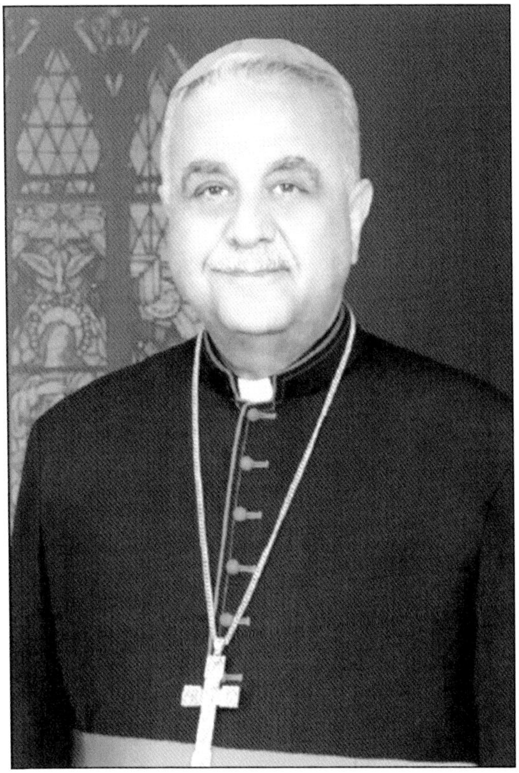

Serving My People. Bishop Bawai Soro was born on March 3, 1954, in Kirkuk, Iraq. He was ordained priest in 1982 and bishop in 1984 in the Assyrian Church of the East. He has a master's in theology from the Catholic University of America and a doctorate in ecclesiology from the Pontifical University of Saint Thomas Aquinas in Rome. After serving over 20 years in the Assyrian Church, he was suspended in 2005 due to his "Catholic tendencies." In 2008, he and some 1,000 Assyrian families, with several priests and deacons, were received by the Catholic Church. On January 11, 2014, Pope Francis appointed him the titular bishop of Foratiana in the service of the Chaldean Catholic Eparchy of Saint Peter. On October 31, 2017, Pope Francis appointed him eparch of Mar Addai in Toronto. In 2020, Pope Francis appointed him consultant for the Congregation for the Oriental Churches. On September 11, 2021, he retired due to medical reasons. Bishop Soro currently resides in San Diego. (Courtesy of Chaldean Catholic Eparchy of Mar Addai.)

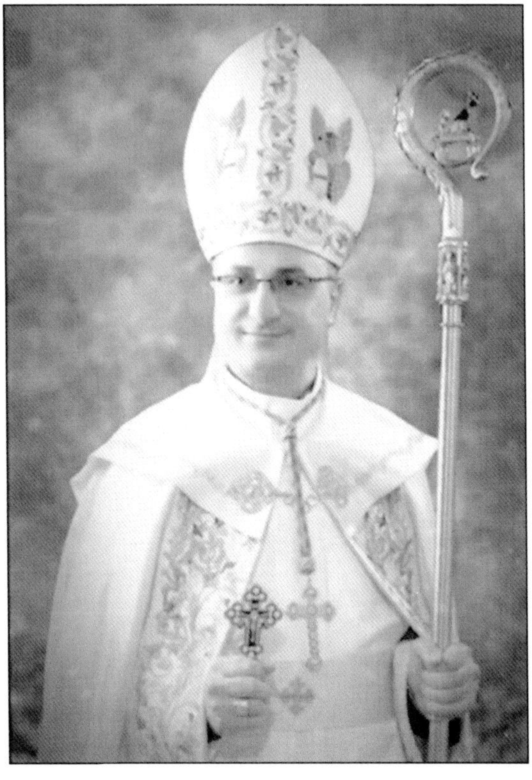

The Youngest Chaldean Bishop to Canada. Robert Saeed Girgis, born in Baghdad on October 23, 1973, earned a veterinary medicine degree in 1996. He was ordained a priest in 2008 by Pope Benedict XVI. On November 18, 2019, he was consecrated bishop by Patriarch Mar Louis Raphael Sako. On September 11, 2021, Pope Francis appointed him the fourth eparch of Mar Addai Chaldean Catholic Eparchy in Canada. (Courtesy of Father John Jwad.)

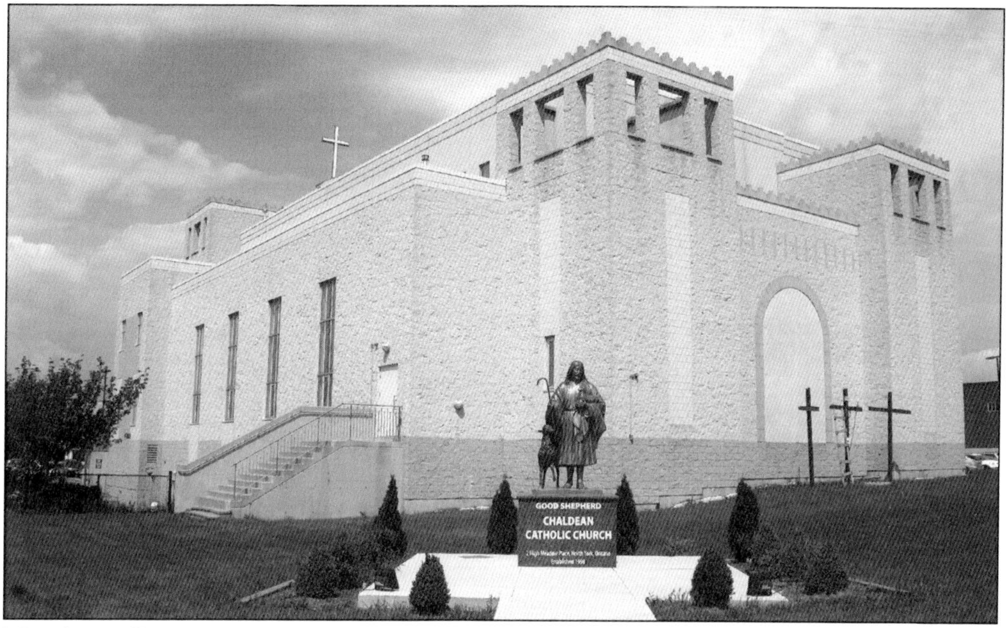

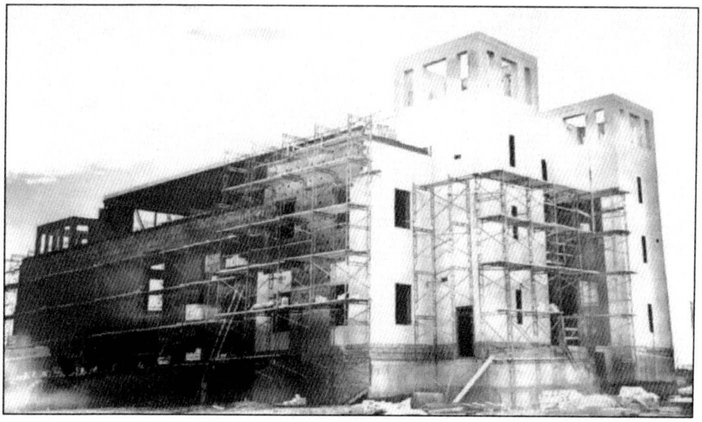

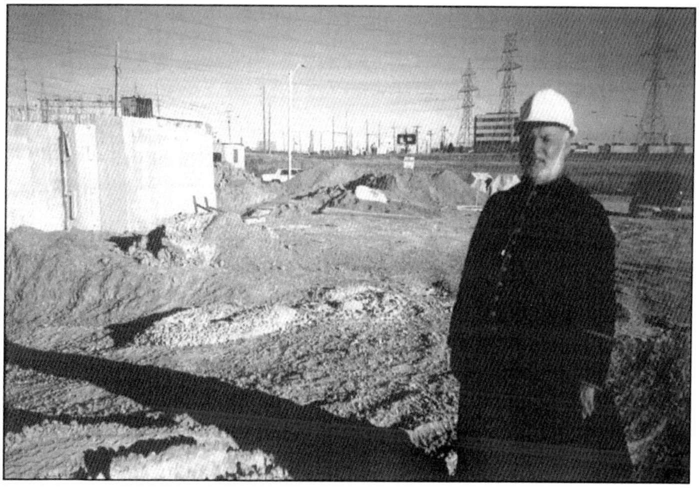

Mar Addai Eparchy in Toronto. On May 28, 2011, after over 10 years of construction, Patriarch Emmanuel III Delly consecrated the altar of Good Shepherd Chaldean Catholic Church, which became a cathedral. By then, there were around 38,000 Chaldean Catholics in Canada served by Archbishop Hanna Zora and four priests. The first Chaldean church in Canada was established after years of renting other churches when Cardinal Aloysius Ambrozic blessed the church ground on March 19, 2000. It is located at 2 High Meadow Place, North York, Ontario. (All, courtesy of Chaldean Catholic Eparchy of Mar Addai.)

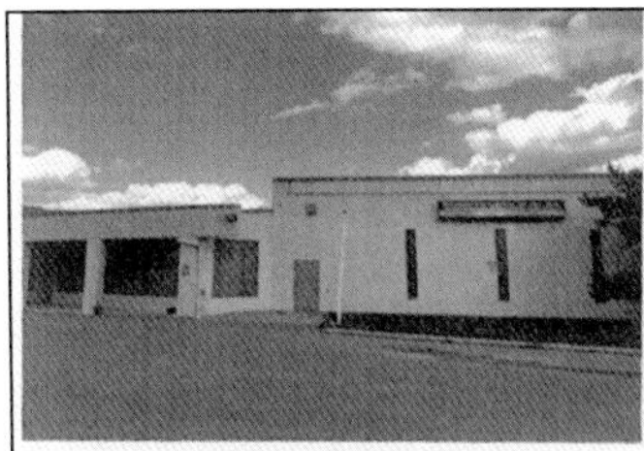

St. Peter Chaldean Catholic Parish

2451 Old Bronte Road.
Oakville, ON. L6H 4J2

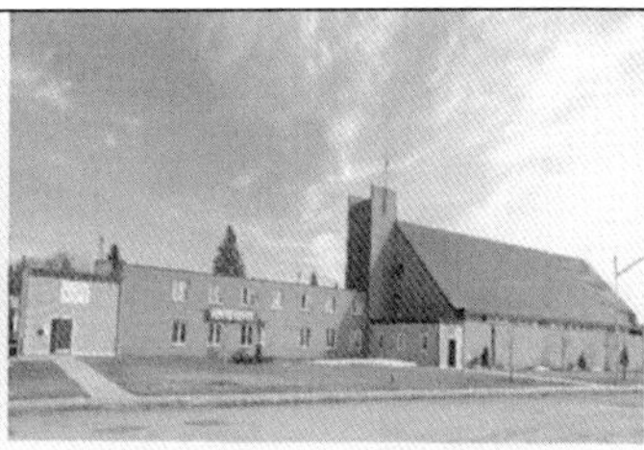

Sacred Heart Chaldean Catholic Church

2101 Lansdowne Ave.
Saskatoon, SK S7J 1G6

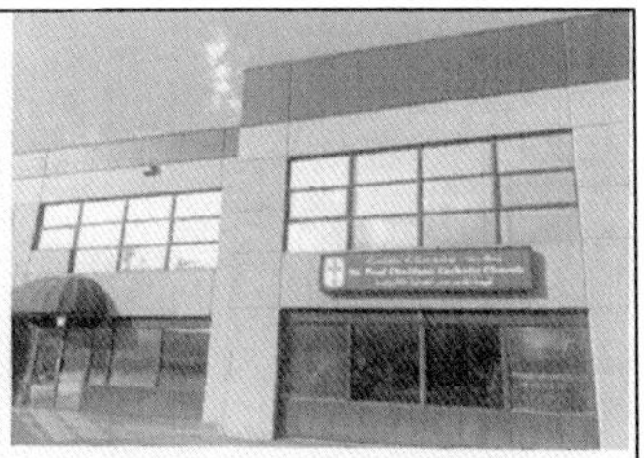

St. Paul Chaldean Catholic Church

101-17957 55th Ave.
Surrey, BC V3S 6C4

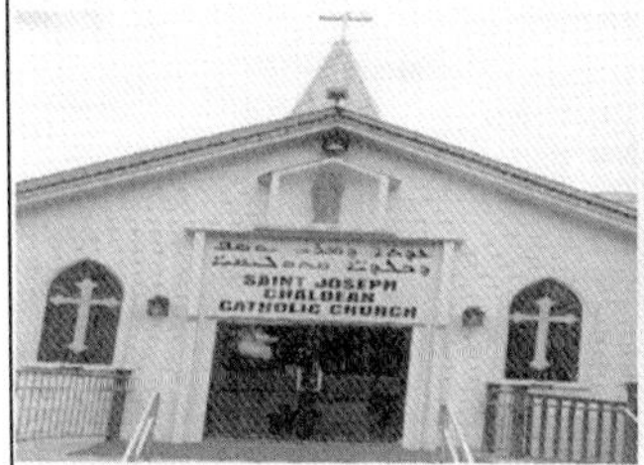

St. Joseph Chaldean Catholic Church

89 Charles St.
London, ON N6H 1H1

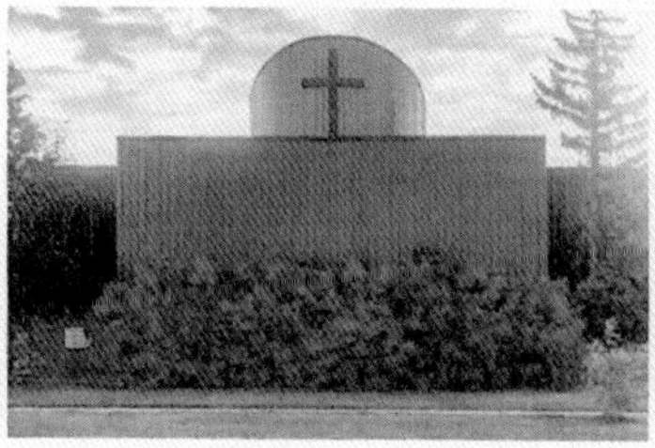

St. Mary Chaldean Catholic Church

1432 19th Street NE
Calgary, AB, Canada
T2E 4Y2

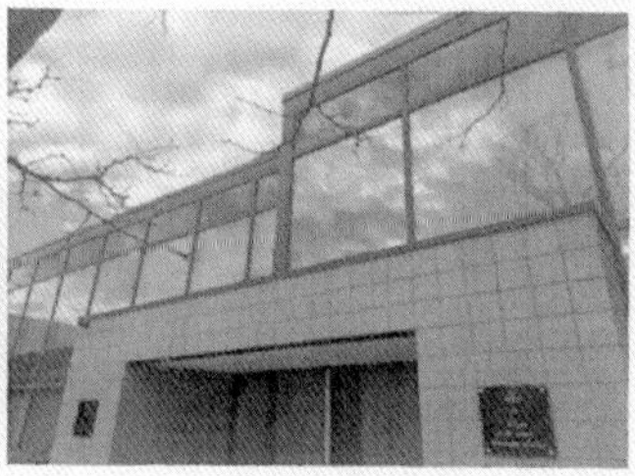

Mar Mari Chaldean Catholic Church

145 Traders Blvd East,
Unit 9-13
Mississauga, ON L4Z 3L3

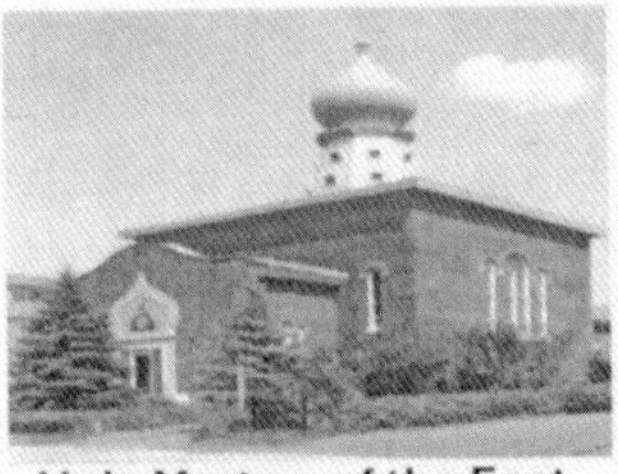

Holy Martyrs of the East Chaldean Catholic Church

44 Rue Guizot (West)
Montreal, QC H2P 1L4

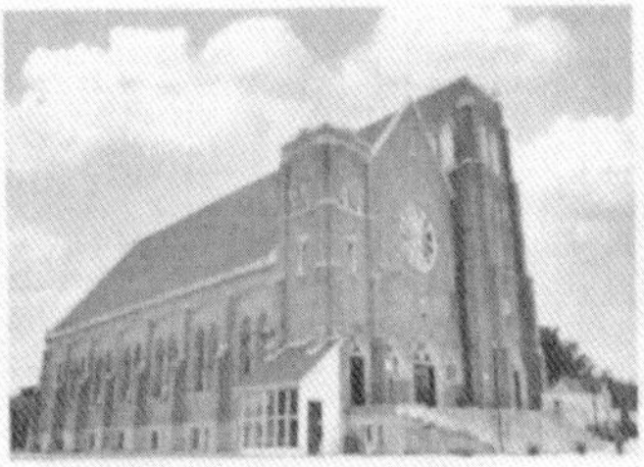

The Holy Family Chaldean Catholic Church

686 Marentette Ave.
Windsor, ON N9A 1Z4

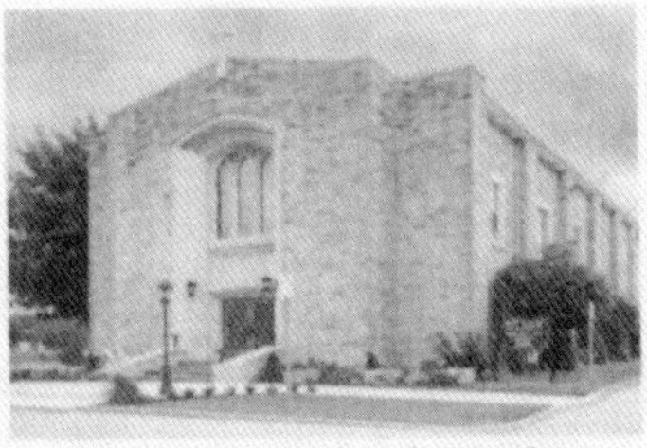

St. Thomas the Apostle Chaldean Catholic Church

506 Templemead Dr.
Hamilton, ON L8W 2H2

CANADA'S CHALDEAN CHURCHES. Above are images and locations of churches within Mar Addai Chaldean Catholic Eparchy. (Both, courtesy of Jacob Bacall.)

Eight

Historic Visit to Iraq by Pope Francis

In 2021, Pope Francis made the first-ever papal visit to Iraq, a country with one of the oldest Christian communities in the world, the purported site of the Garden of Eden, the site of Ur, and the birthplace of Abraham, the patriarch of three religions: Judaism, Christianity, and Islam. Pope John Paul II wanted to visit Ur during his papacy as well as Israel, Jordan, and Palestine, but the visit was cancelled due to differences between the government of Saddam Hussein and representatives of the Holy See, which caused the Iraqi government to prohibit the visit.

On December 7, 2020, Holy See press director Matteo Bruni released a statement confirming that Pope Francis accepted the invitation of the Republic of Iraq and the Chaldean Catholic Church to visit Iraq from March 5 to 8, 2021. The timing of the pontiff's visit was not perfect, considering the pandemic of COVID-19, but if the pope wanted to wait for a better time, his visit might well never take place. Pope Francis was eager and determined to take on the burden of this journey while he was able despite its dense four-day program. Pope Francis sees his spiritual responsibilities as extending to all who live on this earth. He traveled where none of his 265 predecessors ever reached, the birthplace of Abraham, "Ur of the Chaldeans" in the ancient land of Mesopotamia, today's Iraq.

Pope Francis called on the Christian minority (mostly Chaldeans) to not abandon their homeland, as their population has dropped from 1.5 million before the fall of Saddam Hussein in 2003 to less than 250,000 today. Iraqi Chaldeans have endured extreme persecution since the 2003 US-led invasion. In recent years, ISIS drove many from their ancestral homes in Mosul and the cluster of Chaldean villages on the nearby Nineveh Plains.

During his four-day trip, Pope Francis stood amid the rubble of Mosul and held an outdoor mass attended by some 10,000 people in Erbil, the capital of Iraqi Kurdistan, where many Christians sought sanctuary from ISIS. He visited with key Muslims and spiritual leaders, including the reclusive Shia cleric Grand Ayatollah Ali Al-Sistani, and asked for their help in protecting Christians.

"During the stay in the land of our holy prophets, I once more witnessed the disasters of war and the scourge of terrorism and fundamentalism that by disfiguring the image of the creator, manipulates religions in order to reject peaceful coexistence between different ethnic and religious groups and different ideas and cultures," said Pope Francis about his visit.

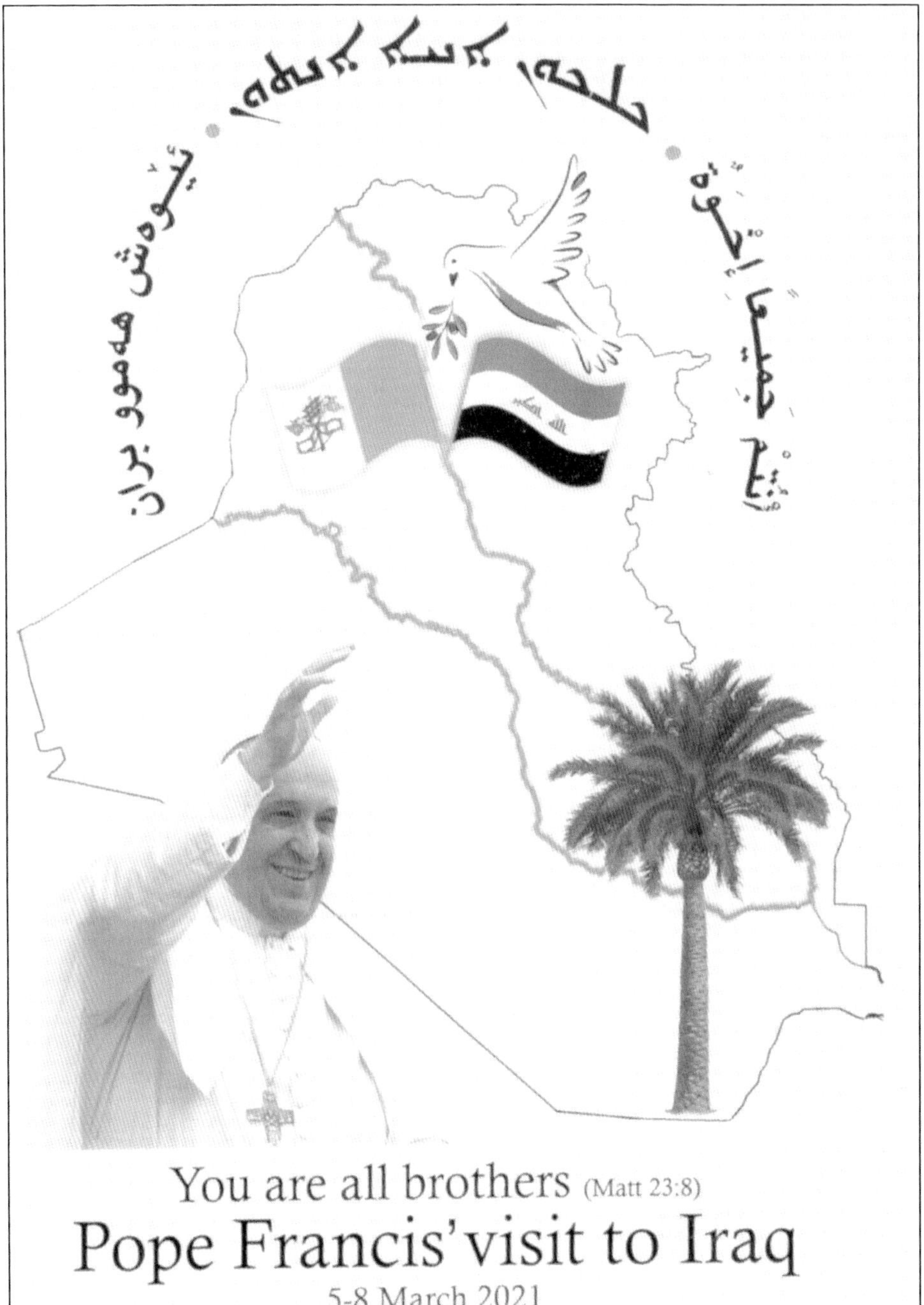

I PROMISED, HERE I COME. This logo was designed to show Pope Francis greeting and blessing a map of Iraq. It includes symbols of Iraq, such as the Tigris and Euphrates Rivers. The white dove carrying an olive branch signifies the desired peace in Iraq. Also featured are the flags of the Vatican and the Republic of Iraq. At the southern part of Iraq stands a palm tree, representing the country's famous dates, which were once the best in the world. At the top of the logo, a quote from the Gospel of Saint Matthew (23:8), "You are all brothers," appears in Arabic, Chaldean, and Kurdish. (Courtesy of Akram F. Kareem.)

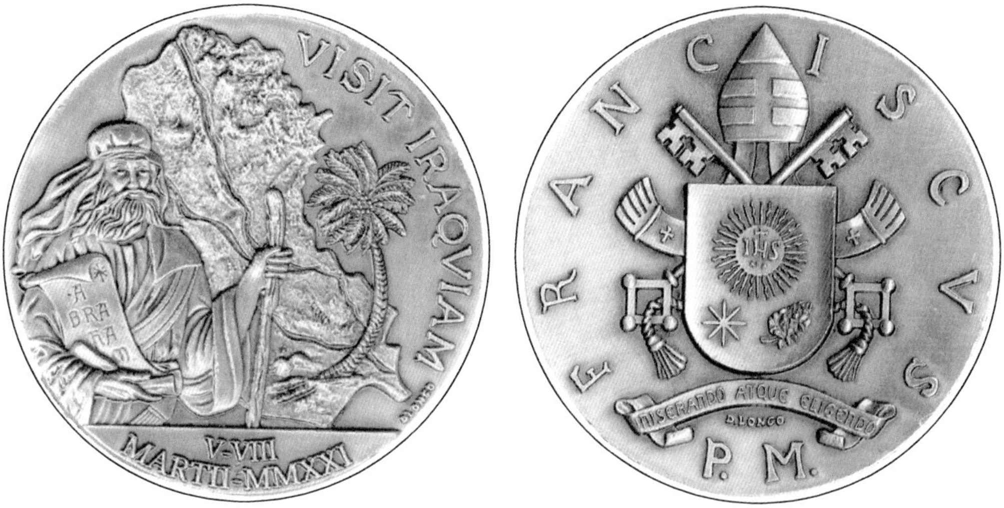

COMMEMORATIVE MEDAL. The Vatican minted a commemorative coin to celebrate Pope Francis visiting Iraq. The front (left) mirrors the official logo and features symbols of Iraq, including the Tigris and Euphrates Rivers and a palm tree. The date of the visit, March 5–8, is inscribed in Latin at the bottom, along with an image of Abraham departing from Ur. On the reverse (right) is the Papal Coat of Arms, representing the keys given to Simon Peter. The crown signifies the pope's triple authority as Father of Kings, Governor of the World, and Vicar of Christ. The Latin inscription *Miserando atque eligendo* translates to "Because he saw him through the eyes of mercy and chose him." This phrase holds personal significance for Pope Francis, who, at the age of 17 in 1953, felt called to the priesthood after experiencing God's mercy during confession on the Feast of Saint Matthew. (Both, courtesy of Father John Jwad.)

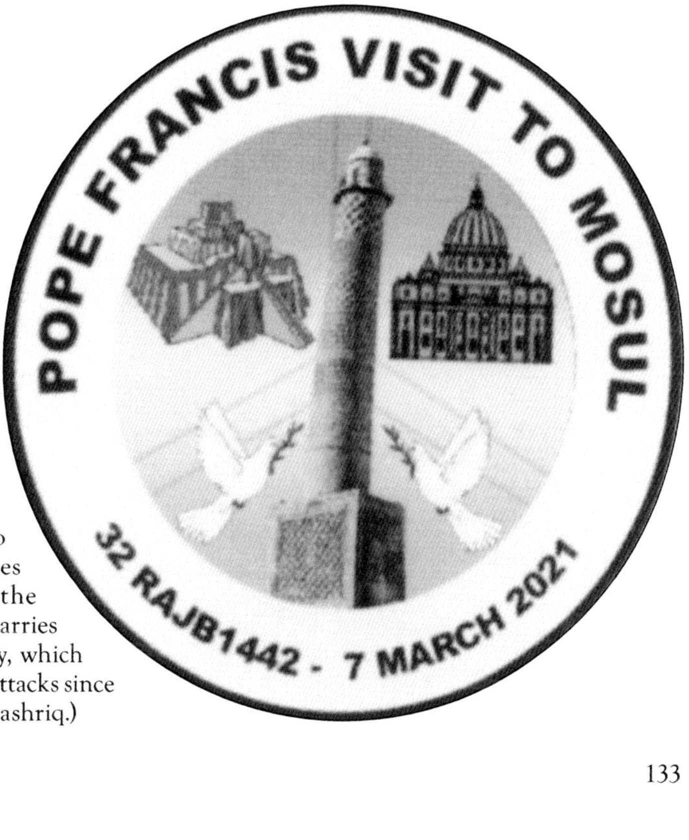

THE MOSUL LOGO. The Mosul logo forms a circle containing three symbols representing the Church of Saint Peter in the Vatican, the historic Ziggurat of Ur, and the humpbacked minaret (*manarat al-hadhba*) of the Great Mosque, which is a symbol of the city of Mosul in the Nineveh Province. Two doves carrying olive branches appear fluttering around the minaret, as if the pope's visit carries a message of peace to this city, which has suffered greatly from ISIS attacks since 2014. (Courtesy of Najm Al-Mashriq.)

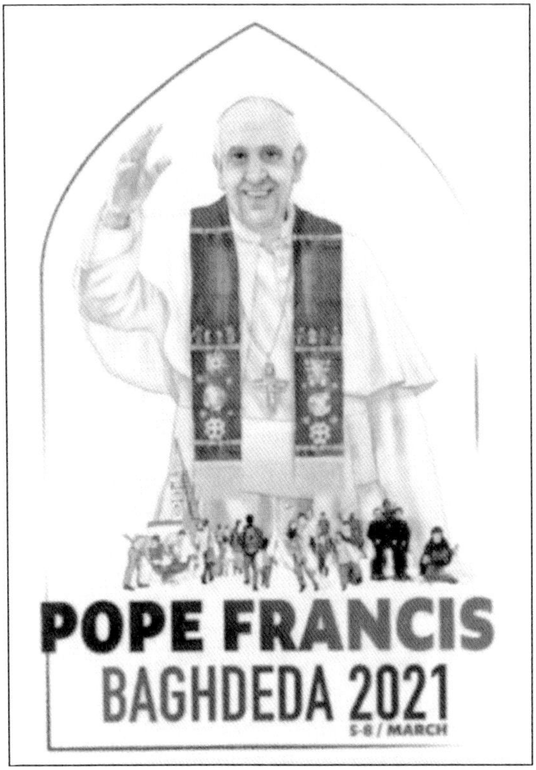

THE BAGHDEDA LOGO. Note a sad mother on the lower right, representing the mothers of martyrs throughout history. Despite her sadness, she continues to work for a living. To the immediate left are images of martyrs, starting with two priests killed by the Ottomans and including thousands of young people who perished in the Iran-Iraq War. The martyrs' depictions conclude with those who lost their lives at the hands of ISIS, symbolizing displacement and return. The most recent event occurred in 2014, when people were forced to leave their homes and churches, represented by crowds emerging from the body of the pope, who symbolizes the universal Church and Christianity. The return is symbolized by the placement of the statue of the Virgin Mary on the Great Church of the Immaculate, serving as a symbol of protection for the city. (Courtesy of Najm Al-Mashriq.)

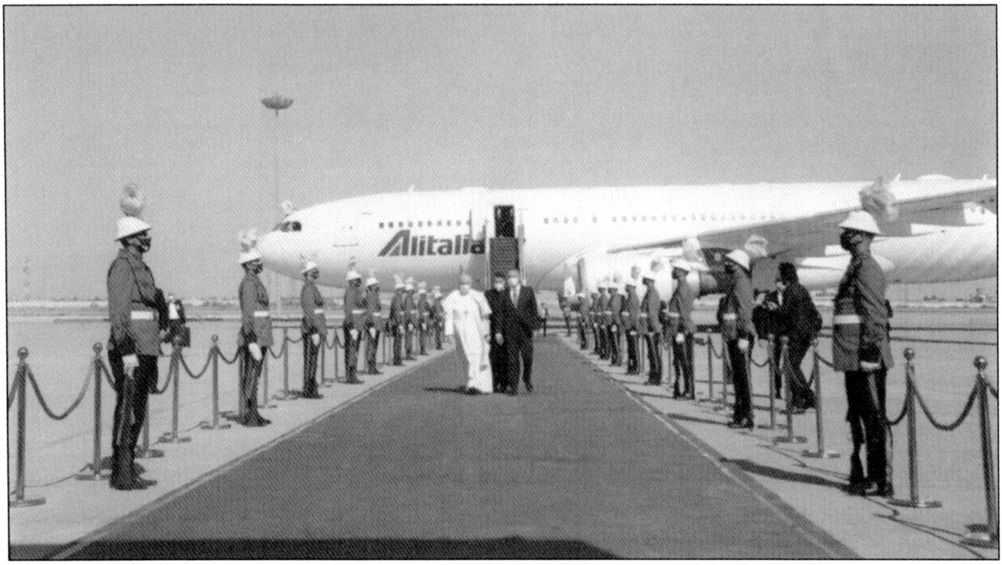

HERE I AM! Upon descending the stairs of the plane, Pope Francis was warmly received by Iraqi prime minister Mustafa Al-Kadhimi and a large delegation of ministers and officials. Welcoming chants echoed in four languages: Arabic (*ahlan wa-sahlan*), Chaldean (*bishina wa-shishlamah*), English (welcome), and Italian (*viva, viva, viva*). This multilingual greeting underscored the diverse cultural and linguistic heritage of Iraq, marking the historic visit of His Holiness. Note the face masks that most are wearing; this visit took place during the COVID-19 pandemic. (Courtesy of Akram F. Kareem.)

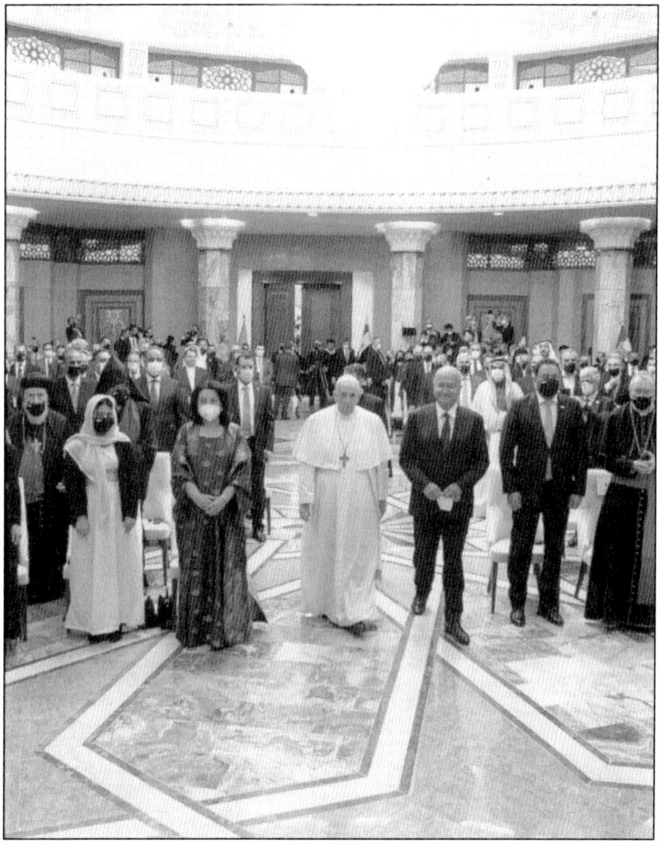

Welcome to Baghdad Palace. On his way to Baghdad Palace, crowds of admirers, both Christian and non-Christian, lined both sides of the road, waving Iraqi and Vatican flags and holding banners to welcome His Holiness. With a heartfelt smile on his face, Pope Francis extended his hand from the car window to greet the enthusiastic crowds. Upon arriving at the door of Baghdad Palace on March 5, 2021, Pope Francis was received by the president of the republic, Dr. Barham Salih, and his wife, Sarbagh Salih. This gesture was notable, as it is rare in Iraq for the wife of the prime minister or president to receive foreign guests. (Courtesy of Akram F. Kareem.)

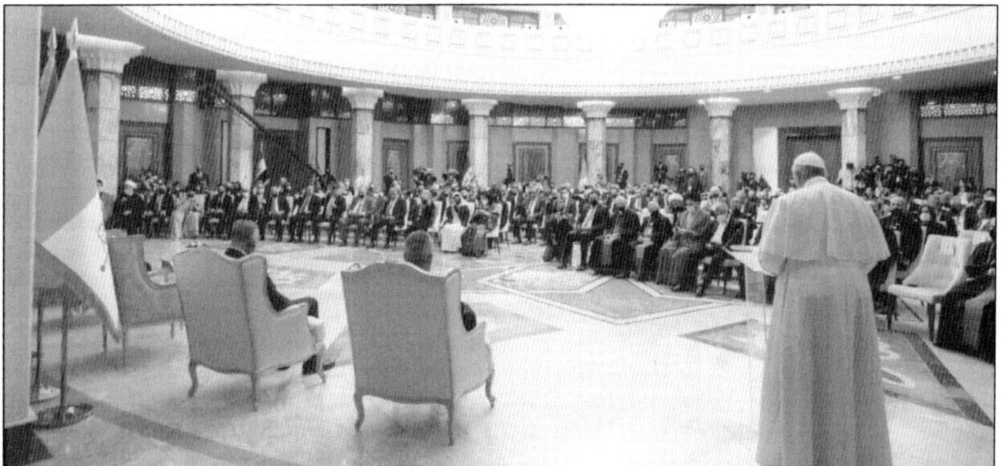

Prince of Peace. Upon his arrival at the presidential palace, Pope Francis was welcomed by Pres. Dr. Barham Salih. After a brief conversation, they proceeded to the main hall, where they met with around 220 guests, including government officials, diplomats, religious leaders, and tribal sheikhs. Pope Francis emphasized his mission as a pilgrim of peace, bringing a message of reconciliation in the name of Jesus Christ, the Prince of Peace. Concluding, he affirmed, "The Catholic Church in Iraq also wants to be a friend to everyone and to cooperate through dialogue in a constructive manner with other religions for the cause of peace." (Courtesy of Akram F. Kareem.)

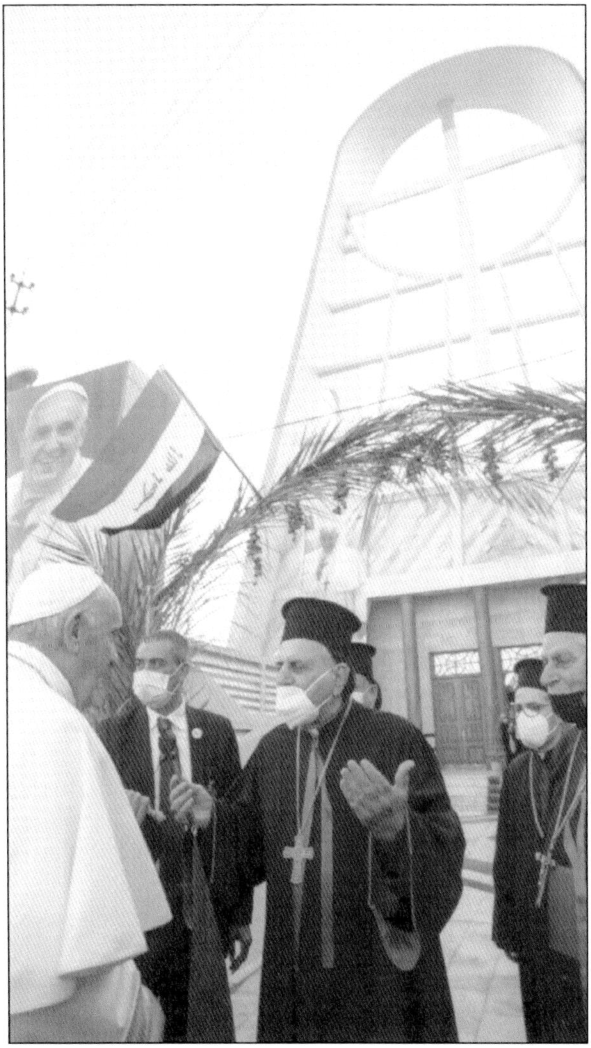

Saydet Al-Najat Cathedral (Our Lady of Deliverance). On the first day of his visit, Pope Francis visited Our Lady of Deliverance Syriac Catholic Church in Baghdad. Greeted by Patriarch Ignatius Youssef III Younan and other clergy, he was moved by the images of the 48 martyrs killed during a terrorist attack on October 31, 2010. The pope signed the golden register book, writing, "I came to Iraq as a repentant pilgrim, longing for faith and peace, calling on God to strengthen His people through the intercession of the Virgin Mary, so we may rebuild the country together as brothers." (Courtesy of Akram F. Kareem.)

Meeting Ayatollah Ali Al-Sistani. On the morning of March 6, 2021, Pope Francis arrived at Najaf Airport. Upon arrival, he was taken to the residence of Grand Ayatollah Ali Al-Sistani. During their 45-minute meeting, he was accompanied by Patriarch Louis Sako and Cardinal Miguel Angel Ayuso, president of the Pontifical Council for Interfaith Dialogue. (Courtesy of Najm Al-Mashriq.)

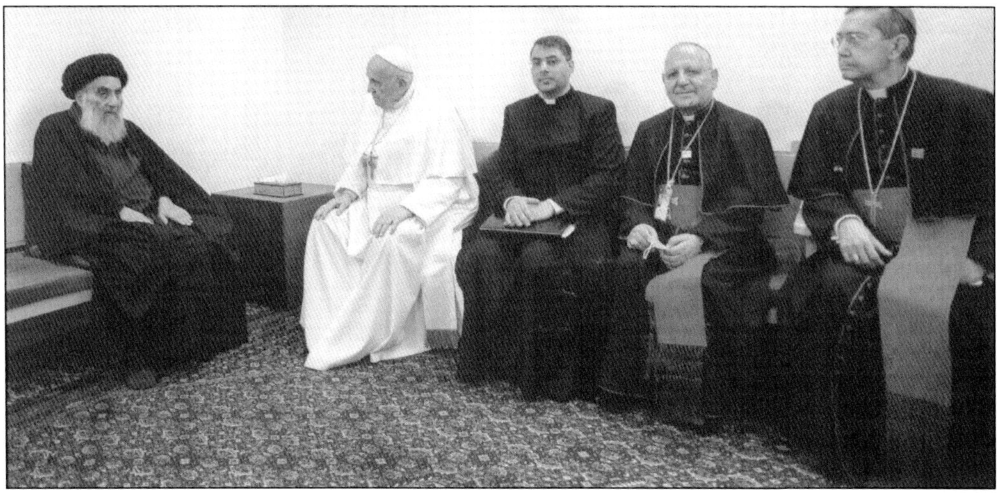

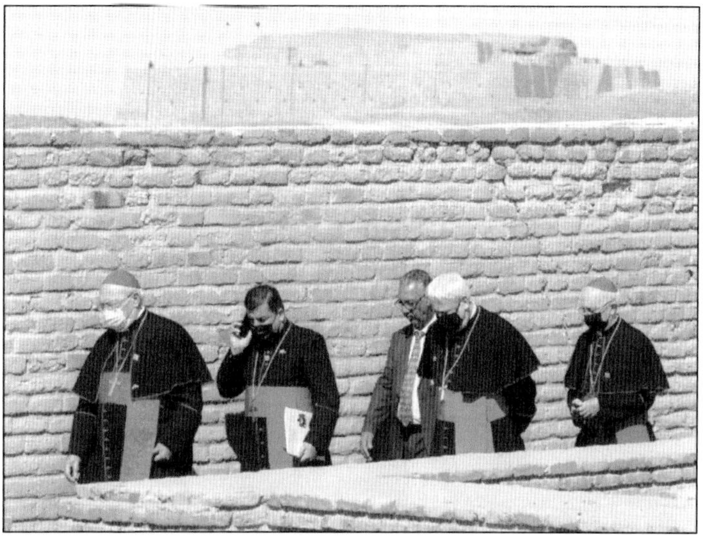

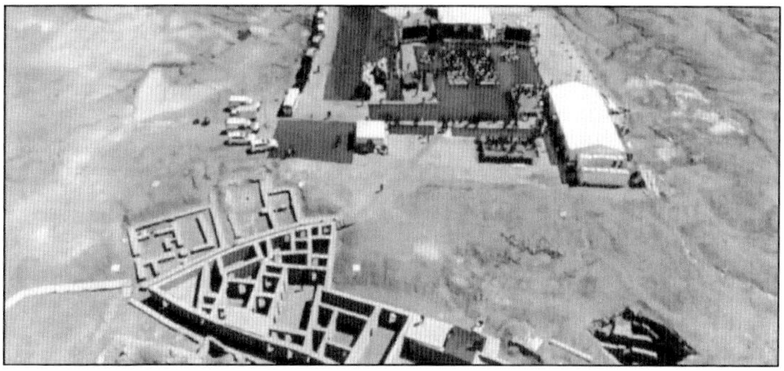

Ur, the Famous Capital of Chaldea. The pope's delegation visited the house of Abraham in Ur, located in southern Iraq's Dhi Qar Province (Nasiriya). This site is mentioned in the Bible and is the birthplace of Abraham, the patriarch of Judaism, Christianity, and Islam. From here, Abraham embarked on his journey to Canaan (Genesis 11:27–31). Bishop Basilio Yaldo, the general coordinator of the papal apostolic visit, is seen here on the phone managing the arrangements. (Both, courtesy of Akram F. Kareem.)

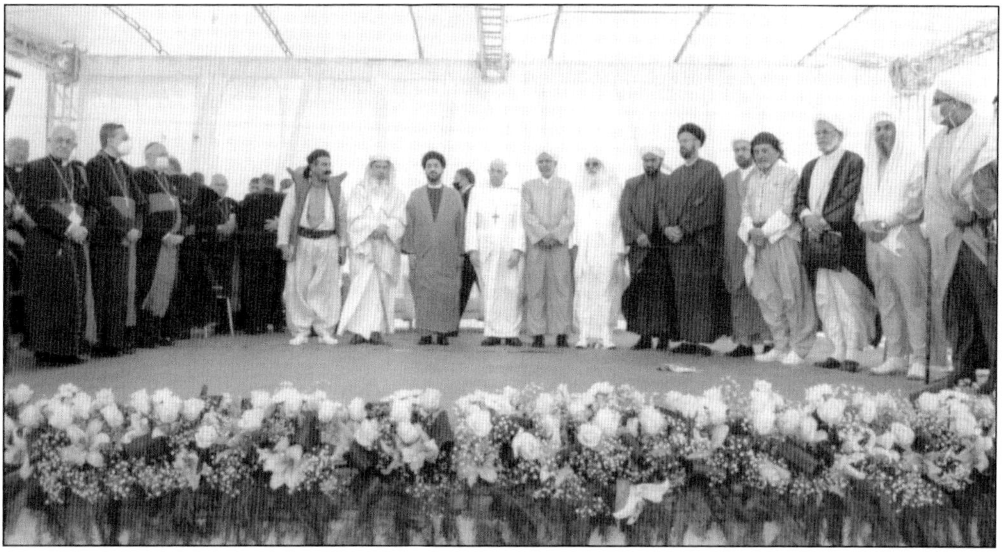

Iraqi Religious Tapestry. The pontiff's visit emphasized the shared heritage of the Abrahamic faiths and the importance of interfaith unity. This historic gathering brought together representatives from various religious traditions, including Islam (Sunni and Shia), Christian, Yazidi, Sabean Mandean, Zoroastrian, and Kakaey. (Courtesy of Akram F. Kareem.)

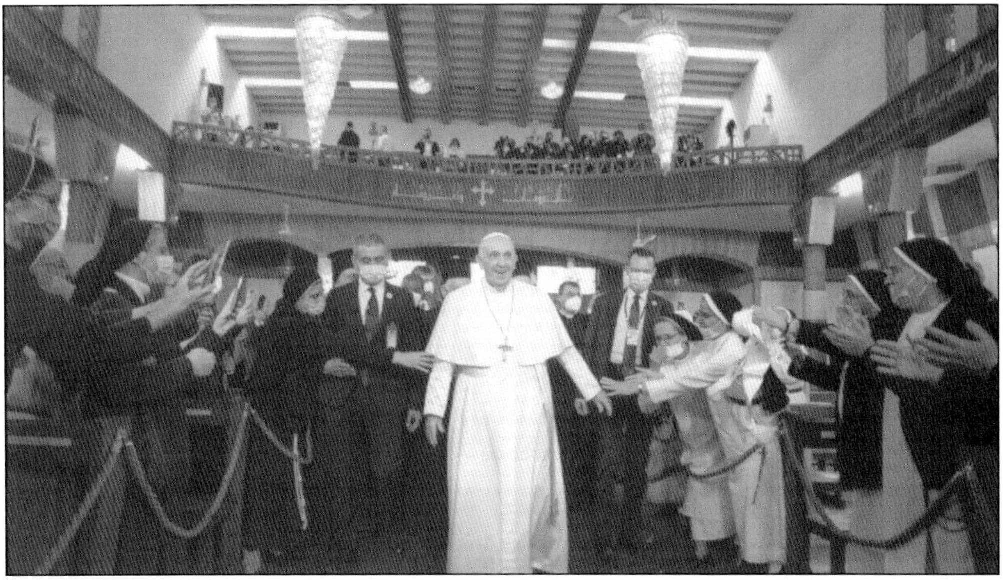

Teshbohta L'Alaha Bamraumeh (Glory to God in the Highest). On Saturday, March 6, 2021, at 5:30 p.m., the convoy of Pope Francis departed from the Papal Embassy in Baghdad to the Chaldean Cathedral of Saint Joseph in Al-Karada, located within Baghdad. For the first time in history, His Holiness celebrated a mass according to the Chaldean Rite of the Church of the East, specifically the Saint Thomas Mass. At exactly 6:00 p.m., church bells rang as the pope entered through the side door overlooking the church courtyard. The mass commenced with the words "teshbohta l'Alaha bamraumeh," chanted in Chaldean by Patriarch Louis Sako. Pope Francis then continued the prayers in Italian, and the congregation sang the hymns "*Lakhu Mara*" and "*Qadisha Alaha*." During his homily, Pope Francis addressed how to respond to challenging situations, noting that in the face of adversity there are two common temptations: flight or anger. He emphasized that neither approach resolves issues. Instead, he highlighted Jesus's example of changing history through the humble power of love and patient witness, urging the faithful to emulate this approach as a means of fulfilling God's promises. (Both, courtesy of Akram F. Kareem.)

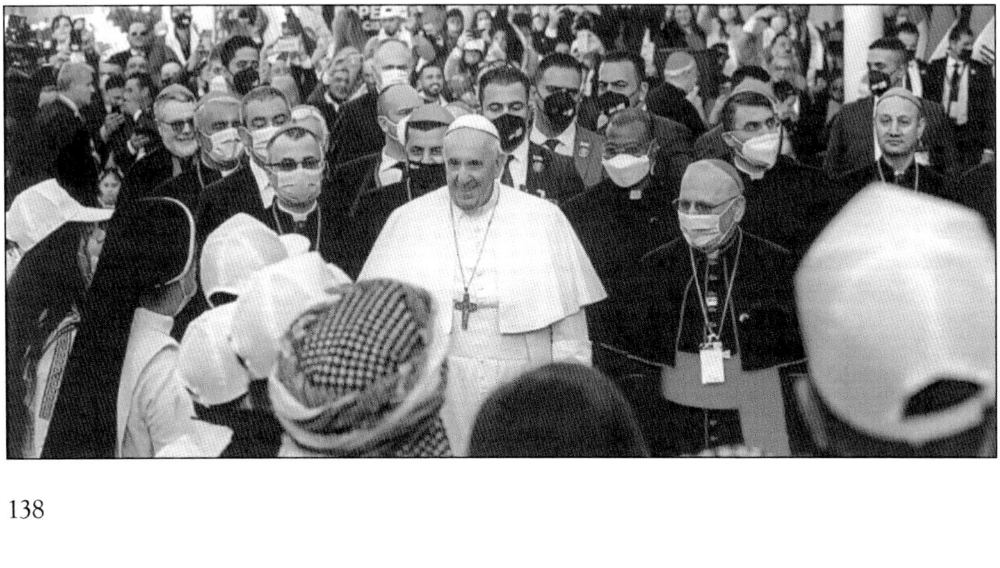

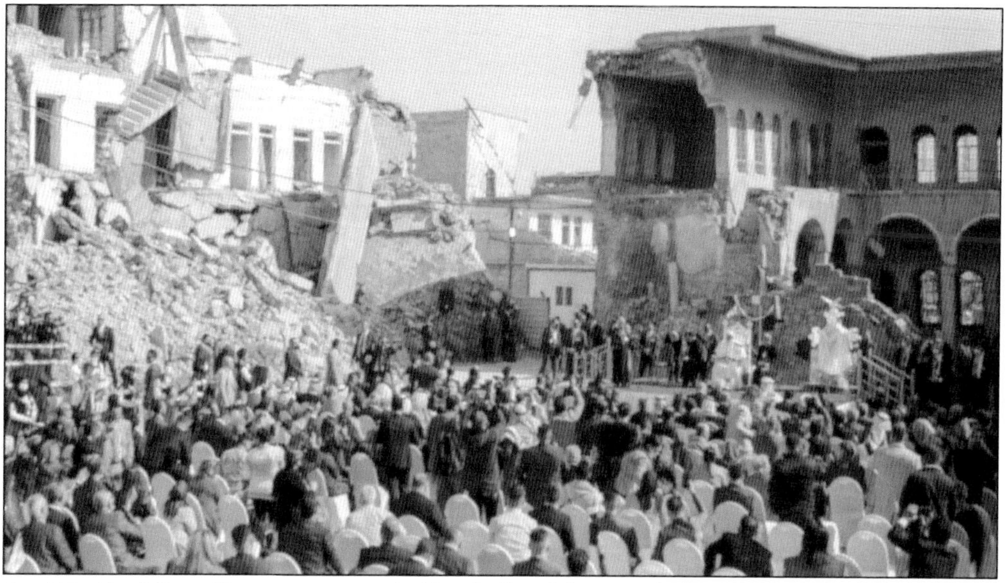

Oh, My God! Pope Francis, surrounded by shells of destroyed churches, leads a prayer for the victims of war at the Hosh Al-Bieaa Church square in Mosul, Iraq, the de facto capital of ISIS. Pictured here are the ruins of the Syriac Catholic Church of the Immaculate Conception (Kanisat Al-Tahira-l-Kubra) in Mosul. (Courtesy of Najm Al-Mashriq.)

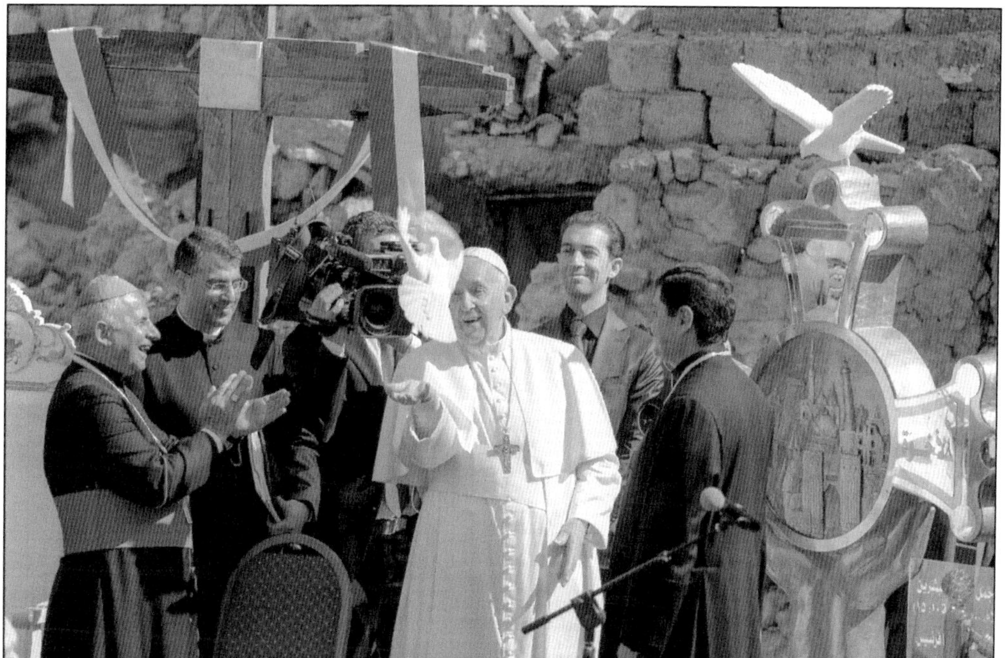

Peace, Peace, Peace. Pope Francis releases a dove as a sign of peace and freedom, joined by the Chaldean Catholic archbishop of Mosul, Najib Mikael Moussa (left), and Father George Ayoub, the pope's interpreter. (Courtesy of Akram F. Kareem.)

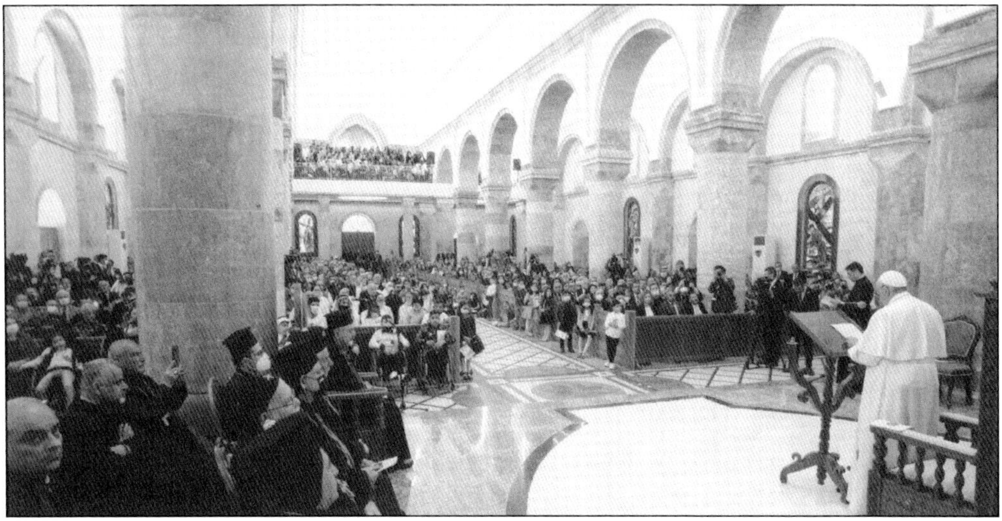

Teshbohta L'Alaha B-Aiteh (Glory Be to God in His Church). Pope Francis arrives to hold a mass at the Grand Immaculate Church in Qaraqosh, Iraq's largest Christian city, in the Nineveh Plains. "The happiness on people's faces in the city of Baghdeda (Qaraqosh) was never seen before on Christian faces in Iraq," wrote a *Chaldean News* reporter in April 2021. "I was crying pretty much the whole time watching the Mass, especially when I heard the ancient chants, *Lakhu Mara d-Kulla mawdenan* and *Qaddysha Alaha*. The chants that we hear every Sunday at church, hearing it there in front of the Pope and hearing parts of the mass and the singing in Aramaic and Syriac, which is the language of Jesus Christ, was just magical," said Crystal Jabiro, who watched the mass in church, in an article for the *National* in March 2021. (Courtesy of Akram F. Kareem.)

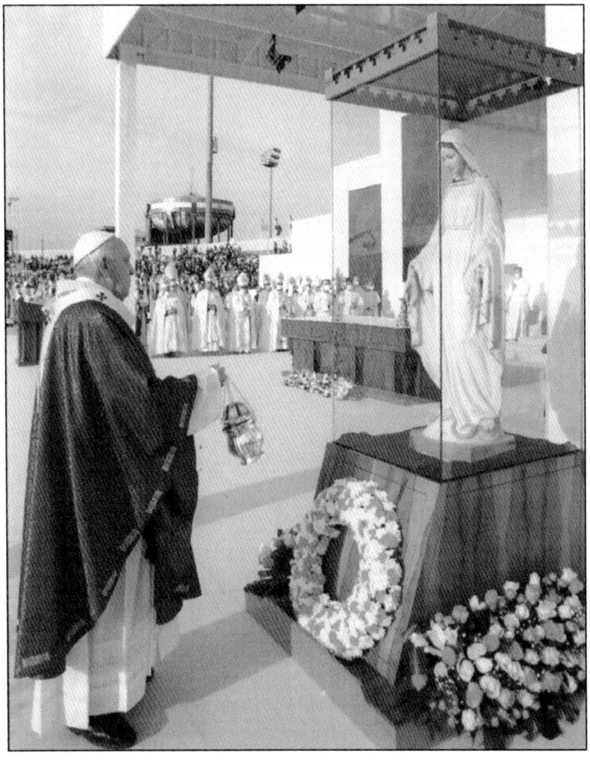

Hail Mary. At the beginning of the mass, Pope Francis incensed and blessed the statue of Our Lady, the Virgin Mary, which had its head and hands smashed by ISIS members during their occupation of the village of Karmulus in the Nineveh Plains in 2014. In his sermon, the pope focused on the Gospel of John 13:2–25, emphasizing the importance of adhering not to human wisdom but to the power of God and following his path, which leads to salvation from every temptation. (Courtesy of Najm Al-Mashriq.)

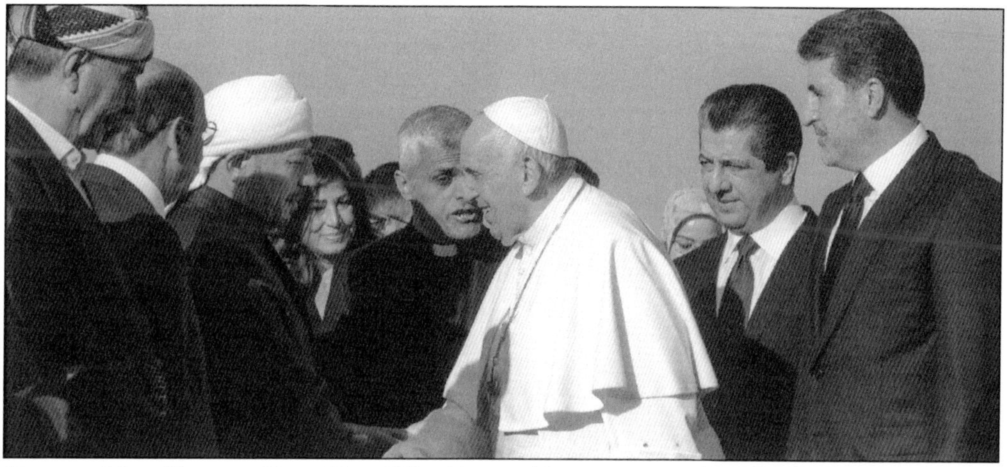

Happy to Meet You, and Your Name? The 84-year-old pope was not done for the day. While he was in Nineveh, more than 10,000 Christians were waiting for him in Erbil's Franso Hariri Stadium, where the excitement was so loud that it could be heard three kilometers away. While the people had come to witness a mass celebrated by the pope, the stadium felt like it was actually a concert, with people singing about their villages and sharing religious hymns. They even brought a *tablat al kas* (goblet drum). Pictured to the right behind His Holiness is Nechirvan Barzani, the president of the Kurdistan region, while next to him is the prime minister of the Kurdistan region, Masrour Barzani, surrounded by others from all parts of the Kurdistan region. (Courtesy of Akram F. Kareem.)

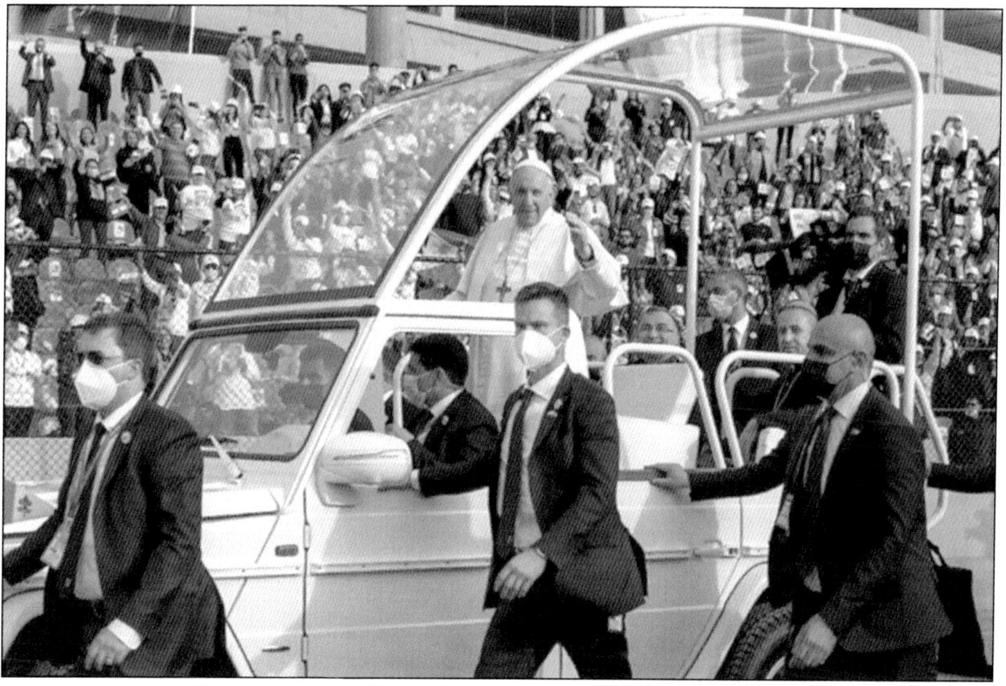

***Shlama Amkhon* (Peace Be with You).** The pope's arrival at Franso Hariri Stadium led to the crowd going wild as he lapped around to give everyone an opportunity to see him closely. The Erbil stadium mass made a significant impression on the pope, who said, "I can see firsthand that the Church in Iraq is alive, that Christ is alive and at work in this, His holy and faithful people." (Courtesy of Akram F. Kareem.)

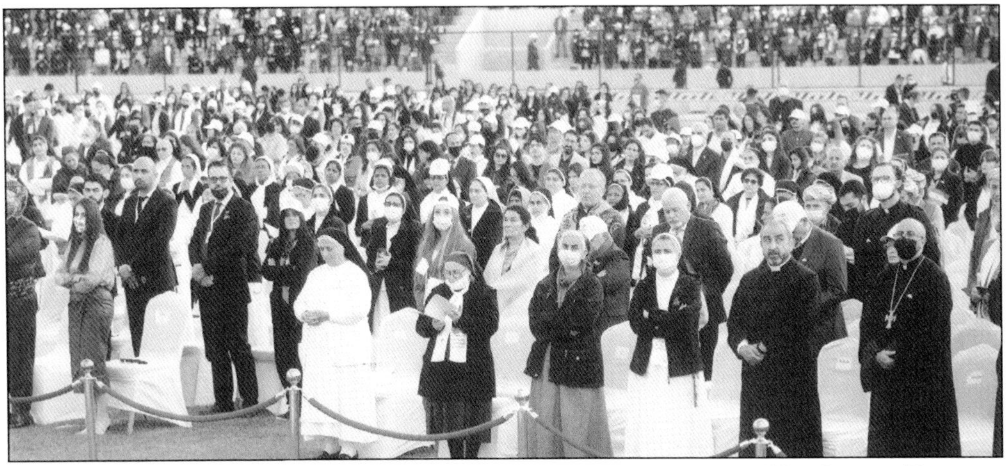

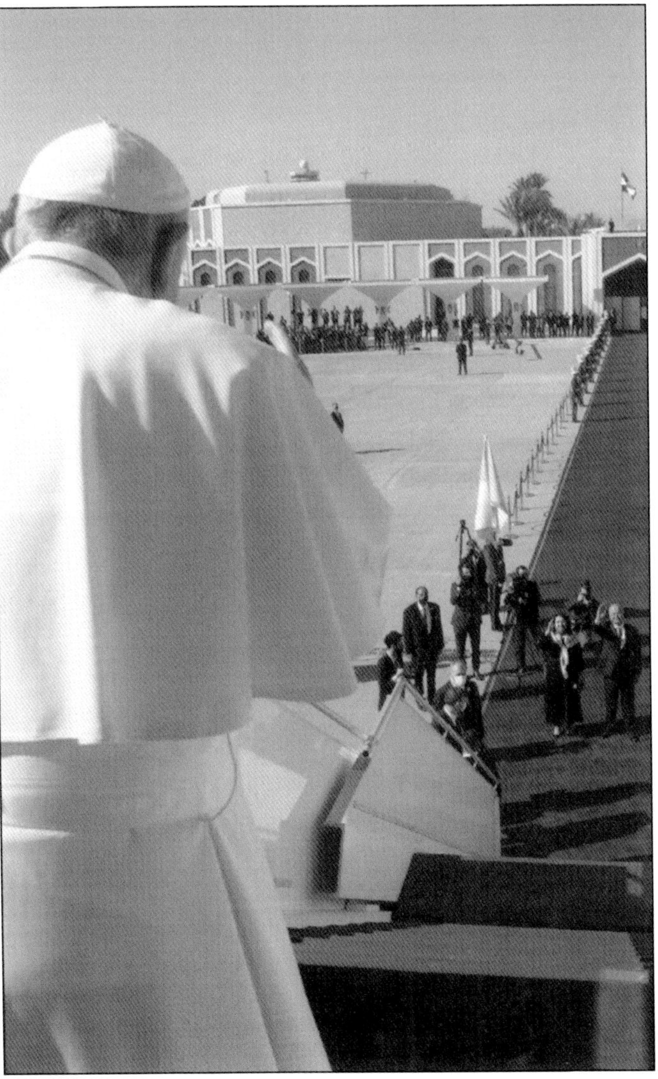

Those Who Live by Faith. Nuns await the arrival of Pope Francis at the Franso Hariri Stadium in Erbil. The mass was held in Italian and comprised of hymns in Arabic and Chaldean, the languages of the local Christian population. Pope Francis concluded the event by saying, "The moment to return to Rome is close approaching, but Iraq will always remain with me and in my heart. I ask all of you, dear brothers and sisters, to work together in unity for a future of peace and prosperity that leaves no one behind and discriminates against no one. I assure you of my prayers for this beloved country. I pray in particular that members of the various religious communities may cooperate with all men and women of good will to strengthen bonds of brotherhood and solidarity in the service of goodness and peace. Peace, peace, peace, thanks! God bless everyone! God bless Iraq! God be with you." (Above, courtesy of Najm Al-Mashriq; below, courtesy of Akram F. Kareem.)

BIBLIOGRAPHY

Adhami, Mohammed M. *Baghdad History: Part One, 762–1917*. Arabic Edition. Al-Mafraq, Jordan: Heba Publishers, 2022.

Al-Banna, George. *History of the Chaldean Patriarchs*. El Cajon, CA: Venus Printing, 2007.

Al-Qazwini, Dr. Jawdat. *Iraq: Images from the Past*. London: Alwarrak Publishing, Ltd., 2003.

Archdiocese of Detroit. *The Michigan Catholic*, September 12, 1980.

Bacall, Jacob. *Chaldeans in Detroit*. Charleston, SC: Arcadia Publishing. 2014.

Bazzi, Father Michael. *Chaldean Nation: Past and Present*. San Diego: Let in the Light Publishing, 2022.

Chaldean News, November 2021.

Dabish, Sam (Shamoun). *The History of the Iraqi Community in America*. Arabic Edition. Baghdad: The Iraqi Printing Press, 1975.

Gill, Anton. *The Rise and Fall of Babylon: Gateway of the Gods*. New York: Metro Books, 2011.

Hassoun, Amer Bader. *The Book of Iraq*. Damascus: Al-Ekha'a Press House, 1995.

Kareem, Akram Faraj Hermiz. *Peace, Peace, Peace*. Published by the author, Amman, Jordan, 2021.

Matar, Selim. *Iraq: Seven Thousand Years of Life*. Beirut: Air P Books Publishing, 2013.

Perry, Bryon. *The Chaldeans*. Troy, MI: Tepel Brothers Printing Company, 2008.

Rassam, Suha. *Christianity in Iraq*. Gloucester, UK: Action Publishing Technology, Ltd., 2005.

Saggs. H.W.F. *Babylonians: Peoples of the Past*. Los Angeles: University of California Press, 2000.

Sako, Patriarch Louis Raphael. *A Historical Overview of the Chaldean Church*. Baghdad: Al-Dewan Printshop, 2020.

Sengstock, Mary C. *Chaldeans in Michigan*. East Lansing: Michigan State University Press, 2005.

Stephen, Louis J. *The Chaldean Directory*. Eastpointe, MI: Nu-Ad Inc., 1998 and 2007 editions.

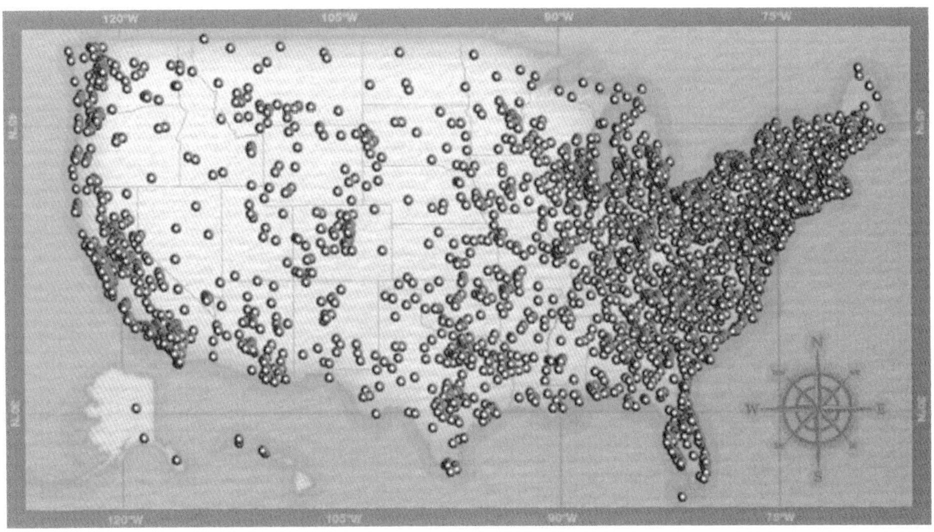